Advance praise f… Life

"As a longtime admirer and user of K… …ed by her passion, drive and commitment in promoting… …ects a full appreciation of history and respect for different cultures."

Carrie Lam
Chief Executive,
Hong Kong Special Administrative Region

"Kai-Yin's aesthetic sensibility of mix-and-match and stylish daring make her outstanding."

Xu Bing
International artist, Beijing

"As outstanding scholar, designer and polymath, Kai-Yin Lo melds and interprets Chinese culture for international understanding and application."

Yue-Sai Kan
Media icon, Shanghai & New York

"Having cooperated with Kai-Yin since the 1980s, I admire her as an artist, who with deep insight and creativity, continues to renew and innovate in jewelry and other spheres of art and design."

Wang Yannan
Co-Founder, China Guardian Auctions, Beijing

"Kai-Yin is an insatiable learner with an intellectual prowess to inquire and synthesise knowledge in tandem with her creative design. Working and traveling with Kai-Yin for more than 20 years, I have been impressed and stimulated by her grand view of Chinese civilisation, the inter-civilisation exchanges and cross-fertilisation, and at the same time her attention to historical details in depth."

Puay-Peng Ho
Professor and Head, Department of Architecture,
National University of Singapore

"I first met Kai-Yin Lo over 30 years ago in Tokyo when she came to promote her exotic yet contemporary jewellery that summed up the essence of East and West, old and contemporary. I was so impressed, as in Japan in those days, we couldn't find any woman like her! After all these years, her jewellery is still my daily accessory. While design is her artistic expression, she is also a great scholar of Chinese and European cross-culture. She is an amazing woman!"

Kazuko Aso

Board member, Asian Cultural Council, Tokyo

"Kai-Yin Lo is passionate in bridging cultures of East and West, cooperating with community, government, education and creative organizations. I am proud to have the sponsored the Central Saint Martins / Kai-Yin Lo Cross-Culture Lectures 2014-2017."

Hans Michael Jebsen

Chairman, Jebsen & Co Ltd., Hong Kong & Denmark

"I have known Kai-Yin Lo since the 1960s and have followed her career with interest and admiration. From being a pioneering designer of jewellery and accessories, she has now become a designer of world recognition. Using her extensive knowledge of European and Chinese history, she has blended in art form the cultures of East and West. She has done this at a time when our connected world, particularly in the fields of politics and business, recognizes the vital importance of the creative industries in enhancing cross-cultural understanding and international cooperation."

Sir Henry Keswick

Chairman Emeritus, Jardine Matheson Holdings Ltd.,
London & Hong Kong

DESIGNING A LIFE

A CROSS-CULTURAL JOURNEY

KAI-YIN LO

BLACKSMITH BOOKS

For my loving family and cherished friends
who inspire and sustain me,
and whose support I treasure.

ISBN 978-988-79638-3-7

Published by Blacksmith Books
Unit 26, 19/F, Block B, Wah Lok Industrial Centre,
37-41 Shan Mei Street, Fo Tan, Hong Kong

Tel: (+852) 2877 7899
www.blacksmithbooks.com

Book design by Vincent Vi
Cover by Carol Norton

This is a tale of self-discovery, of bravery and foolishness, of business successes and mistakes, all the time inspired and guided by a deep curiosity and respect for culture and the interchange and inter-influence of East and West. My goal has always been to project and define a distinctive approach in all I do.

KAI-YIN LO

CONTENTS

PART III

FOREWORD

I first encountered Kai-Yin Lo some fifteen years ago when I was Dean of Fashion, Textiles and Jewelry at Central Saint Martins (CSM). She arrived on our doorstep offering to share with our jewellery design students her experiences of a particular and specialist area of the jewellery world that she had pioneered. It soon became clear that this was just one facet of this highly educated, enterprising, energetic and passionate polymath. After I became head of the whole college, the relationship with CSM developed and deepened and even after my retirement she continues to be a greatly valued friend to both of us, generous with her time, her extensive global network, and her knowledge. Not only does she contribute her learning to CSM but she has also held Visiting Professorships in such leading institutions as Tsinghua University in Beijing, and the Central Academy of Fine Arts, Beijing. Her fascination with Chinese culture has led her to co-author and/or edit four books on historical aspects of artifacts and living patterns in Chinese life. Her role in creating and maintaining her own design business was recognized in 2007 by the award of 'World Leading Chinese Designer' from the Hong Kong Design Centre.

It is the development of this business that is at the core of her creative reputation. Growing out of her initial collecting and assembling of Chinese and Central Asian semi-precious ornaments and artifacts, she began to establish a market for unusual antique pieces that were neither costume nor fine jewellery. She identified a market for the discerning stylish client who wanted intriguing pieces of both quality and craftsmanship at accessible prices. Building on this she also pioneered the introduction of coloured stones cut and carved by traditional craftsmen in Asia. She has continued to seek out craftspeople and deploy their skills across a range of products for the contemporary world, thus preserving these ancient crafts for the future.

Kai-Yin has been a dedicated lobbyist for culture in Hong Kong for many years, tirelessly championing the city's growth as the Asian centre of the art market, promoting the appreciation and value of good design, and the importance of creative thinking within the education system. She has travelled the world and devoted many hours to countless boards and committees in pursuit of these aims. Her ability to cajole is relentless, almost shameless, and she is without doubt the arch persuader. If she believed in it, she could truly sell ice to the Eskimos.

She has been promising to write this book for some years. It shares the story of her journey from a comfortable Hong Kong childhood through her life-defining education in Britain and America to the tough times when suddenly she had to make her own way in the world. It is the story of enterprise and imagination, of finding a deep vein of creativity within herself, of luck and friendship, married always to a keen instinct for the market.

Her recollections of Hong Kong in the mid-twentieth century capture a community and social structure on the brink of change, and her years in America, New York in particular, reflect the dynamism and ambition that she, through a combination of vision and desperation, was able to harness to establish her business. Her experiences in Japan reflected the tension between peoples created by politics that she advocates can be ameliorated by knowledge and respect for one another's cultures.

A passion for history together with her fascination with the interplay of cultures East and West are the backdrop to her life and give this book its unique perspective. They inform and define all her activities — successes and disappointments — that have become the threads that form the fabric of Kai-Yin's life journey shared in this book. We are invited to join her in the highs and lows and twists and turns of the life of an independent Chinese woman in the global world of the late twentieth and early twenty-first centuries.

Jane Rapley
Professor Emerita
Central Saint Martins UAL

PROLOGUE

CARTIER NEW YORK

It was a brisk April day in New York City in the late 1970s. I had been living in the city for several months, looking for a way to create a future for myself, perhaps for a means to correct the past, but most certainly for a way to earn enough money to live on – more than my monthly pay that netted after tax US$475 from my job as a public affairs assistant at Time Inc. My chosen path was design, specifically the design of jewelry, but New York is a big and unforgiving city, and months of tramping the streets with a bag in my hand, offering my items to the many stores in uptown Manhattan, had elicited nothing more than polite smiles and the patronizing comment, 'That's interesting, but not for us'.

I was a young woman from Hong Kong who had recently seen her family lose a fortune and fall on hard times. Instead of the future I suppose I had long expected as an offspring of the well-to-do, my first job as a newspaper reporter was not promising. A later job as Assistant Public Relations Officer at the relatively new Mandarin Hotel that opened in 1963 afforded me a chance to be connected to the wider world. In the course of my work, I had the occasion to meet the famous and the distinguished – film director David Lean, writer Graham Greene and explorer Thor Heyerdahl, to name a few. My stroke of good fortune was meeting James Linen III, Chairman of the Executive Committee of Time Inc. at The Mandarin. He offered me a job in New York and so it was that I found myself in the Big Apple, occupying an upscale apartment at 470 Park Avenue on the corner of 57th Street, provided by another kind friend I had met on the job at The Mandarin. The daily commute between Time's midtown offices and that apartment created the opportunity I needed – one that prepared me for my next career.

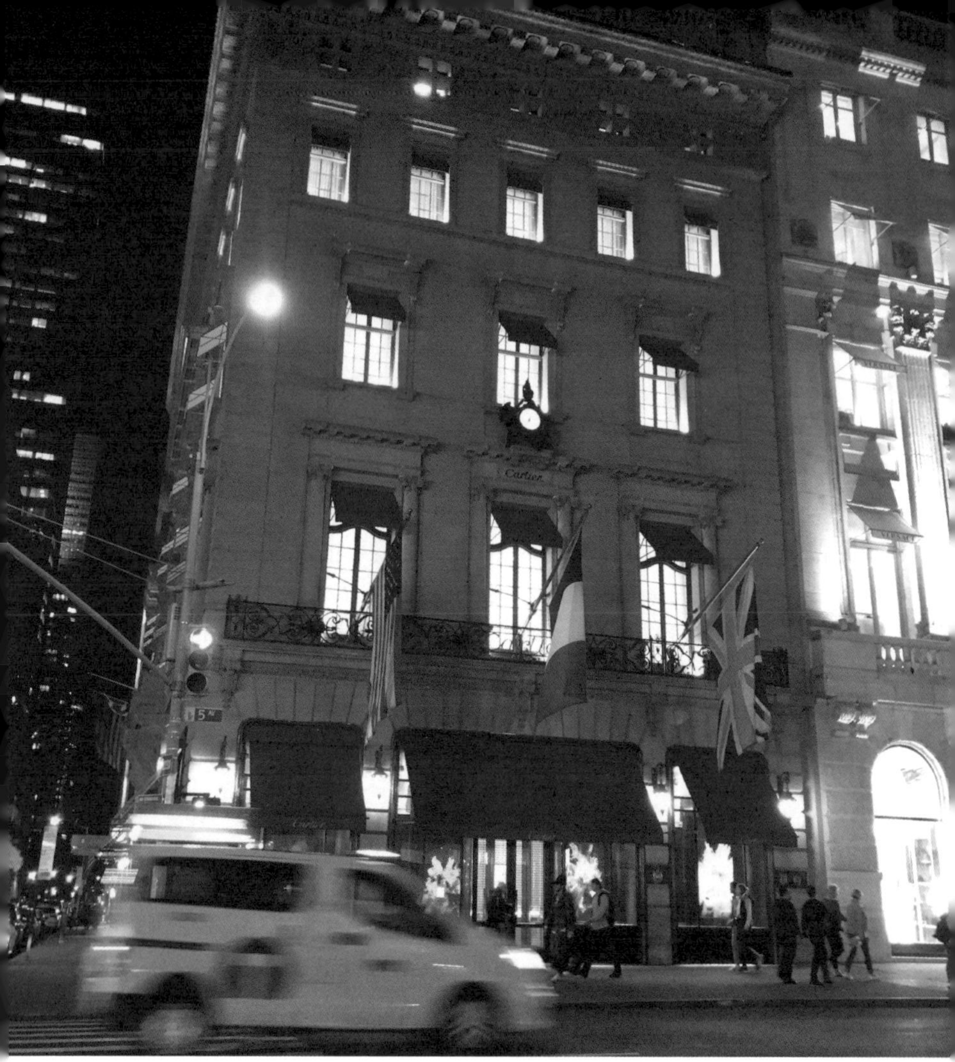

Cartier New York. Built in 1904, declared a landmark in 1984

Every day, I walked west along 57th Street, turned the corner into Fifth Avenue, looked into the alluring vitrines at Tiffany's and continued south along the avenue, which was dotted with the most luxurious retail stores in the world, the headquarters of some of the world's best-known corporations, and filled with sophisticated well-to-do shoppers. The next landmarks I passed were the high-end department stores Bonwit Teller, then Saks Fifth Avenue, and then Rockefeller Center. At 51st Street, I would turn right and walk west to the corner of Sixth Avenue, and the Time-Life Building, where I worked.

New York was the style capital of the world, and I studied the merchandise in each of the shop windows that I passed, and sometimes went in and browsed the counter displays, gazing at the accessories laid out to entice well-heeled New York shoppers. These were shops selling the latest fashionable items to the elite. The depth of the culture that these items and stores represented was a huge inspiration for me. And of course, the designs. Every day as I walked, my brain was working, searching for what I could offer to these people that they didn't already have. Once in a while I would take refuge in St Patrick's Cathedral to ease my anxiety and recharge my strength. Time was moving on and I was desperately hoping that the jewelry designs I had been working on would interest someone soon.

As usual on that day in April, I had samples of my jewelry collection with me, and a specific destination in mind — the Cartier store on the corner of 52nd Street and Fifth Avenue, the center of Midtown. Over the months, I had considered the different levels of the jewelry market and decided the best way for me to gain entrée was to concentrate on the high-end stores. I had developed two ranges of jewelry, a line of eye-catching necklaces with Chinese and Central Asian antique components, and a range of necklaces with coordinating earrings in colorful semi-precious stones set in sterling silver. The latter were affordable and particularly easy to coordinate with fashion. And there were other sales channel possibilities — department stores, costume jewelry boutiques and more 'progressive' places like Henri Bendel, a store with a unique collection offering Western antiques as well as accessories. But something pushed me to aspire to the top of the jewelry and accessories retail chain.

As it happened, it was the last year that Cartier New York was operated independently from its Paris corporate parent, and what happened to me that day could never happen now. The Cartier store was, and is, magnificent. Entering was a breathtaking experience; the grand limestone mansion was built in 1904 and quite rightly declared a New York landmark in 1984. Grace Kelly had shopped there, and so had Jackie Kennedy. Pierre Cartier, the grandson of the founder, had established the New York store and named it

Cartier's American Artworks. It represented the pinnacle of the traditional jewelry and accessories trade that I aspired to join. Around that time, some investors were looking to take over Cartier and reinvigorate it; another old family going through troubled times. The investors, Silvermatch, bought Cartier Paris and soon after took control of Cartier New York and Cartier London, and many of its practices were abandoned, including the one that allowed unknown designers such as myself to have a chance.

'Open Vendor Day', which took place once every ten days, was the kind of opportunity that could only happen in America. I queued up at Cartier on such a day, when a would-be vendor could walk in and meet with a buyer to make a sales pitch. When my turn came, Mr Charles Dishman, the General Manager, viewed the twelve necklaces I showed to him, each of them coordinated assemblies of Chinese antique beads and curiosities. I had gone to New York armed with US$5,000 as seed money, and a drawer-full of antique Chinese and Central Asian beads and carvings, small items made of ivory, bronze and antique jade, ornaments dating back many centuries, and 'finger pleasers', as they were called by the collectors and literati of old China and Japan. These I had obtained on my trips to Hong Kong's Cat Street. But, I thought, why not enhance their specialness with coordinating elements and make them a part of everyday life as pieces of adornment? That was the thinking behind the items that I showed him. And after requesting some modifications, lessening, in my view, their attractiveness, he accepted ten pieces out of the twelve.

I was launched! It was serendipity. And it was luck. The time was right for something different and exciting in the world of high-end accessories. Bold designs, old meets new, East meets West. That Cartier experience, it turned out, was ultimately just a one-off, but the joy and encouragement I gained from having a collection accepted by Cartier provided me with the confidence and drive to continue to create more pieces to adorn people with taste. As David Pilling, Asian Editor of the *Financial Times*, once wrote, 'She makes history wearable.' And consciously or unconsciously, that is what I did.

I have designed many things, but more than anything I have devoted energy and love in taking exquisite, meaningful and forgotten items from the past, the disparate and overlooked leftovers of beautiful artistic creations of bygone eras, and repurposing them, allowing them to live again in a reinterpreted arrangement that is modern and wearable and therefore enhances life. That has been my focus and my proud achievement.

Seeing the limited appeal of antique pieces — partly due to their relatively high cost — I soon turned to designing a new range of jewelry using natural and colorful, but not expensive, semi-precious stones. The success of this new range of semi-precious jewelry made my name in the U.S., the U.K., Japan, Singapore and Hong Kong. Suzy Menkes, the influential style critic for the *International Herald Tribune*, wrote on May 7, 1992: 'She bridges the gap between precious and fashion jewelry — she is a pioneer.'

That was what I had set out to do. I saw a need for this direction for jewelry — colorful, real and affordable — and grasped an opportunity to provide what working women needed. But I also wanted to be successful in an independent and unique way. I wanted to be different.

My life as a designer has followed a very unusual trajectory for a young woman from Hong Kong. I was schooled in English Medieval and European Renaissance history, and only later discovered my own heritage while collecting Chinese artifacts and ornaments, learning about the origins and background of these pieces and coordinating them into wearable art. What was it that drove me to carry that bag containing coordinated antique ornaments to sell around New York? The short answer is that I had to make a living after my family reversal of fortune. But I also believed in my goal and mission, and that my designs would serve a good purpose in life. Worthy antique pieces would be given a new spirit and be repurposed back to contemporary life. And the semi-precious range that I created, well-coordinated and interpreted, did come to initiate a new language of 'affordable luxury' in accessories to enhance both fashion and our lives.

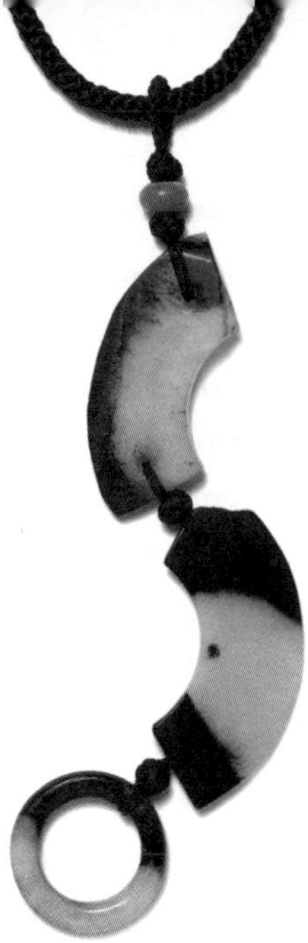

PART I

'The path to success is talent, creativity, and drive.
Often creativity is a balance of skills, beliefs,
and experimentation…along with a certain daring.'

—Jane Rapley

FAMILY & GROWING UP

1

Family & Growing Up

The story of my family, like that of many families in Hong Kong, is of an escape from the villages of the Pearl River delta in southern China — escape to a city offering opportunity and growth, and administered by a laissez-faire government that allowed new arrivals to just get on with building their lives, as long as they kept their place.

My grandfather, Lo Yu Tong (羅玉堂), was born in 1885 in a small village in Saichiu, near the Pearl River estuary. Family lore relates that my grandfather arrived in Hong Kong around the age of ten in 1895 and attended Queen's College, at the time the only school in the British colony where Chinese could learn English. A number of Chinese who attended Queen's College rose to prominent positions in the Legislative Council and in banking and commerce. Many of the details of his early years, of how he built his business, are now lost, but we do know that he founded a trading company in Central District off Queen's Road Central, in a narrow alley called Chiu Lung Street — the "Street of Bright Prosperity". It runs parallel to Pedder Street, which in those days was close to being the western boundary of British colonial Hong Kong. To the west of that were Chinese people, Chinese businesses and almost no Europeans. We owned a building at 19 Chiu Lung Street called Nga Men Chiu Loong Hong (雅文超隆行), and later my father ran a trading company from there, and my mother had a travel agency in the same building. They have wrecked the street now in many ways with rebuilding, but still I go there often. I feel a connection; it is like having a small communion with my grandfather and my parents.

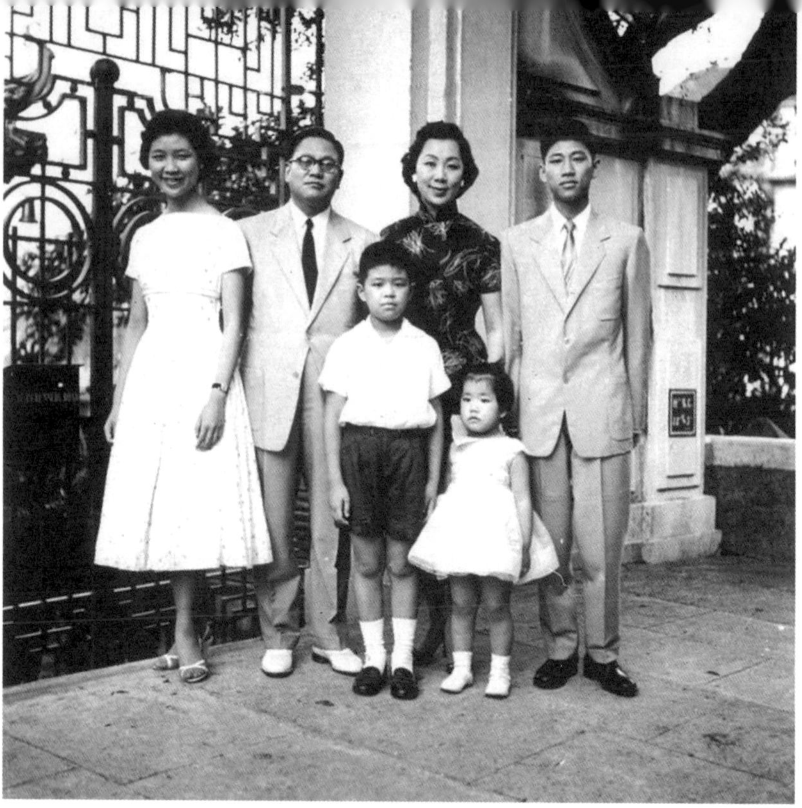

The Lo family in 1955:
father, mother, me, Robert and younger Anthony and Marina

Grandfather was an ambitious man, and in the early years of the twentieth century, Hong Kong business offered opportunities for those who grasped them. He expanded fast and soon achieved the position of comprador for the Hong Kong branch of a major British bank. Compradors were a strange kind of 'go-between' or 'fixer' for European businessmen who would not understand the whys and wherefores of getting things done in Hong Kong and the other treaty ports in China. These foreign bankers and traders with such firms as Butterfield & Swire and Jardine Matheson did not learn the local language or customs and instead relied heavily on the indispensable go-between compradors, many of whom became wealthy and influential as a result. The comprador go-betweens typically took a percentage of all deals, purchases and sales by the company they worked with, and also might often arrange parallel deals, leveraging their positions to their own direct benefit. But they took a proportion of the risk, too, and if a deal went wrong, they would suffer. It was a practice that one day would have implications for my family.

My grandfather, followed by my father, held the post of Comprador at the Mercantile Bank of India, London and China (有利銀行), one of the British Empire's important financial institutions, until it was taken over by the Hongkong and Shanghai Banking Corporation (today's HSBC) in 1959. He made enough money from his trading operations to build a very large house for his family at 17-19 Kennedy Road, or 'Second Road', the highest level on which Chinese were allowed to live. There was a saying that 'Dogs and Chinamen could not advance beyond this level', and from there up to the Peak was reserved for the British and other foreigners. His friends were some of the most successful Chinese businessmen in Hong Kong. His close friend, Lee Hysan, erected the grandest compound on Kennedy Road and bought a lot of land in Causeway Bay which later turned out to be very valuable.

In the 1930s, my grandfather founded a brand of cologne and toiletries called 'Baak Ga Lee', and I remember when I was young going to his quite sizeable shop, beyond the Western Market, close to the Wing On Department Store on Des Voeux Road. That cologne was redolent of old Hong Kong, or maybe old Hong Kong was redolent with it. Cologne was very important in those days, especially in the hot summer, and the top brand was Kwong Sang Hong's Two Girls Brand, whose advertisements in the 1930s featured twin sisters in cheongsams. But ours was also a popular brand. I have vague but wonderful memories of that shop and the odors that pervaded it, so much a part of those far-off days of another Hong Kong before I left to go to school in England.

My father was born in 1912 in Hong Kong, and my mother was born around 1920 in the port city of Swatow (Shantou), one of the first opium shipment points along the China coast in the early 19th century. It was opened as a Treaty Port in the 1840s after the first Opium War and it remained an important city well into the 20th century. My mother's grandfather was for a time during the 19th century the governor of Swatow, but she did not like to talk too much about her family history because it was a typical story of a family in abrupt decline. She had no birth certificate, but I do know that her father attended Columbia University in New York, and that a close relative once served as Chinese ambassador to Washington, D.C. Again, in another age.

My maternal grandmother came from a family that was well educated. One prominent member of the family was Mr Ho Kai who was instrumental in the founding of the former Hong Kong Kai Tak airport, which was partly named after him. But over the years, the grandeur faded for that family too. My grandfather, my mother's father, did no work for the last twenty-five years of his life; as a result, he had no money and provided no support for the family. They lived in Spring Garden Lane in Wanchai, in a narrow house of four stories plus an attic, down the hill from our family mansion. My mother's aunt was Dr. Eleanor Thom, who in 1924 became the third woman to graduate from the University of Hong Kong. I believe she was the first Hong Kong woman to get a Ph.D. from Columbia University. She later became a senior official in the Hong Kong Education Department, and we all used to look up to her. She was very bossy, but she liked me because I was a good student and she helped to find me, and my brothers and sister too, places in schools in England.

My paternal grandfather's Number One son was by his concubine. In the spirit of generosity and largesse, my grandmother welcomed this firstborn as Number One son, giving him legitimacy. Number Two son was my father. The number three child was a daughter, the one and only daughter, and my only aunt. She married Patrick Luk, whose father was the Chief Secretary of T.V. Soong, China's finance minister for many years, brother-in-law of Chiang Kai-shek and a member of the Nationalist government through the war against Japan and until the communist takeover in 1949. Patrick Luk was a man of great savoir-faire and his sister, Christina Luk, was a famed beauty. She married Harold Lee, the grandson of Lee Hysan, my grandfather's good friend. The Lee family continues to be very prominent and their Hysan Development Company still owns a huge portion of Causeway Bay, including the Lee Gardens area and the Lee Theatre.

Then came Number Three son, who lived most of his life in America. He joined the U.S. Air Force but moved back to Hong Kong in his later years. Number Five son, my Number Five Uncle — all Chinese families are organized strictly by hierarchy and rank, and people refer to each other as such, not by name— died young.

Number Six, meanwhile, studied in Lingnan University in Canton (Guangzhou), where grandfather also had a huge mansion. I went there once when I was very young and marveled at the size of it. I remember the house so well. It was a typical Cantonese residence with a series of rooms: a vestibule, a spacious room where the footmen would hang around, then a main entry room that could park sedan 'carriages', and then a main parlor. It was a Chinese-style mansion unlike our Western-style mansion on Kennedy Road.

Number Six uncle later joined the People's Liberation Army and went to fight in the Korean War. His girlfriend was the middle of three sisters whose names were Cheung Kong-yat, Cheung Luen-so and Cheung Ding-mei, which meant respectively 'Fight the Japanese', 'Alliance with the Soviet Union' and 'Conquer the Americans'. He married 'Fight the Japanese'. He used to tell the story of how one night he was stationed on a hilltop in North Korea with the wind so piercing that he decided there and then to get out of the army. He found a way to go back to school in Guangzhou, and in the 1970s somehow made it to Germany and joined the faculty of a university in Munich. He married a German woman and finally got his qualification as a pediatrician in Glasgow, Scotland, and died in Munich.

My senior uncle, the Number One son by the concubine, married the daughter of the man who had the mansion opposite ours at 19 Kennedy Road. He was a leading collector of antiques. Our house was filled with these so-called antiques, most of which turned out to be fakes or not 'of the period' when it came time to divide all the stuff up. But then we were always full of hope. Number One son had five sons and three daughters, eight children in all, while we were just four. In the end, that branch all settled in Canada.

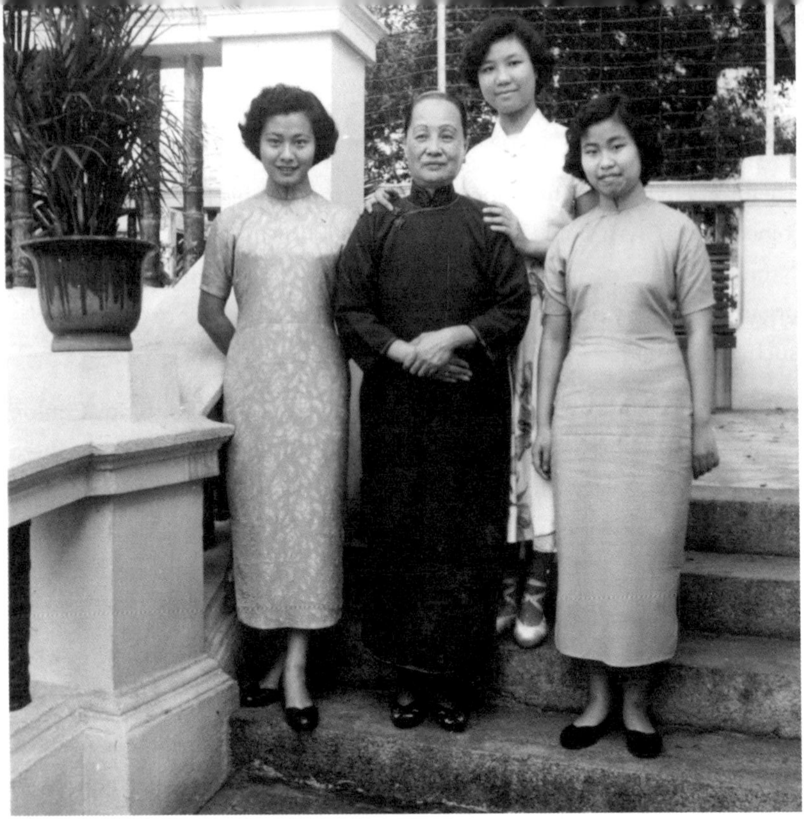

Grandma with her bound feet,
standing near the front entrance of the house, 1954,
with me on the left and two cousins on the right

When I was young and living in that great mansion, we ate on most days with Grandfather. The other branch had their meals separately. When there was a family gathering, for instance for Grandmother's or Grandfather's birthday, there would be at least two or three large round tables sitting ten people each, and there were always a lot of relatives who wanted to come because my grandfather was wealthy and would give generous *lai see* packets. When grandfather was presiding, we were not allowed to speak. 'You don't speak when you sleep and you don't speak when you eat,' was the directive. It was all very stern. We all had to behave. I remember our grandparents sitting on both sides of their *kang*, a traditional wooden dais. Grandpa would be lying on the *kang*, not to be disturbed, while Grandma was always sitting there, always in the same position, which allowed her to see all movements on that floor.

The Lo family today is composed of four generations, as fixed by my grandfather. The family motto was decreed to be 'Hing Kai Ga Xing', meaning something like 'to enhance the family's reputation'. And these four words were and are used to fix the middle names of all people in the family depending upon their generation, which was a common practice in old China, particularly with prominent families. The four generations started with my father's generation, for whom the middle name was always Hing. My father was called Lo Hing-kwong and the brothers were Lo Hing-lung, Lo Hing-ban and Lo Hing-keung. I am of the 'Kai' generation — I am Kai-Yin, my brothers are Kai-Leung and Kai-Yiu and my sister is Kai-Man. 'Ga' is for the next generation, and we haven't got into the 'Xing' generation yet. But those four words — Hing Kai Ga Xing — provide in their way the framework and reflect the aspirations of the family.

My memories of childhood are of a 'complicated' family. We were a big family with lots of stories, intrigues and tensions. There were separate quarters for each branch of the family, derived from the two wives. We tried to maintain a peaceful and harmonious front. For the times, that arrangement was normal; a standard big Chinese family with all sorts of pressures but trying to maintain harmony while the grandparents were alive.

My father, while 'Number Two Son', was the first son born to grandfather's legitimate wife, so he and we, his four children, were eligible to occupy the top floor adjacent to our grandparents' quarters. In our generation, the eldest is Robert and I am number two. Robert and I are very close. I never married — that's just the way it has turned out — while Robert is married to lovely Sally who is English, born in London. They have two adorable daughters and four grandchildren, whom I love. Sally was the bravest girl because she came out to live in Hong Kong after marrying Robert, living in that huge house, in a completely alien world. She didn't know a soul in Hong Kong.

My next brother, Anthony, first went to Millfield, an independent 'upper crust' school in Somerset, England. Then after our change in circumstances, he worked his way through college at McGill University in Montreal, ran a restaurant for a time and later became an investment banker. Lastly there is Marina, the youngest. She went to the same convent school as I did in England, and became an active school prefect, atoning for all my shortcomings as a non-participant in school activities. Both Anthony and Marina grew up basically in Canada, another world, while Robert and I remained in the twin orbits of England and Hong Kong.

You will notice that all of them have English names. I was once given the name Sally but I didn't like it, and when I went to the U.K. I always asked people to call me Kai-Yin. It was my decision to not use my English name. I cannot explain why I did so, but in retrospect I suppose it was a signal of respect for the Chinese culture of which we were a part, no matter how much we strove to be English or international. For me, as a cross-cultural scholar, I all the more cherish my Chinese name, which means 'to open up all that is beautiful and good'.

OUR BIG HOUSE

2

Our Big House

By 1914, my grandfather had made enough money to build our grand family mansion on Kennedy Road, a winding east-west road halfway up the mountainside on Hong Kong Island that fronts northwards above the crowded streets below. It was just the first level up the hill, and it was the highest point at which Chinese were then allowed

The façade of the Lo residence, built in 1914

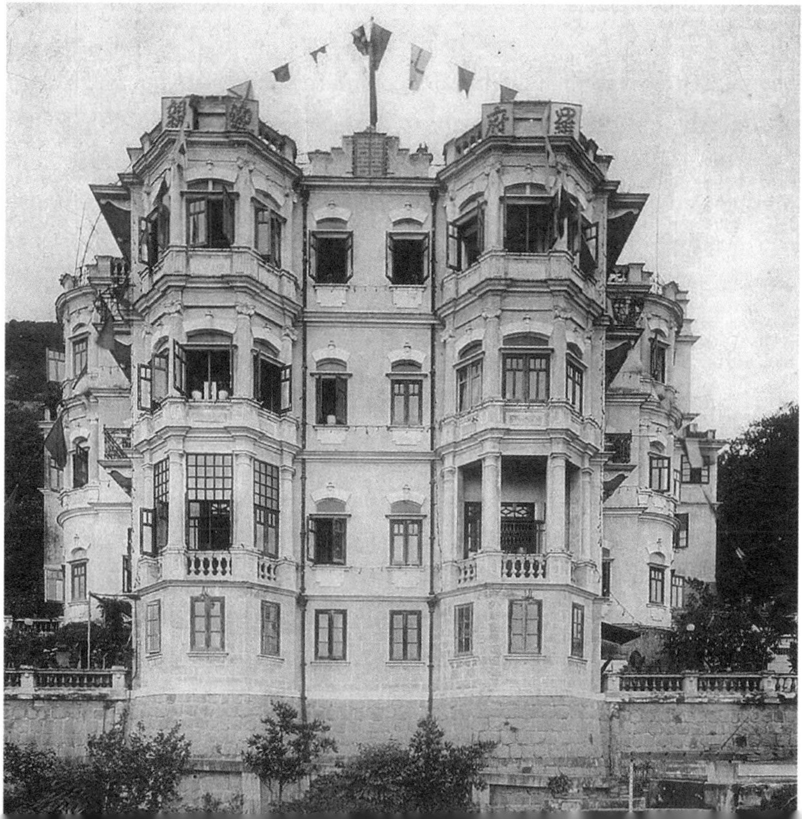

to live. The Lo house was one of a number of great homes built by wealthy Chinese merchants and businessmen along the road – the Second Road, as it was called – and also along Conduit Road at about the same level up the hill but on the other side of Garden Road, the main thoroughfare to the Peak. Only one of those great mansions is left today as I write – the Ngan mansion, which is derelict. But in those early decades of the twentieth century, the prominent Chinese families of Hong Kong all lived along Kennedy Road and on Conduit Road on the same level.

In all sorts of ways, conscious and unconscious, our ancestral house and what it stood for has impacted my life. The scale it represented, the traditions it encompassed, the social status it implied. And its loss, too. Our house was constructed between the years 1914 and 1918 in an unusual but nevertheless grand fashion. It was complex in structure with three formal stories, a roof garden and two side extensions, each with a small garden. The two giant wings on either side of the main building were each four stories high, plus an expansive and beautiful roof which offered panoramic views of Wanchai below and the harbor and Kowloon beyond. There were two giant water ceramic containers on the roof in case of fire. Oh God, the very thought of it, to think that we could quench a fire with that amount of water! At the very bottom of the structure were pigsties and quarters for the servants. Below that, to the north of the house and heading down the steep hill towards the streets of Wanchai, were our layered gardens, which were extensive. The lowest part of the house would have been about halfway down the 253 steps from Kennedy Road to Queen's Road East. The main entrance to the mansion was a grand gate on Kennedy Road with another shorter set of steps leading down to the front door of the mansion, on the third story of the main structure.

The two wings, east and west, each had different street numbers. My grandmother and grandfather lived on the fourth level at number 19 while we lived at number 17 on the same level. My father being the eldest son by grandmother meant we were eligible to share the same floor as our grandparents. These strict hierarchical rules applied to all those who lived in that house through all the decades, right through to the mid-1970s.

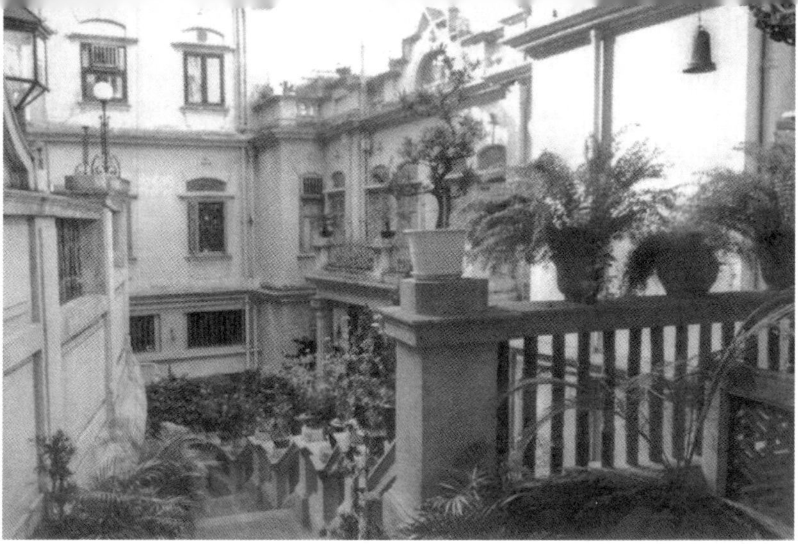

The interior garden leading to the third floor of the big house

In between the two wings, nestling between the grand façade and Kennedy Road, was a small courtyard, and there were gardens on the sides, and an adjunct at the back. We had a magnificent magnolia tree just behind the kitchens. The mansion, in short, was a world unto itself.

At the age of fourteen, when I had proved myself to be a good student, I moved out of the room shared with my brother and was given my own room. I was studious and my grades were always good, and my grandfather was proud of me, and always kind. It was a traditional Chinese family, but I was favored despite being a girl. When I got into Cambridge, they were so proud of me.

I moved into a small annex room above the kitchen, and I was allowed to decorate it, and make it my own little place. That meant a great deal to me, and it was the first time I had the opportunity to display some sort of design sense. I was already interested in *chinoiserie* — Europe's interpretation of Chinese design — and that was in a way to be the theme of my room. Blue was my preferred color in those days, and light blue was the dominant color of the room. It had to be light blue. Medium blue represents death in Chinese tradition — it is the color found at funerals. But light blue was safe. I slept there and read there until I left for school in the U.K. Now, I don't use blue because my fortune-teller forbids me. These days, shades of red are my color, and who can say how fate and good fortune really work?

Later, when I came back from England, I convinced my grandfather to allow me to move out of that room and convert the small set of rooms above the garage into a mews apartment. Again, I did all the decorating myself, and to this day I am still proud of its decor.

On the third floor of the big house, in from the main entrance, were large and quite gloomy reception rooms furnished with dark wooden furniture. Then, down one flight of stairs, the second floor was occupied by the eldest son's large family with seven children; they had both sides of one floor and also part of the basement.

For a long time after the house was sold and everything changed, family members blamed father for the loss of the family fortune. For some time, as I was building my brand, many of them also thought I was too high-profile. There was uneasiness about it. But in the end, in our various ways, we all turned out well enough. My second cousin, Kai-Hei, an architect,

Front entrance of the Lo family house at 17-19 Kennedy Road

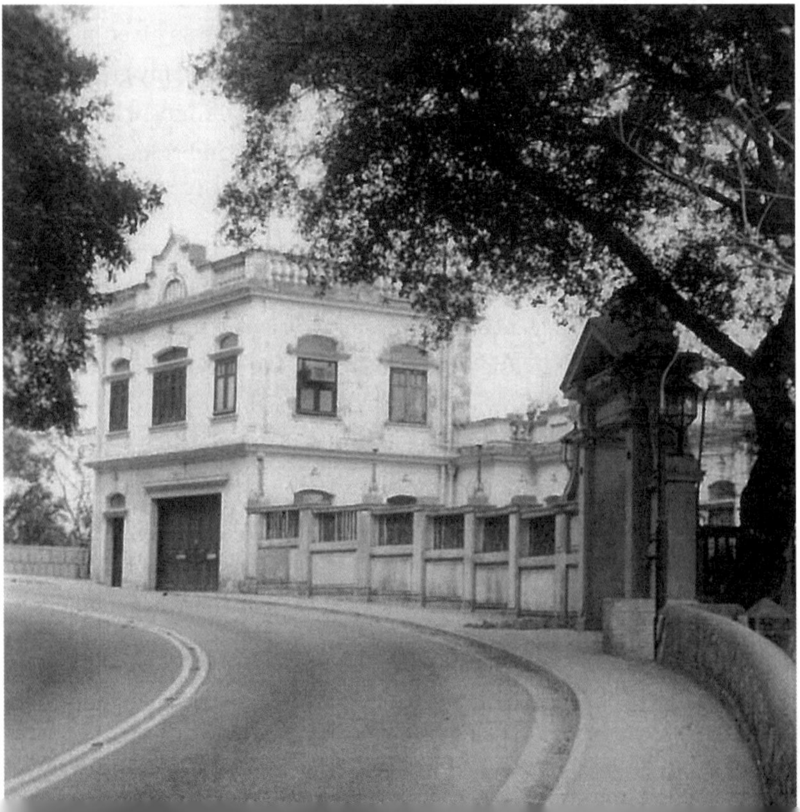

was the mediator, and my younger brother Anthony contributed to a better relationship. They both lived in Canada, and they have some kind of affinity.

They play golf together. So, in recent years we have taken the trouble to organize periodic meals and meetings as members of one big family, and the tensions now seem so long ago. The past is finally the past. I hope the bond of family will continue to strengthen.

Life on Kennedy Road amongst the large houses erected by the successful Chinese merchants was rich and interesting and we, the children of the Chinese elite, had total freedom to run around and explore. Everything we wanted or needed, including my primary school, St Francis Co-educational School, was close by. Next to us to the west was a huge bamboo grove, I remember. Then further along Kennedy Road came Tung Chi College, a middle school, which was set up in the 1930s.

The biggest family mansion on Kennedy Road was that of the Lee family, the descendants of Lee Hysan who also controlled much of the real estate below us on Queen's Road East as well as in Causeway Bay. And next to our house on the eastern side was the Wu family mansion and estate. After our family fortunes collapsed, Gordon Wu, the owner of Hopewell Holdings, bought our house and the land it sat on. He wanted to buy Mrs Wu's vast garden and house as well but she refused to sell it and also for a long time refused to die. But they waited and eventually, of course, she did die. Hopewell Centre was built on the land that had been our mansion and garden, and today you can walk off Kennedy Road onto the seventeenth floor of the Hopewell Tower and take the elevator down to ground level. That is a public thoroughfare down to Queen's Road East, which is a passage I often take, as do many others who want a shortcut. But I understand they plan to expand and redevelop the existing Hopewell Centre into what will be the biggest single structure on Hong Kong Island. Hopewell Holdings, owned by Gordon Wu and his family, will own all the land from our old house to as far along as St. Francis' Canossian College, and then a great edifice will be erected, and historic Kennedy Road will be a massive thoroughfare. Any vestige of old Hong Kong will be gone. At least in my mind's eye, I can still see our mansion, the sloping gardens and the bamboo grove next door.

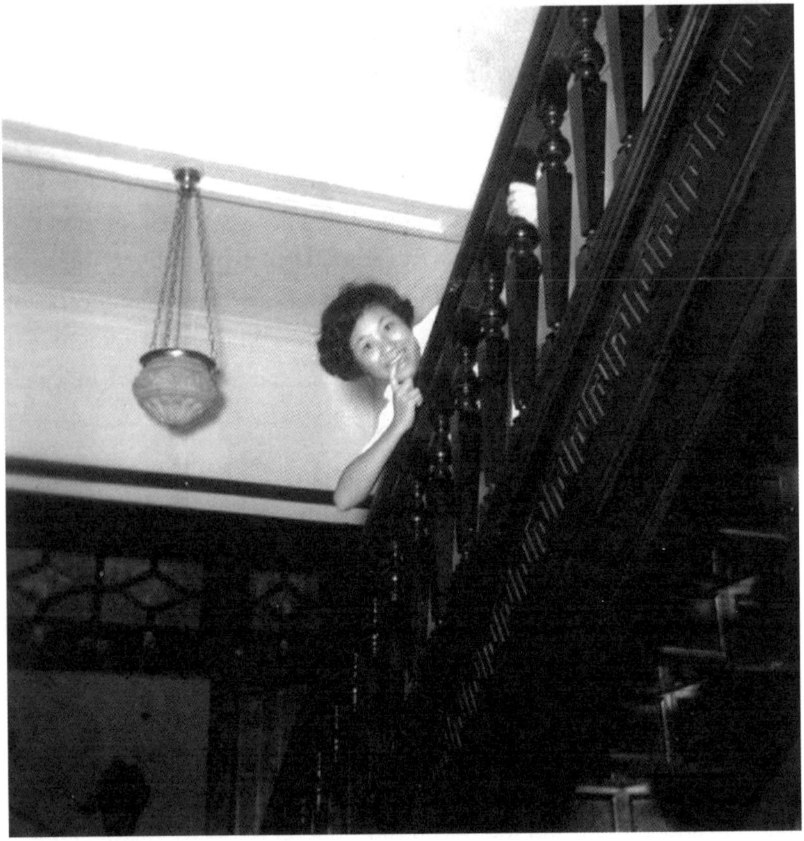

On the long staircase running up to the fourth floor of our house

OLD HONG KONG & WANCHAI

3

Old Hong Kong & Wanchai

Hong Kong is the most extraordinary and unlikely mixture of cultures, and I am a product of that mix. The Cantonese 'Lingnan' culture dominates – Cantonese in essence but more – and there are so many other strands visible in the tapestry of this city. The English colonial influence was of course very strong, and the international trade and finance which the British colonial administration welcomed and encouraged attracted and nurtured people like my grandfather and many others, particularly after the turn of the century; and most significantly from the 1960s onwards when the manufacturing class grew powerful and increasingly entrepreneurial, converting the land on which their factories were built into huge housing developments and prospering with it.

Hong Kong is a very special place. It used to be called 'a borrowed place on borrowed time,' a phrase attributed to journalist Richard Hughes, and it was and to some extent remains an anomaly. The interplay between southern Chinese culture and colonial British culture was pronounced. Chinese culture pulls in one direction and the framework of the political system, which influenced the social system created fundamentally by the British, pulls in the other. An interesting historical example of the ironies was the fiftieth jubilee anniversary of Queen Victoria's coronation in 1887. The British residents of the Colony decided that the moment should be marked in some way and held a meeting to discuss proposals from which the Chinese were excluded. The final decision – to create a park in the Queen's name – failed to come to fruition. The Chinese community then held their own meeting. One prominent Chinese businessman declared that the Chinese traders and merchants in the Colony 'ought to take some steps to show their gratitude for the protection afforded them,' and the meeting decided to mark the anniversary by funding and founding a Chinese Chamber of Commerce in honor of Her Majesty, an institution that after undergoing transformation is still operating. The British, meanwhile, managed to come up with a memorial statue. The lesson is that the British provided the law and order and framework but it was the energy and entrepreneurship of the Chinese that made Hong Kong what it became.

The British established themselves in Hong Kong in the 1840s, with the commercial heart of the colony in today's Central and military encampments and a naval base just to the east in today's Admiralty. So many of the old buildings in central Hong Kong have now been demolished, but there is still a sense of the past on the streets, retaining a trace of the world I knew when I was growing up. Reclamation has gradually moved the shoreline north into the harbor and halfway to Kowloon, or so it seems. But the feel of the city overall, and the international sense of style and dynamism that was evident in that small area of central Hong Kong, is very much evident today. The energy on Pedder Street and the surrounding area and the bustle of the markets of Wanchai have not changed much in all these many decades until recently.

Hong Kong in the 1950s and 1960s was a city with a population of three or four million people. Once home to nothing more than fishing villages on the south China coast, mercantile values sharpened by British colonial discipline and efficiency contributed to growth and prosperity. The waterfront area in Central around The Mandarin is vitally important to the history of Hong Kong. Until well into the twentieth century, the Chinese were effectively barred from this area, and could live and establish businesses only to the east of the British military — in Wanchai and beyond — or to the west, beyond Pedder Street. Aberdeen Street was once the line of demarcation. Chinese were not allowed to tread and certainly not to build east of this point. The basement of PMQ on Aberdeen Street shows a stone bearing this sign.

My grandfather operated in both areas, buying property and running businesses both to the west and to the east of Central. The hillsides above Wanchai were also opened to Chinese, but only up to the level of Kennedy Road where our home was situated, and on Conduit Road, about the same distance up the hill to the west. After that, it was Europeans-only territory.

Hong Kong has been a part of my life in all sorts of ways, big and small, from the beginning. But amazingly in terms of my jewelry design business, race and culture have been for the most part almost irrelevant. I became a brand first in the city of New York, and then spread throughout the United States, then to Singapore, Japan and London and other international markets. I suppose it is because I worked hard to make the designs international from a style and cultural perspective, with only a hint of Oriental flavor, making the designs distinctive and highly wearable.

The streets of Wanchai also contain much history: so much that is relevant in terms of understanding how Hong Kong came to be, and the dynamic connection between the staid British colonials in Central and the Chinese and their specialized shops of seal carvers and book makers and various

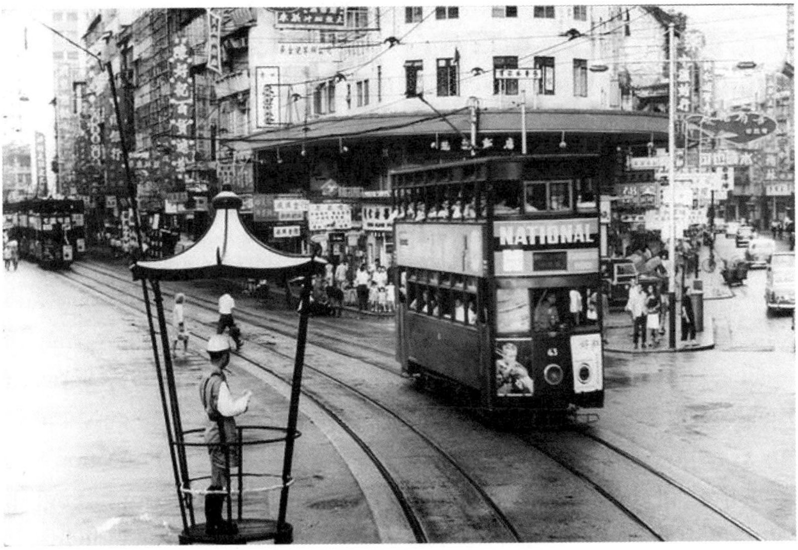

Wanchai scene: it could be today, except for the policeman's kiosk

small businesses that operated in the teeming alleys and byways on either side of Queen's Road East, the main road in the Wanchai area. Until the 1920s, the tram track along Johnston Road was the harbor's edge, and on the northern side of the road was a mass of sampans and lighters, ships loaded with goods from China, a scene exploding with activity. The roads leading south off Johnston Road up the incline towards Queen's Road East — Ship Street, Amoy Street and the rest — were filled with the hustle and bustle of shops selling items servicing the ships. Still further up the hill is a maze of smaller streets, including Schooner Street and Star Street. And above that Kennedy Road. The stone steps next to our house, on which we used to run up and down to Queen's Road East (I believe there were 253 of them), are still there. Near the school I attended, now renamed St Francis' Canossian College, there was another set of steps connecting Kennedy Road and Queen's Road East below. Most of the other children walked up those steps to get to school from the warrens of Wanchai. But not me. I walked to school along Kennedy Road.

Still further up the hill is Nam Koo Terrace, not far from our old family home, which includes a famous 'ghost house' that was a dormitory for St Francis students and, for a time during the war, barracks for the Japanese army. Gordon Wu, the real estate entrepreneur, I gather, chose it to be the second phase of Hopewell Centre, but the plan was scrapped after residents strongly objected, and it remains today an historical site and a testament to how healthy Hong Kong remains as a society. Those in power do not always get things the way they want them.

St Francis' Canossian College was founded in 1869 by a group of Italian nuns, the Canossian Daughters of Charity, as a hospital, orphanage and school combined, and they did such a good job that the government assigned them the land on which the school still operates, between Kennedy Road and the level below. Most of the pupils were girls, but in my era, there were already some boys also in attendance. Education was in both English and Chinese, but for me it was the basis of my English education. The alumni of the school include many significant individuals in Hong Kong society, including quite a number of politicians, amongst them our Chief Executive Carrie Lam.

Our family may have been wealthy, but we were not among the wealthiest in Hong Kong by a long way. The Ngan family opposite operated the China Motor Bus Company. Then there was the powerful Lee family. We used to go to the Lee mansion every Chinese New Year to pay our respects because Lee Hysan had been my grandfather's very good friend. They say Lee made his fortune by buying Jardine Matheson's land holdings in Causeway Bay, amongst many deals. He was killed in 1928 at the age of just thirty-six, shot in Central by assassins who approached him on the street. One of the assassins was immediately killed and the other escaped to China. Supposedly my grandfather saw it happen. The family story is that grandfather and Lee had lunch together every day for some fifteen years.

As my father grew up, he followed my grandfather all the time, shadowing him to learn the comprador business. For a long, long time he walked three steps behind my grandfather. Mr Lee, by contrast, sent his sons abroad to be educated. He had four wives, and Number One son, Richard Lee, was by the second wife. Richard went to the U.K. and later became a very prominent person in Hong Kong society, serving on the Legislative and Executive Councils in the 1950s and 1960s. He died in 1983. Number Three son was Harold Lee and he attended Pembroke College at Oxford and was extremely urbane, speaking English with a pronounced upper-crust British accent. He had no wish to be part of the Hong Kong government, and the Taipan of Jardine Matheson, Hugh Barton, asked Harold to be the first chairman of The Mandarin Hotel, which was wise because he had exactly the right stature and appeal. It was Harold who chose the name The Mandarin for the hotel. And in his role as chairman of The Mandarin, he indirectly gave me my big chance in life to be connected with the wider world.

Lee Hysan's Number Four son, J.S., was a scholar who went to Yenching University in Beijing, parts of which were later merged into Peking University, and was a classmate of the furniture scholar Wang Shixiang who wrote a thoughtful inscription in beautiful calligraphy in my furniture book, *Classical and Vernacular Chinese Furniture in the Living Environment* (1998), about which more later. J.S. was a noted scholar who amassed a very fine collection of Chinese paintings and antiques and was instrumental in founding the Chinese University of Hong Kong. He donated part of his collection to the university museum. When I launched my furniture book, I asked J.S. to officiate at the launch event, although he never liked the limelight. I asked him to do it for his old friend, my father, and his classmate Wang Shixiang who wrote the foreword for the book, and he did.

But to go back to Harold Lee, he married Christina Lee, a sister of Patrick Luk who was the husband of our aunt. Christina was a great beauty who had attended Mills College in California. Her grace and savoir-faire well complemented her husband's stature.

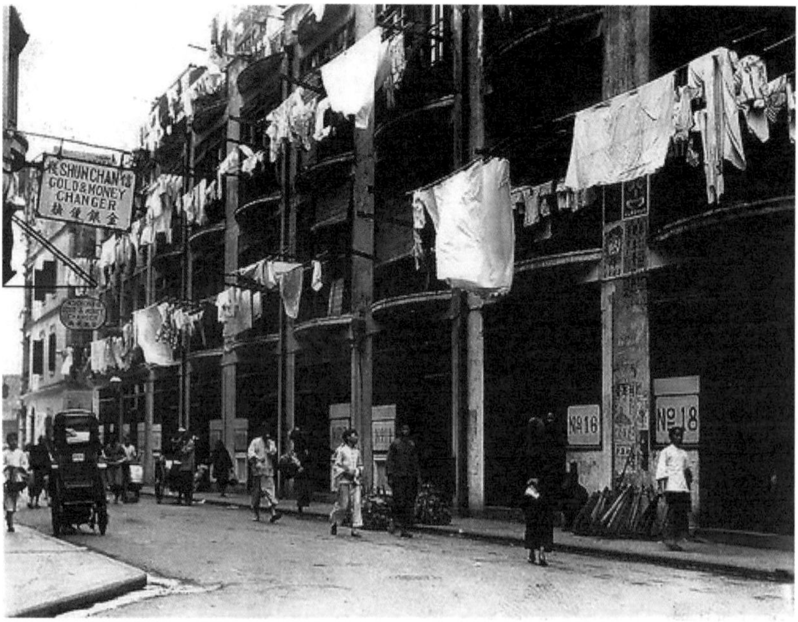

A Wanchai street scene near where mother's family lived on Spring Garden Lane

When we went over to the Lee mansion at Chinese New Year, I looked at it and marveled at its vastness, even compared to ours. It was special to experience the grandeur of the rooms and gardens. They had fancy friends, including Larry Yung, later head of the CITIC Group in Hong Kong, and son of the first 'red capitalist' in post-1949 China, Rong Yiren. His glamorous wife was famous for her jewelry. I used to marvel at her – thinking, wow, even her handbag was sewn with real jade! That was a source of my aspiration and inspiration for a long time, except that I wanted to modernize such traditional accessories. We saw these fancy people only once a year, but going to the big Lee house meant a great deal and left a deep impression on me. I am not sure that it impacted on me directly, but later, when I was trying hard to 'better' myself, the image of those people must have been somewhere on the edge of my mind.

U.K. EDUCATION

4

U.K. Education

It was the tradition in Hong Kong then, and is still the practice now, that the wealthy families would send their children abroad for education. We were still in the thrall of England, and so for my brother Robert and I, it was the U.K. The younger set of siblings, Anthony and Marina, went to Canada for most of their university education, although they attended secondary schools in England.

In Hong Kong, I did my first years of secondary education at Maryknoll School, and always achieved good results. But I usually performed poorly at exams because I was so nervous. At that time of sitting through school-leaving examinations, my vision was affected. I couldn't even see during the critical tests. I passed the O-levels but did not take the A-level examinations. I left Maryknoll School early and was sent at the age of fifteen to a convent boarding school in England — the Convent of the Holy Child Jesus — located in a small village in Sussex called Mayfield with just one main street. Auntie Eleanor, my great-aunt, found the school for me, and another school for brother Robert in Taunton, Somerset.

It was my first time away from home, and the experience was not privileged like the boarding school experience is for children now. It was like you were put in there and abandoned… you did not come back for years. I was homesick, I hated being away from Hong Kong, and I was so lonely even though the nuns were good to me. In fact, as I was the first Chinese student in that school, I was given a room to myself. But I was so stressed. It was truly traumatic. I looked at the schedule and thought, 'Wow, three more years to go, one year before the O-Level exams and then two years to A-Levels. I decided I had better do it quickly, and the fastest way to get out of there was to pass the required subjects in as short a time as possible and take the Oxbridge entrance examination.

In the end, I pushed three years of study into one and a half. I did nothing but work. I was a recluse because I studied so hard. I never really participated in school activities, saying my health was delicate, and it was a pretty Spartan existence for all. I had a curtained alcove in my room, and I pinned a heavy blanket to the movable curtain which acted as a partition, so that the light from my lamp could not be seen in the hall after 9:30 lights-out. When I left school, I weighed just 86 pounds. Getting into university was my sole goal while I was at the convent school. I wanted to get out of that place as soon as I could. My sister later went there as well. She was a good student, got good grades, and was also a good leader and became school prefect. She absolutely atoned for all my sins.

During school holidays, we stayed in a four-story house in West Kensington owned by an English couple, Mr and Mrs Glover, who had lived in Malaya. Apart from brother Robert and I, there were three other children from abroad — Ming Lai Lim from Singapore; Alfred Lau, the son of a prominent doctor in Hong Kong; and Pashupati Rana, the grandson of the last Maharajah of Nepal, who later became a senior minister in the Nepalese government through the 1980s and 1990s. I have lost track of Ming Lai and Alfred, but Pashupati Rana has kept in contact with us all these years. Pashu's wife is the aunt of the present Maharajah of Gwalior, and I attended the wedding of the young prince in Delhi where he rode into the festive grounds on a white elephant. Later on, when I was at Cambridge, brother Robert and I were parked during the holidays with a former senior manager of the Mercantile Bank who had a flat in London, in Belsize Park. I suppose we helped to pay the rent for him.

The fastest way out of the convent school for me was the Oxford and Cambridge examinations. I think they have changed things now, but then, if you passed the exams, you could have the chance of entering either University. I studied all night every night in that self-erected closet and the hard work paid off. I passed the university examinations. They required a classical language and a modern language, and for the classical language I attempted Chinese, while for the modern language I swatted at French. The latter I learnt in record time. My Chinese is still not that great, but it served me well enough to pass the Classical Chinese papers of the entrance examination, otherwise I would have to learn Latin. I also learned enough French to somehow pass that as well, and I was accepted into both Oxford and Cambridge.

I chose Cambridge because it was prettier. I was seventeen years old. I was accepted at Girton College for Women, one of the two women's colleges in the university at that time and the more famous of the two (from the mid-1980s Girton became co-educational, and now at alumni meetings I see more men than women).

Before the academic year began, I attended a private language school in Lausanne to learn French for four or five months, and then moved into Girton College. The fact is that at the university I did not study hard and was not a very good student, largely because it had been such a trial getting there. I was exhausted.

At school in Hong Kong, I was always a good student. Never number one, but always within the top five or six. It was partly because in a big family you are expected to do well, and with all the tensions that existed in the house with the cousins, or other siblings, there was pressure of many kinds. Also, Grandfather was the big patriarch and he liked children who did well at school because he wasn't well educated at all. Auntie Eleanor was very proud of how fast I finished school and made it into Cambridge. We all looked up to her, although I decided early on that I didn't want to be like her. I thought it would be so dry to be an academic or an educationalist.

When I was at school, I wanted to read geography at university. Actually, I would have preferred to read literature, but my English was not good enough. I remember we studied Charles Dickens' novel *Great Expectations*, and I had to look up every third word on the first two pages. But the history mistress at Convent of the Holy Child Jesus, Mother Helena, was nice to me and had an influence on me, and so I chose history. My subject at Cambridge, then, was Medieval European and English history. I could have taken courses in history on Asia as well, but I was too lazy to take the train from Cambridge to London. I chose medieval English history because Dr. Ullman, the Regis Professor at Cambridge, was arguably the leading medieval historian in the U.K. From him, I learned all about monastic orders and medieval strongholds and that was why it meant so much to me when I went to Syria in 2008 and saw the Coptic relics and the grandest Crusader castle, Krak des Chevaliers, because I knew the background.

I enjoyed being at Cambridge, perhaps enjoyed it too much. Initially, I didn't work very hard and instead socialized and wasted too much time. We had a little clique of friends at Girton College. Some were English girls and some foreigners, but I tended to mostly mix with Asians, people from India and the Middle East. My closest friends were Goha Ebrahimzadeh who is Persian, now living in the USA, and Mary Dyson who is South African, now living in Paris. I still see them both occasionally. There was Alastair Hamilton, who was half-Italian. His father was the well-regarded publisher Hamish Hamilton, and through Alastair I met many literary people and came into contact with the continental elite. I think I tended to bond more with Europeans and Asians. The English people I knew were mostly from the upper class. They were quite nice to me. There was dinner once in a while at the London house of Sir John Keswick, Jardine Matheson's Taipan, where I met many Asian students studying in the U.K.

I only went down to London now and then, as I didn't have many friends there. But I remember one who became very well known — Lucia Santa Cruz from Chile, who was friends with Prince Charles. Her father was ambassador, so I went to the Chilean embassy on Eton Terrace quite often. There was John Tusa, who later became head of the BBC World Service and the first Chancellor of the University of the Arts. And Henry Keswick — who became the supremo Taipan of Jardine Matheson, taking the company to new heights — and his wonderful wife Tessa, who have remained firm friends ever since. When in London, I stayed at the house my grandfather bought for my brother and I, a modern Georgian-style house in Kensington near Holland Park.

Girton College was a long way out of town, which had big repercussions because I could not ride a bicycle. I never learned, and to this day I still cannot ride a bike. I took the bus into town, and later on my grandfather gave me a car as a kind of reward for having got into Cambridge. That car caused a lot of trouble.

Cambridge was wonderful. I had worked so hard to get in and my grandfather was so proud that he said when I returned to Hong Kong, he would let me live in the new flat above the garage, right on Kennedy Road. I was thrilled to be allowed to redecorate it.

By my second year, I was relatively settled in Cambridge and studying quite hard when something unfortunate happened. One of my good friends at Cambridge was Abdullah Alireza from Saudi Arabia; he and his Harrovian

Abdullah Alireza from Saudi Arabia was my good friend in Cambridge

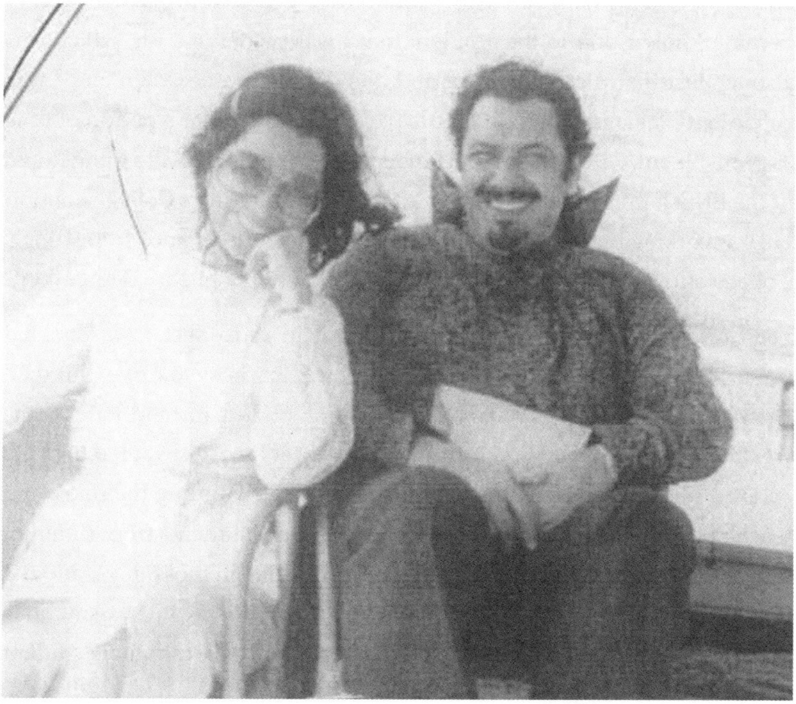

classmate Tony Kornerwere with me all the time. Another good friend who was at Oxford was Karamat Jar, the grandson of the Nizam of Hyderabad, who had also been at Harrow. The fabled old Nizam supposedly died of malnutrition because he was too miserly to eat properly, even though the Hyderabad jewels were considered the greatest such collection in the world after the English crown jewels. I still maintain contact with Princess Esra, the divorced wife of the last Nizam and Karamat's sister-in-law. She has helped to rebuild Hyderabad, and I hope to make a trip there when she is in residence.

One day, Abdullah, Tony and I got in my car to drive to Oxford to see Karamat. I owned the car, but I could not drive and did not have a license, so Abdullah drove. On the way back from Oxford, we had an accident just outside the confines of the university and the car ended up in a ditch by the road. I do not remember precisely what happened. I was in the back seat. No one was hurt, but the police were involved, and it changed my life. We had left Cambridge without approval, which was not permitted and which, it turned out, was grounds for heavy reprimand. Also, it became known due to the accident that I was owner of a car, which was also against the rules. After a period, the decision came down and I was 'rusticated', meaning I had to take leave of Cambridge for a period of time as punishment. Girton College arranged a pass for me at the Reading Room of the British Museum and I could attend classes at King's College London. I liked working in the Reading Room within a short distance from King's College and decided to transfer to King's and got my history degree there.

The accident was stupid and careless, but in retrospect I was treated unfairly. I did have the car and I did not have a license to drive, but then again, I didn't drive it. I mixed a good deal with Indians and with Arabs, wealthy people of color, and I suppose the powers-that-be wanted to make an example of a wealthy foreign student who was flaunting the rules, and teach people a lesson not to be extravagant. Many students from different backgrounds were breaking the car ownership rule in those days, and the decision was in its way an expression of racism, elitism and sexism. They couldn't take action against a rich Indian or Middle Eastern male student, whereas I was an easy target.

Nothing happened to Abdullah, of course. I have remained in touch with him, and we meet occasionally on my trips to London. Initially, I also kept in touch with Karamat and his wife Essin. The princely family has the tradition of marrying Turks and Theroshiva, grandmother of Karamat, was a granddaughter of the last Sultan of Turkey. Therosheva was very grand. I was once invited to Hyderabad House in London to lunch and I could not quite maneuver the knife and fork in the required English way, and so I put down the knife and in the American way transferred the fork to my right hand. Therosheva looked at me severely and said, 'You lift your fork up with your left hand and poke at the meat!' Only the English way was acceptable. Later on, the stern façade evaporated into affable friendship.

Punting on the River Cam by King's College and Chapel, Cambridge

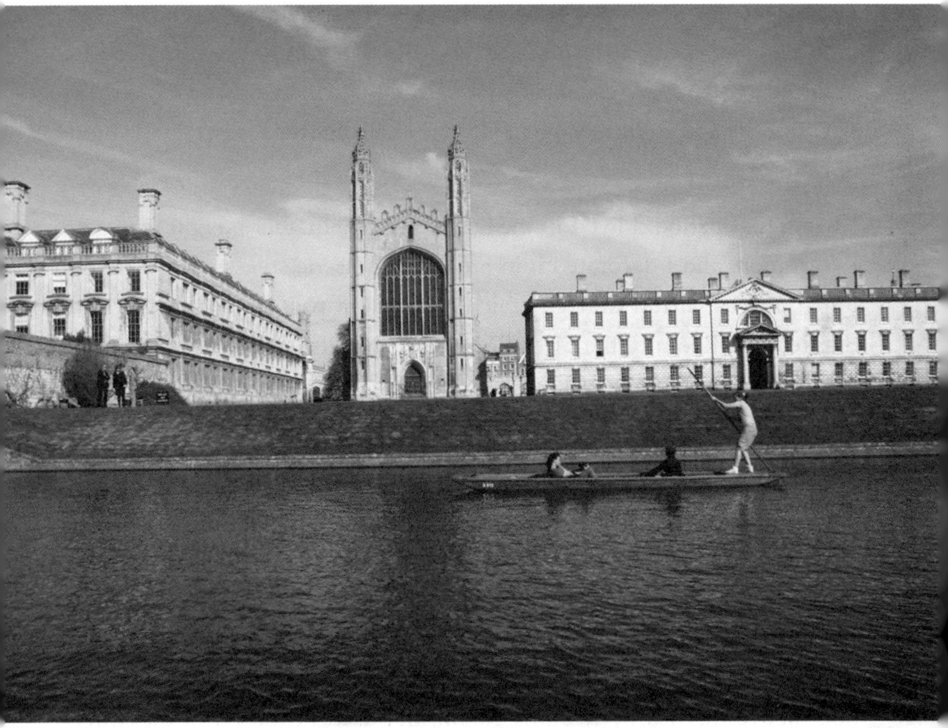

At King's College, I studied Tudor early Renaissance history, and I basically spent most of my time in the Reading Room learning early modern English history — Henry VII, Henry VIII and down to Elizabeth I. For many years, I regretted studying Medieval European history in such depth because it left me basically ignorant of Chinese history. But now I am pleased that I was able to have that as a base, because it gave me the opportunity to absorb the knowledge and scholarship that made me what I am today — a cross-cultural historian, enabling me to merit the position of being the first Visiting Professor, Cross Culture, at Central Saint Martins, University of the Arts London.

I was so settled working at the Reading Room, a thirty-minute walk from King's College London, that I asked to be transferred to the History Faculty to complete my degree there. I am pleased that I changed my subject from medieval history to the exciting days of the English and European Renaissance, which was a time of the flowering of the arts, and also of inquiry, competition, consumption and discovery in the sciences and in medicine, when the West was rising to dominate the world economically, scientifically and culturally, but had yet to challenge the mature civilization of China.

During that period, I lived in the house my grandfather bought for us in Kensington, and I decorated it in French chinoiserie style with a Chinese touch. It was Girton College which arranged a pass for me to work in the Reading Room of the British Museum with its leather padded desks with ample pullout extensions, and I used to sit looking up at the glass dome while on all sides flanked by mid-blue leather divisions filled with books. In 1995, Norman Foster transformed the library and outside area into the great glass dome we see today. The books of the Reading Room were transferred to the British Library and the top of the dome houses restaurants and, around it, exhibition galleries.

The impression of the Long Gallery on the north side of the British Museum remains particularly vivid in my memory. It was in the Long Gallery, a floor above the nearby Reading Room, that I was exposed to the 'three color' pottery sculptures of the Tang dynasty (618-906AD) and the white and 'shadow blue-green' ceramics of the Song dynasty (907-1270AD). Then housed nearby in Bedford Square was the great Percival David collection of Tang, Song and ceramics. The idea was planted in me that hopefully one day I would be able to handle and possess similar pieces. At that time, white ceramics rarely appeared on the open market and Chinese collectors focused on the more ornate wares of the Ming and Qing dynasties.

I also did odd jobs at an interior decorating firm, Trollope and Sons, on Halcomb Street, Belgravia. I had always been rather arty, always had a sense of design and an innate fertile aesthetic sense. And on returning to Hong Kong, my grandfather allowed me to occupy the mews flat above the garage, which I decorated in a way which again fed off my distilled interpretation of subdued chinoiserie.

That short apprenticeship at Trollope's wound up serving me well. The employment record in London provided valuable proof of my connection with the U.K. and helped immensely with my application for a British passport in 1997 when most of Hong Kong was scrambling for a foreign passport.

CHANGE IN FAMILY FORTUNES

5

Change in Family Fortunes

In 1967, my grandfather, the man who had built our world, was still alive, but he was bedridden and incapacitated, and no longer actively participating in the business. My father was the Comprador at the Mercantile Bank and also in charge of the family businesses and assets, when suddenly everything went wrong.

China was in upheaval; the Cultural Revolution was spilling over into Hong Kong with riots in the streets as Chinese communist activists tried to destabilize the Colony. It seemed as if the end was near and that the Red Guards and the People's Liberation Army would come over the border any day. The stock market tumbled, property prices plummeted, and everything spiraled down. And it was at that moment that the Comprador of the Mercantile Bank, my father, desperately needed cash.

The trigger for the calamity that befell us was an unfortunate commitment that my father made on a guarantee. The deal went bad, and he had to cover the difference. As I understand it, there was an Indonesian client for whom my father set up the guarantee for the purchase of a plane, and the plane crashed into the sea and the Mercantile Bank was the guarantor. We children were all abroad studying, so we didn't know too much about what was happening. My elder brother Robert, an accountant, was rushed home from the U.K. to deal with the mess and it was he who sat through the meetings, being ground down by the questions from the rest of the family about what had happened. I had a grand plan to study in Florence, but instead I had to return to Hong Kong to find work. As for me, with a history degree, what could I have done to help? For a short time, I worked as a reporter on the *South China Morning Post* newspaper, covering the law courts, trying to help make ends meet.

Our family owned a corner building down below our house in Wanchai, opposite Spring Garden Lane, and also buildings on Electric Road in North Point. And there was the cologne shop beyond the Western Market. My grandfather also owned some buildings along the tram tracks on Johnston Road opposite Southorn Playground in Wanchai. Property prices fell by 50 to 60 per cent as a result of the political turmoil. The guarantee put up by the Comprador was substantial, and the smaller holdings were not sufficient to cover the debt. So, we were without options but to sell our biggest asset; the family house had to go too. It was sold to Hopewell Holdings in 1972.

Now in much reduced circumstances, each of us had to figure out our own way to rebuild our lives, and to make ends meet. The life of privilege we had lived ended abruptly. We had to learn to earn our keep. Robert and I stayed in Hong Kong while younger brother Anthony and sister Marina went to Canada, where they worked their way through college — Anthony at McGill in Montreal and Marina at York University in Toronto.

In the middle of the crisis, my father became ill and just gave up. The riots ended and by 1970 the markets had recovered somewhat, but it was too late to save our family house on Kennedy Road, and the family had to evacuate. It was a huge operation after so many decades of living there. All the servants were discharged, some of whom had worked for the family for thirty years and more. I lost my little mews house next to the big gate and my favorite amah retired back to her home village in Shun Tak, the county in Guangdong from which many of our domestics came.

Father became a permanent invalid and it was many years before he passed on. Mother, on the other hand, went out to work. I asked my brother, 'How are we going to live?' The answer: it became my mother's responsibility, and ours. She was wonderful. She just sold things constantly. I remember one time I saw her go to a pawnshop to sell a big diamond ring, which she sold for a song. I could not tell if it was her engagement ring, but whatever it was, it presumably helped to keep us afloat for a while. Mother devised a way to keep the family together. She herself came from a grand family that had also fallen on hard times and come to a similar fate as ours. She was infinitely resourceful, brave and upbeat, empowered by her Catholic faith and her own optimism. She provided the strength when grandfather and father became ill, and she was always planning the best for her children, endeavoring to provide us with good education and the opportunity to improve and succeed. She was wonderful and always resourceful, even though she had suffered a great deal because her father was abusive. She went to Maryknoll School, as I did. For years, she was the cheerful and much-loved chair of Maryknoll Old Girls' Association. She had such a large heart and was very adaptable. Above all, she coped.

In the aftermath of the collapse, mother took a job at Towngas Cookery School in 1980 and became quite a famous and beloved cooking teacher. The housewives who attended her classes said that she combined philosophy and common sense with her cooking. She also taught at the YWCA on Garden Road and was active with the many causes at the association. She had a creative approach to cooking, which seemed to me to distill the essence of humanity, and I hope I have something of the same in me.

When she passed away after a long illness on February 14, 2016, we believe she was 96 years old, but she did not have a birth certificate. For years she had not been able to communicate. We thought that she could hear a bit, but there was no reaction. But before that, I was fortunate to have had the chance to have many mother-daughter conversations with her, for which I am grateful. It was said that she was not practical, but this was a woman who had not grown up as a working person, and when disaster struck and circumstances required her to do so, she bravely faced her problems. My father died fifteen years before her, after having been in a vegetative state for a long period. We deeply thank Dr. Bell Tse, Hong Kong's top geriatrician and heart specialist, who looked after both of our parents.

My mother was hazy about certain things, but she had good common sense, and saw to it that her children received good education. She went

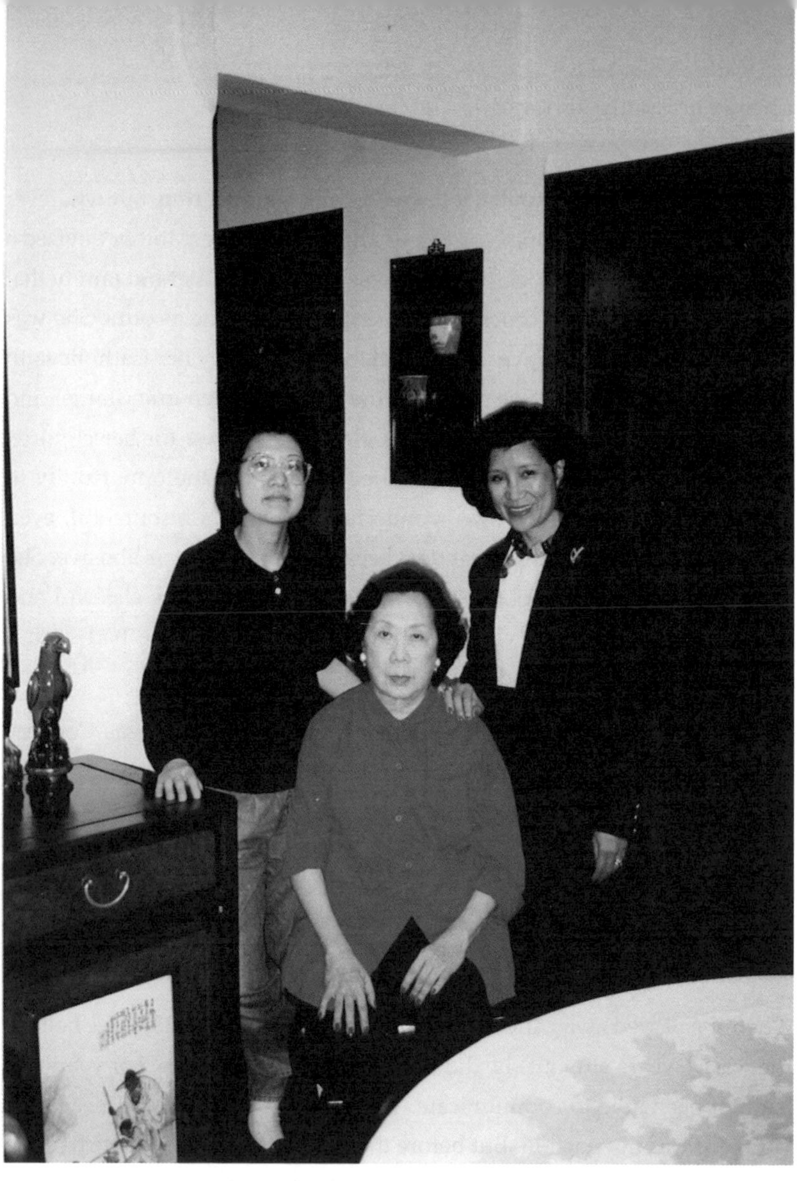

Marina and me with mother, 1970

to England several times when I was studying there, the first time when she and my father took me to boarding school. I cherish the photographs of me with my parents outside the Houses of Parliament when we first landed in London. When I emerged from school in England looking so thin, my mother was alarmed. And when I came back to Hong Kong after studying history in Cambridge and London, she wanted me to become a teacher. After studying history, what else do you do? Teach or become a journalist. But she didn't push it, and left me to go where I wanted to go. She did not object to me going to the United States, living in New York and starting a new life. And when I started building the jewelry business, she was very proud. With my first pay from The Mandarin, I bought her a piece of jewelry, a colored stone ring, bluish-green, a small token of my love and appreciation for being a wonderful mother. She would not allow herself to spend money. It cost me about HK$3,000 at a time when I was making HK$4,000 a month. I bought it from S. H. Chan, a shop in The Mandarin shopping arcade that later on became, through the owner's daughter Joanna, instrumental in working out with me the technique for setting semi-precious jewelry in sterling silver plated in 18k gold, a process that required challenging metalworking skills.

In fact, it was working at The Mandarin that provided the answers to many of my challenges.

Father and me by the Houses of Parliament during our first week in London

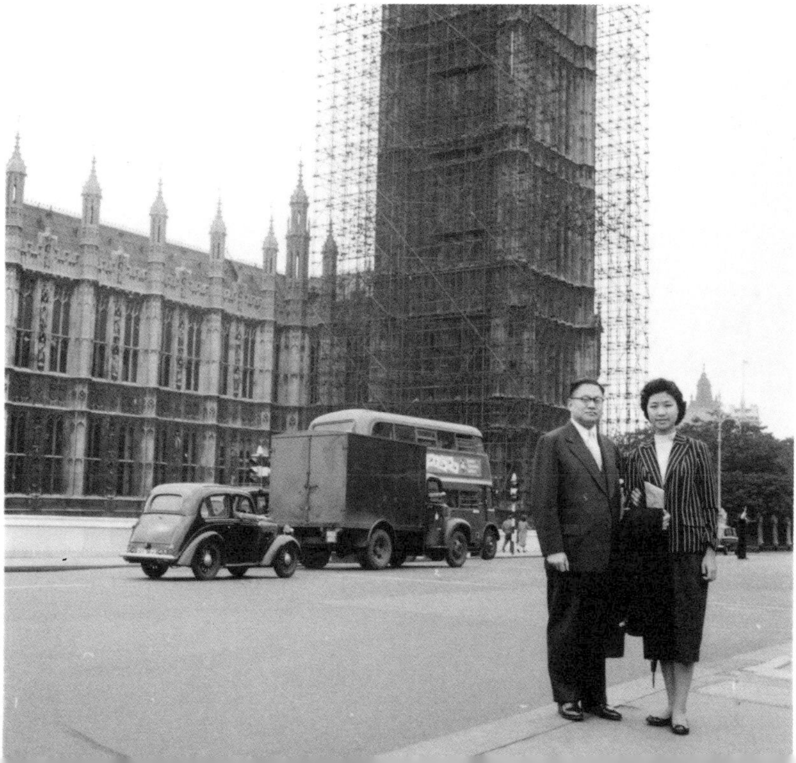

6

Return to Hong Kong

There are three places on the planet with which I feel a particularly strong affinity, two of them in Hong Kong: Central district, the business and commercial hub of the city and also for my career, and Wanchai where my family was based for so many decades. The third is New York, Midtown Manhattan, where I found my path to the future.

On returning to Hong Kong from England after years of studying history, I had no idea what I was supposed to do. Was I going to be a teacher? The thought did not appeal to me, but what else could I manage with the education that I had? Following my short and uninspiring reporting career, I found myself working at The Mandarin Hotel as Assistant Public Relations Officer.

The Mandarin was built on the site of the old Queen's Building, on what had been, until not long before, the waterfront. The site was originally going to be occupied by an updated 'Queen's Building'. Hugh Barton, at the time the Taipan, the head of the venerable trading firm Jardine Matheson, founded in 1832, made an unusual but wise decision that the site would be used to build a first-class hotel, something that Hong Kong Island lacked, even though the site would have made much more money had it been used for an office building. Barton had the foresight to appreciate that Hong Kong needed a five-star hotel.

It was an enormously influential decision.

The Mandarin opened in 1963 and at twenty-seven stories it was then the tallest building in the Colony. Jardines and Hong Kong Land, which

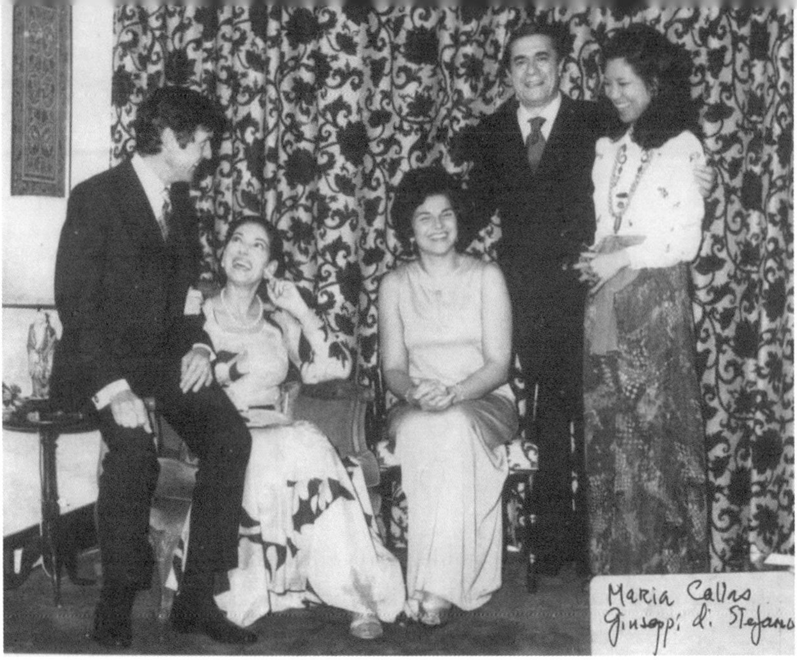

A glittering galaxy at The Mandarin:
General Manager Peter Stafford, supreme diva Maria Callas,
tenor Giuseppe Di Stefano and wife, and me

owned it, decided from the beginning that The Mandarin was to be of the highest standard. The leading hotel in Hong Kong at the time was the Peninsula, across the harbor in Kowloon. Hong Kong Island simply had no international-level hotel.

No expense was spared on the construction of the interior. The new hotel was reputed to be the first in Asia to have a bath in every guestroom. The plan, reflected in the hotel's name, was to project a sense of Asian distinction and elegance. The Mandarin was listed in *Fortune* magazine as one of ten great hotels in the world. And I think I may have played a role in making that happen.

Working at The Mandarin, I was the ever-ready runner assisting my boss, Maggie Christiansen, an Englishwoman married to an army officer, who did not know much about Hong Kong nor about things Chinese. I was the filler-in. I was fortunate to meet and serve many visiting VIPs, including the celebrated writers Graham Greene and John Le Carré; filmmaker David Lean; Thor Heyerdahl, the pioneering sailor of Kon Tiki fame; and the supreme diva Maria Callas and celebrated tenor Giuseppe di Stefano. And on and on. I was hired to be alert, accommodating and useful, whether taking them to Cat Street for antique shopping or for a spin on the harbor. Richard Nixon came twice with his old friend Bebe Rebozo and I gave them a guided tour around Central Hong Kong. Nixon was so impressed with me that he offered me a job in the USA! But it was also around that time that I received another job offer in the United States, which turned out to be a better choice.

Being back in Hong Kong after eight years abroad meant adjusting to a way of life I was no longer accustomed to. I missed the museums and exhibitions, music and dance performances that were so easy to access in London and other European capitals. Having been schooled in English and European medieval history, my knowledge of Chinese history and culture was only slightly better than what I had learned at school in Hong Kong in my early teens.

But I returned to Hong Kong with a determination to understand my own heritage. I consciously chose the path of engaging Chinese history through art, antiques and culture. This coincided with the opening up of China in the 1970s when all kinds of wonderful objects hitherto unknown and unavailable began to find their way onto Hong Kong's markets. Artifacts started to dribble out even in the early 1970s through Macau and other channels, and I was determined to collect as many pieces as I could afford. At that time my knowledge of Chinese art forms was rudimentary, and I used to roam around Cat Street and Hollywood Road with their many antique shops and stands, looking at art and buying pieces that caught my eye (in those days, antiques were affordable even by my standard!) while at the same time learning what I could about the background of the artifacts. Very often I would tag along with seasoned collectors who also frequented the area, especially on the weekends, and there would be other aspirant collectors like me who wanted to understand and appreciate the traditions and history from which these antiques emerged.

I decided to reassemble and 're-shape' the beads and other ornamental objects I bought to fashion pieces of jewelry that could be worn every day, and that would also look modern, coordinate with fashion, and be enjoyed as 'living' adornments that would enhance daily life. Why let these beautiful historical objects sit in a glass curio cabinet or be pillowed in an embroidered box when they could be worn daily? This was actually, in retrospect, a neat segue from studying history. My work was enlivening history and scholarship into creative design. And this work also allowed me to escape what was looming as an inevitability — a career as a researcher or teacher.

The items that were then appearing in Hong Kong's antique market were truly extraordinary: bronzes, jades, semi-precious stone carvings — ancient artworks from the Shang dynasty (1500-1050BC) and the Zhou dynasty (1050-221BC); pottery figures from the Han (206BC-220AD) and the Six Dynasties period (206BC-581AD) through the Tang period (618-907AD). Just imagine being able to obtain objects similar in age and not that inferior in quality to the iconic pieces on display at the Metropolitan Museum in New York or the British Museum and the Victoria & Albert Museum in London!

Where did these pieces come from? They had clearly been smuggled out of China, but from where and how had they made it over the border, we could not know. If the Cat Street dealers knew, they weren't telling. In particular, it was the smaller objects that attracted my interest — exquisite metal ornaments with green patina, some with traces of gold on the surface, intricately chiseled small jade, agate, crystal, turquoise and colored stone carvings that appeared in increasing quantity on the antique market for the first time. Later I learned that they were not turquoise stones but amazonite, still vibrant with color, placed in tombs along with gilt bronze pieces as burial accompaniments, all surprisingly intact with a patina that only old age could provide. Very often in good condition, these burial accompaniments were aptly called 'Adornments for Eternity' (the name given to the extensive and authoritative Mengdiexuan collection amassed by two Hong Kong collectors, Kenneth and Betty Chu, between 1973 and 1990).

With my modest budget, I would spend every Saturday morning or early afternoon prowling the shops and stands on Cat Street and Hollywood

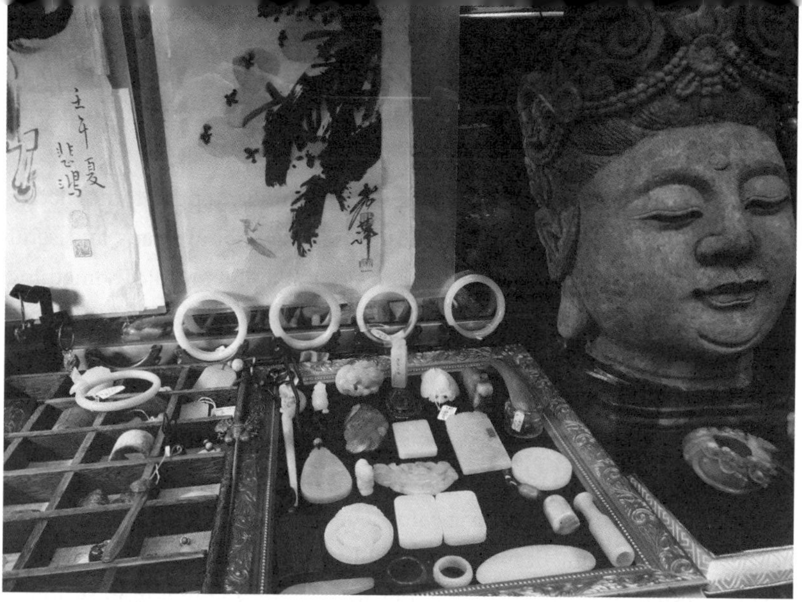

A window on Cat Street with a new flow of artefacts from China

Road, eagerly awaiting the arrivals of new finds. I would then rush off to find references in books and spend the rest of the weekend reading about them and researching my new discoveries. Then I finalized the decision to purchase, which I would make on the following Monday or Tuesday. I would share information with a small band of fellow enthusiasts who frequently did the rounds of the same area and we would pick the brains of the more seasoned collectors and scholars who were generous enough to share knowledge in true scholarly tradition. I would badger this small group of collectors, which included Victor Shaw, Run-Run Shaw's nephew, who was generous with sharing, and also Simon Kwan and James Watt.

James at that time was teaching Chinese history at the Chinese University of Hong Kong. Speaking with an Oxford accent, he was learned, and magnanimous with his time and scholarship. He later went to the United States and became the chief curator of the Chinese department at Boston Museum, and later occupied a senior curatorial position at the Metropolitan Museum. He was a forerunner in detecting the choicest and rarest pieces, interpreting the new findings, and one of the first to expand our knowledge of Chinese jade. I remember when I was at university in England, I would go to the Victoria & Albert Museum in London and look at that famous Eumorfopoulos Han horse (named after a British collector surnamed Eumorfopoulos). For the first time, back home prowling along Cat Street, I found antiquities of similar quality.

So, I followed these eager collectors. I lacked their depth of knowledge of many antique pieces, but I did educate myself about beads and semi-precious stone carvings and decided to make them into something wearable. I thought it would be interesting to string together bits of history that were completely unrelated. And this was how I spent my weekends, usually on Cat Street, mostly by myself. Other collectors were lurking around as well. Being a novice, I was fortunate to have had the benefit of not being encumbered by formal learning in the classical tradition, which valued each piece for its intrinsic value. I had no background at all in terms of the traditional practices of scholarship or how to value each piece. I was interested, instead, in displaying them with a contemporary touch, making them wearable, allowing them to become part of everyday life. In mixing pieces from different periods, harmonious juxtaposition was essential. And these pieces cost no more than HK$500-1,000 on average at the time. I remember one Christmas, I bought fifteen round white jade *bi* at HK$100-150 each and used them as Christmas presents. Today they would be worth significant amounts.

This was my opportunity to understand everyday objects from another age, rendered with great finesse and skill, that collectors and the antique trade regard as artifacts. I came to realize that they documented China's heritage, skills, innovation and artistry — its civilization. I was particularly interested in the small carvings executed in a variety of semi-precious stones — besides jade, primarily agate, turquoise, amazonite, lapis lazuli and crystal, and of course nephrite jade. It took some time to learn how to differentiate between different kinds of jade (and which kinds were rarer and more sought-after) and the different kinds of semi-precious stones used for decoration for thousands of years.

Everything was inexpensive, partly because not many people had the knowledge to date these pieces properly. Dating often relied on the burial sites from which these pieces came, and gravediggers often would not release such information. I made necklaces and pendants with items that one can date to more than five thousand years ago.

It was a brave new world of discovery and learning about China via objects of daily use, and an induction into a new area of the historian's craft. Scholarship in China even now is compartmentalized into archaeology (those who dig) and research (those who spend their lives working on the things dug up). Often the artifacts remain in the research institutes for decades unless a museum has the interest and inclination to display them. I vividly recall what a struggle it was to drag the Liangzhu artifacts from a research institute located in Zhejiang where they were being studied, to the newly-opened Shanghai Museum nearby, which wanted to house and exhibit them as historical representations of the 5,000-year culture of Zhejiang province. But there were few people back then who were able to put these pieces into historical, technical and artistic contexts. Thus, the field was open for experts from China and other parts of the world to formulate new interpretations of the freshly available materials.

As a result of the emergence of these cultural treasures over the past seventy years, the social, economic and artistic history of China has been rewritten. I am referring not to the imperial and aristocratic holdings which are well documented in China and in world museums like the British Museum, the Metropolitan Museum in New York, the Nezu Museum in Tokyo and of course the Palace Museums in Taipei and Beijing, but to the 'newly excavated' collections and items which emerged via the 'private routes' opened up through Hong Kong and Macau in the 1970s.

I also came to acquire a deep interest in, and possibly sufficient knowledge to appreciate, the refinement and value of Chinese porcelain and other antiques. In 1972, an opportune meeting in the Lockhart Lounge on the 25th floor of The Mandarin — with Julian Thompson, head of the Chinese Department at Sotheby's London and famed expert of Chinese porcelain, and the celebrated collector and art dealer Edward Chow, stopping in Hong Kong on their way to visit a special blue and white ceramic exhibition in Tokyo — led to further explorations of staging the first Sotheby's auction in Hong Kong. I was keen that this first auction would take place at The Mandarin — what an opportunity for exposure for the hotel! So, in 1973, the first Sotheby's auction took place in the Harbour Room on the second floor of The Mandarin. It was an historic occasion as a bowl from the Chenghua period of the Ming Dynasty (1465-1487AD) was auctioned, setting a world record for a piece of Ming porcelain. I still recall the image of the bowl being held high on the podium for all to see.

For me, it was not only a good public relations coup, further exposing The Mandarin to world consciousness, but also a step towards establishing Hong Kong as an important center for trading and auctioning Chinese works of art. This development had great implications and influence.

OFF TO NEW YORK

7

Off to New York

I met my benefactor and good friend Jim Linen through chairman Harold Lee at The Mandarin. At that time, after having been president and chairman of Time Inc., James A. Linen III occupied the post of chairman of the company's executive committee. He was a wonderful man with an easy, accessible style and generous nature that made you feel important and respected. The first thing about him that struck me was his relaxed demeanor, so unexpected for a high-level American CEO. His two sons also became good friends with my brothers — it is a relationship that our family cherish.

Harold Lee, Chairman of The Mandarin, and James A. Linen III, Chairman of Time Inc's Executive Committee – the key to a new future!

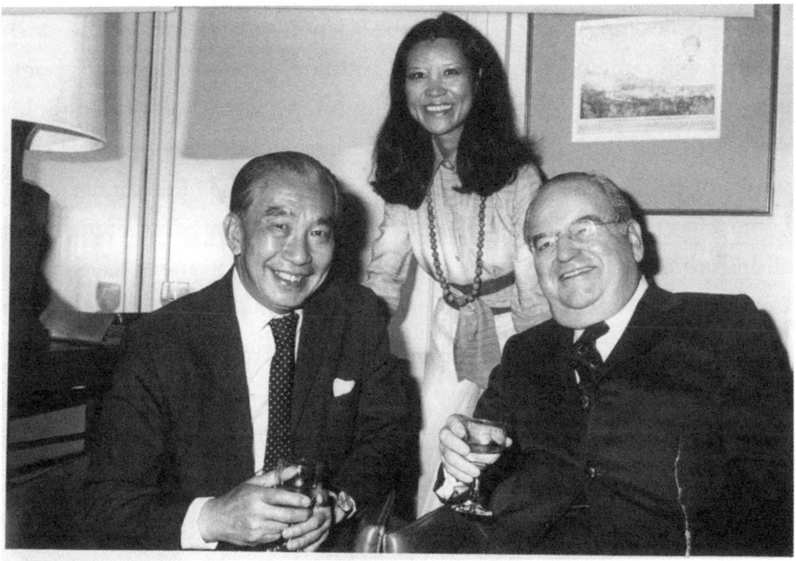

Jim's father had been a missionary in China at the same time as Henry Luce's father. A regular visitor to The Mandarin, Jim was often on his way to Thailand, a country he loved. I performed odd jobs for him on his frequent trips to Hong Kong and he took me under his wing. It was a big opportunity and good training, and thanks to dear Jim and his family I came to believe in the values of the Americans and their great country. Americans with that level of success often exhibit a spirit of largesse and a relaxed personal style that makes junior people feel reassured and encouraged.

One day Jim surprised me by asking, 'Would you like to work in New York? We will find you a post in Public Affairs.' I of course jumped at the opportunity. 'Why not!' I replied immediately. But it was not easy to get a work visa. In the end, I secured one that required an exit from the U.S. every six months, which turned out to be a blessing when I later set myself up with a fledgling jewelry business.

Thus, I found myself in New York. I was lucky. Without that break, I would not have wound up where I did, and doing what I do. America, at the time, offered limitless opportunities — for challenges, for newness and experiments that dared you to grasp, develop and overcome.

Thanks to Jim and his family, and the open and friendly people I met, I came to believe in America. American society resonated for me. The Linen family I will remember forever with gratitude. Jim took me to his home in Greenwich, Connecticut, a sprawling house where I got to know his three sons and two daughters. The experience was an eye-opener. I shall never forget the first time he invited me to Christmas Eve dinner at his home. His entire extended family showed up, all twenty-four of them and all in formal attire. They made a huge impression on me — celebrating Christmas in a traditional way that was not unlike the family gatherings at home in Hong Kong for Chinese New Year. Everyone had to make a speech. It took forever.

This was my first American family experience. What struck me most was how different it was from what I observed with the English. The Western

'Old World' values were present in both places, but the expression of it in the American context was quite different, much warmer and almost exuberant. Jim represented to me all that is good in Americans.

I saw quite a lot of Jim in Time's New York offices, and he looked after me. But of course he was on the forty-eighth floor of the corporate headquarters while I was circulating down below. There was not really a permanent job for me to do, as it turned out. I was first put to work in the documentary television division, then in the public affairs department. Finally, I wound up reporting to then-publisher, Henry Luce Jr; that is, Hank Luce, the son of the founder. He also had a house in London just around the corner from the American Embassy on Brook Street. As I had to exit the country every few months, on one occasion I went to London and visited their home. His wife liked me. While there, I heard that *Fortune* magazine was sending a photographer to cover the Peninsula Hotel in Hong Kong, and I asked the editor to take a look at The Mandarin.

'Just give The Mandarin a chance, it's a wonderful new hotel!' I urged. My suggestion resulted in a profile of The Mandarin in *Fortune* as one of the '10 Best Hotels in the World'. That was indeed a great boost!

I am a great believer in serendipity. How do we cultivate or stumble into the grace of finding what we are not consciously seeking? I arrived in New York with little money and a bag of ancient metal ornaments and jade carvings, and that was the beginning of my future. I was lucky in so many ways, being in the right place at the right time, full of energy, ideas, hope and optimism. The energy of New York City inspired me to think of ways to bring all my skills, interests, fantasies and opportunities together to create a future for myself.

That collection I sold to Cartier was of re-mounted old odd items, but I soon found the audience for this type of jewelry was very limited. Also, frankly, I didn't want to part with many of the things I had collected and had repurposed. So, while still working at Time, I started to create the designs that incorporated semi-precious stones.

So, I was roaming around New York with a satchel, showing my wares, which now included semi-precious stones. I lived on Park Avenue in an apartment owned by a Bulgarian lady named Babushka who I had met along with her boyfriend Eddie Hand at The Mandarin. He was from Detroit, terribly expansive and extravagant. Babushka was good looking, a Central European beauty, dark-haired, white skin, voluptuous body, quite tall. She was very nice to me and had this compact and convenient apartment that Eddie had bought for her. It was not big, just two rooms. But it was Park Avenue at 57th Street! One day she moved out of the apartment and in with Eddie and said to me, 'You can stay here.' So I did. For six months, I walked to work every morning thinking, 'What can I do better beyond surviving?'

My horizon was expanded at Time Inc. and even though I did not have much to do at work except odd jobs, I did gain an insight into the workings of a big media operation. They also sent me on a wonderful trip to Iran. *Fortune* magazine organized big trips with American businessmen, and I was an 'assistant and bag carrier' for the corporate presidents on that trip. So many private planes! I have never seen so much caviar in all my life. But on the trip, I learned a lot about the lives of the big corporate players, which proved useful. In Persepolis, I confess I picked up a little piece of stone off the ground and pocketed it. I was looking at things on that trip from an historical point of view rather than in terms of design. My whole designer career had not really begun at that point.

Back roaming the streets of New York, I was still glued to the storefront windows of Fifth Avenue and the mesmerizing displays of jewelry made of gold, expensive diamonds and other jewels beyond the grasp of all but a handful of people. Off the famed avenues, I also saw window displays for the lower end of the market, the imitations and costume pieces which were far more prevalent. Kenneth J. Lane was the kingpin of costume jewelry design, using dyed glass set in base metal. However, his prices were not inexpensive due to his brand name.

There was nothing in between fake materials and expensive gemstones. And I said to myself, there is a need for something that is not so serious and expensive and also not fake. Surely there was a niche for a more 'authentic' look, for accessories made of real materials such as natural stones that were multicolored, attractive, wearable and affordable.

The sense of jewelry and its role as an adornment was very different in the West from what it was in Asia where, when you go out to a dinner, you put on your finery. Not so much in the West, where people would often wear expensive clothes matched with a necklace of glass baubles set in base metal. And I thought, that needed fixing. It was clear that New Yorkers appreciated fine jewelry but even there, people were not in the habit of wearing expensive jewelry, for security and other reasons. Americans liked ornaments, and in terms of precious stones, this would be costly, so the jewelry was all kept in a safe and women usually did not have the time nor inclination to retrieve it and wear it. The way jewelry is worn in Asia is different. In our part of the world, even for a birthday party, you wear your little jade pendant, some small piece of fine jewelry. Jewelry means a great deal in India, in the Malayan and Thai cultures and in old China. It is a part of everyday life, and I think it was that role for jewelry that I wanted to introduce to the West, and it required a brand-new direction in designing ornaments.

Ornaments and accessories since the earliest times have been worn as a distinguishing mark of rank and decorative significance. Why not, I thought, coordinate the disparate antique pieces in my possession, mellowed with patina, from a bygone heritage, and reconfigure and adapt them, giving them a new energy and relevance?

Antiques made wearable by positioning them in a harmonious combination became the first range. I liked to wear real things; I didn't want to wear costume jewelry. The second range was composed of semi-precious stones and at that time also incorporated ivory. I saw the skills of the ivory carvers in Hong Kong, and made use of their intricate skills to carve color stones. The first collection consisted of pendants suspended on leather or braided cords. I have always stressed pendants because they are less formal in look. I devised a cord system ending with knots based on the traditional button fastening from the Chinese cheongsam.

I was highly motivated as I was challenged to survive and do well, and to create. And that phase of lugging that bag around New York with my pieces in it lasted for a very long time. I once checked with the Hong Kong fashion designer Vivienne Tam and she said she did the same walk for a long time too! And yes, I used to sometimes park myself in St. Patrick's Cathedral when I needed solace and to recharge. I am not baptized but having attended convent schools all my life, I do believe in God.

I once read that innovation is not all hard work or dumb luck, it's mostly about paying attention. How can we find what we are not consciously seeking? The British belle-lettrist Horace Walpole recounted a tale in 1754 about three Persian princes from the Isle of Serendip who possessed superpowers of observation. Walpole concluded that this old tale contained a crucial idea about human genius. 'As their highnesses travelled, they were always making discoveries, by accident and sagacity, of things they were not in quest of.' And he proposed a new word, 'serendipity,' to describe this experience. Walpole was suggesting that serendipity was a skill rather than a random stroke of good luck.

Do we then create our own serendipity? These days, we may identify serendipity as the powers of perception, the dawning of an idea that develops into multiple realizations to be grasped, harnessed and formulated into something new. For me, it could be a combination of something based on an original gut feeling or notion to be modified and developed into a new guise and meaning.

I am grateful to the people who opened up and gave me a chance, but I am more grateful for the American system. Where else could you just queue up at a top-flight store and the general manager would see you? But it happened regularly in those stores in that era. Sadly, my association with Cartier lasted for just that one season. The new ownership of the company decided that only Paris-designed items would be sold. That was why I created my semi-precious collection, which turned out to be more influential — and made my name.

In Hong Kong, I asked my friend Joanna Chan at the jewelry shop on the mezzanine floor of The Mandarin to help me to experiment with setting semi-precious stones and ivory pieces in sterling silver, then later in 18k gold-plated silver. I also used ivory and semi-precious stone carvings in 'international' styles for the Western market. These were assembled or fashioned into particular shapes by workmen, some of whom came from the declining ivory trade. In my initial collections, a lot of elements were held together by gold wire, which was an untraditional way of securing the pieces. I also devised a clasp with a section of a knot inspired by my travels in Asia which I used for many, many years, and which became something of a signature for me. I am thankful to Joanna for helping me with my then-unproven jewelry business venture.

'What good is it,' I thought, 'having these completely disparate pieces of jade, turquoise and lapis lazuli lying around?' The traditional scholar would with great ceremony take out a piece encased in embroidered cloth and would share his knowledge of the piece with like-minded collectors, then put it back and close the lid. I said, 'No. I want these things to be part of my everyday life.'

So, I mounted these colorful stones, many of which came from South America and some from South East Asia, and just beginning to find their way to Hong Kong. I succeeded in recruiting skilled carvers to work these semi-precious stones. They were centered around Wellington Street in Central. I started with amethyst and red agate shipped from South America and lapis lazuli from Afghanistan. Later on, I bought blocks of stones at jewelry fairs in Hong Kong.

When I handed over the first block to these carvers, I had no clients in mind, just an idea that this other class of jewelry could work in Midtown Manhattan. I asked them to use their proven skills to carve intricate shapes, interlocking rings and links, for instance. The carving of such shapes based on old skills created such amazement in New York. I also used ivory sparingly in my works in those days as we weren't as conservation-minded as we are today. I haven't used ivory in many years. Nor coral. Coral used to be abundant, and it was a favorite material which I used to design beads and drops with floral motifs made by skilled Taiwan cutters familiar with the material. Now, with the coral reefs getting polluted, the price is high and the coral is full of white spots. What climate change and pollution have done to our environment!

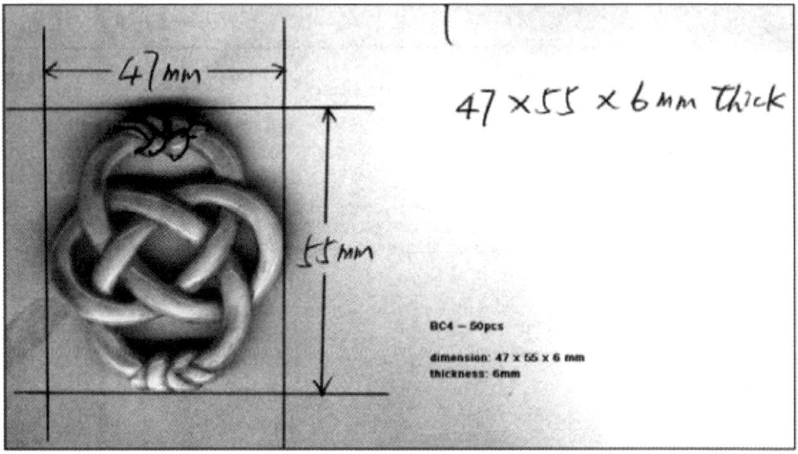

A representative knot first rendered in ivory. When the material was banned, the knots were carved with ox bone and semi-precious stone

Setting carved ivory and semi-precious stone pieces in new or contemporary styles and shapes, as opposed to the usual Buddhas and the familiar forms, was a new page. Charms as ornamentation are a Western tradition that I played to. I did a Celtic cross, a fish with a silver tail, heart shapes in several renditions, ivory balls with two or three movable layers dating from the Ming period that showed off the carvers' skill, first developed in the Ming dynasty. I was always making use of traditional shapes and techniques in fresh ways, instilling a contemporary touch. The charms weren't too expensive, which meant that the client could purchase one, two or more over time and collect them onto a bundle of charms. I would add a dash of color to the charms with stone beads, or with coral which has been a favorite element in European jewelry since the 18th century or earlier.

Before long, I had a small but enthusiastic following. But I needed to find a way to develop a bigger audience. I was groping towards formulating an affordable, popular range of jewelry that would appeal to working women.

The tempo and lifestyle in New York made me aware that there was a need for jewelry that accessorized and coordinated with fashion. It had to be real, colorful and, above all, affordable. How I carved out the niche that I did was the result of observing women's lifestyle, taste and needs. I matched this with the carving skills of artisans in Hong Kong that enabled me to create and realize this unique line of jewelry that bore my personality and look. My study of history, I think, also helped me in observing the social trends and behavior in New York, Los Angeles, Houston and other major American cities.

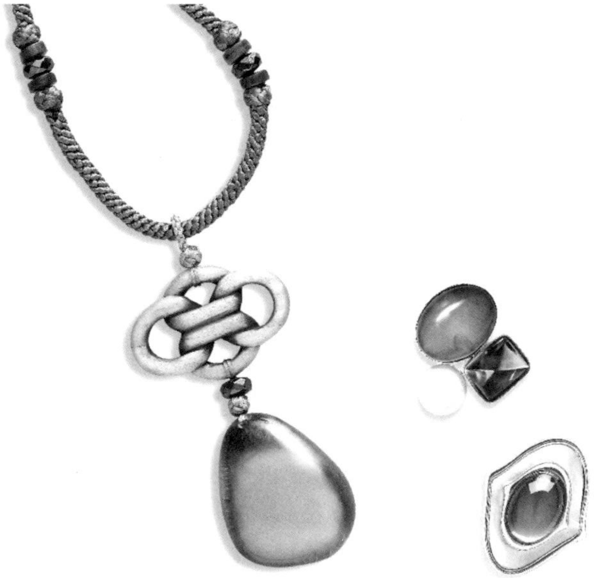

The signature Kai-Yin Lo look with semi-precious stones (and a lot of amber) set in sterling silver 18k gold vermeil

It was always possible it wouldn't have worked. It was a mad leap in many ways. But it did work, and I'm very grateful to the United States for making it possible. The United States is a country that almost compulsively needs new things. In Europe and the U.K., I doubt if institutions would allow Open Days when vendors could queue up to show their wares and be given a viewing and an opportunity for a break. In fact, it works both ways — the vendor gets a chance to show, and the store opensup opportunities to see a wider range of items on offer.

I moved out of Babushka's apartment on Park Avenue and into another place on Park Avenue — I was always a Park Avenue girl — thanks to Pablo Manzoni, a beautician at Elizabeth Arden. Pablo knew many rich women because he fixed their faces, and he lived at 521 Park Avenue in a big and very ornate apartment. I rented a room at the back, close to the kitchen, and stayed there for two years. The move also marked my entrée to the world of New York society, and many of its members were to become my clients.

I first 'met' my dear friend Elsa Peretti via the telephone when she called Pablo. Elsa of Tiffany fame is one of the few contemporary designers, and possibly the only jewelry designer, to have been given a retrospective at the British Museum. Elsa called the apartment regularly and so did Maria Callas, with whom I had the happy chance to speak a couple of times!

Over the years, Elsa and I became good friends, and she was generous enough to allow me to rent her spare New York apartment from 2008 to 2012. When Tiffany launched the Peretti jewelry line in Shanghai, Elsa, who never liked the fanfare of promotion, wanted her stalwarts to support her, and that included the manufacturer of her stones in Hong Kong, Patrick Chu and his son. Except for the obligatory speeches, she mostly hung around with us. She then came to Hong Kong and visited my apartment, where I kept a showroom. Imagine, she bought jewelry from me! Three strands of butterfly keshi pearl (which reminded her of the Japan she loved) all worn together, as she has a long neck!

In March 2015, I was part of the Hong Kong Design Centre delegation visiting Barcelona, and I stayed in her spacious apartment in a 1930s building filled with memorabilia and her designs. It was a joy to walk on the original floor tiles intricately patterned to fit every turn and corner in the apartment. Elsa had ornaments and memorabilia neatly placed to tell stories. It was a great treat and wonderful tribute to a woman of immaculate taste.

While in Barcelona I took the opportunity to visit the nearby 14th-century village comprising eight to ten houses that she had taken pains to restore.

Again, what a joy it was to experience a preserved and revived cluster of late medieval houses and to occupy one of them! Elsa had installed a small museum exhibiting a collection of Chinese white ceramics from the Song Dynasty, Japanese screens, and some of her well-known designs for Tiffany. Elsa is far more famous than me, and she had the talent and good fortune to have been backed by Tiffany. I take comfort in being assured that it is talent – and grasping opportunity – that leads to recognition and success.

But the irony is that my success in life is thanks to a guy from Detroit with a rather murky past who bought a well-positioned apartment for his girlfriend, and in a lesser way to a beautician named Pablo who rented me a room in prime Park Avenue. Whenever I go to New York, I still go past that building on Park Avenue and 57th Street. It was so important for me. It gave me a well-positioned base from which to grow and learn. I was so lucky. I could have ended up in Queens and beyond.

BUILDING THE BUSINESS

8

Building the Business

My problem was how to get the collection into the stores. And it was again Jim Linen who helped me. Among the guests on the *Fortune* magazine corporate trip to Iran were Ralph Lazarus, Chairman of Federated Department Stores, a great buddy of Jim's. Federated owned Bloomingdale's, I. Magnin and many other department stores, so when I had put together a small collection of necklaces and earrings using semi-precious stones, I went to Jim and said, 'Jim, I'd appreciate your help. Can you make some introductions?'

'Sure,' he said. 'I'll call up Ralph Lazarus.'

And he did. Mr Lazarus responded promptly, and the next thing I knew, I received a call from a woman named Rose Wells.

'Hello, Kai-Yin, I am the chief merchandiser for Federated,' she said. 'I'm very busy, and I'm on my way to California, but as Mr Lazarus made the introduction, you can come and see me at our headquarters at Federated. My only available time is 7 a.m., tomorrow morning.'

Of course, I went to see her.

'Very interesting,' she said, looking over the pieces. 'I will introduce you to the right people.'

I then met the chief merchandising director of Bloomingdale's, who had only some advice for me.

'Your things,' he said, 'should be up-market.'

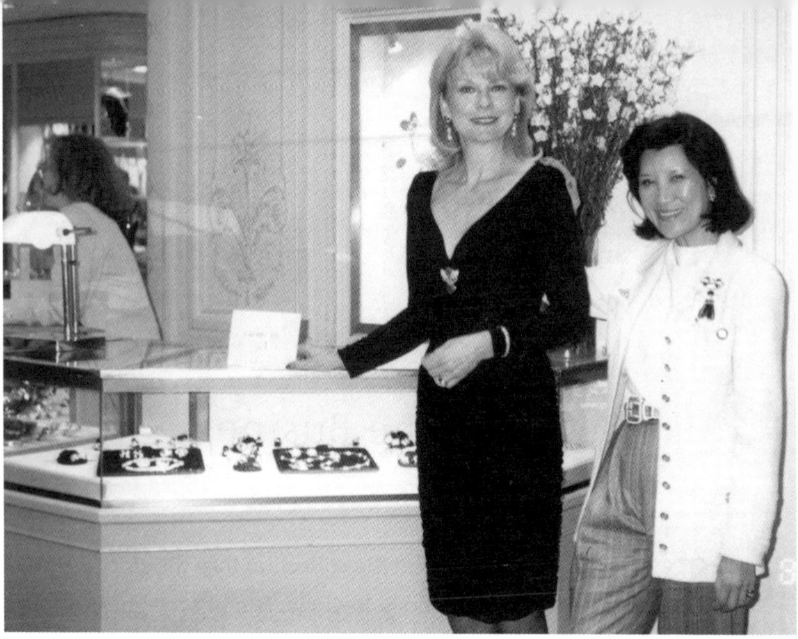

My counter at Bergdorf Goodman, New York's premier store, in 1985

'You don't buy?' I asked in surprise.

'No, I don't buy, I look,' he stressed.

Getting to the buyers — that was the challenge. But in the end, Bloomingdale's agreed to test a batch of a dozen items in their New York store. It must have gone quite well, because they came back with another order and put my jewelry in three more stores.

The leading department stores in New York in those days were Bergdorf Goodman, Saks Fifth Avenue and Bloomingdale's. The chief merchandising manager at Bloomingdale's introduced me to the head of the accessories division who then referred me to the buyer. The buyer was actually in Hong Kong and I met him in his room at — where else? — The Mandarin. I showed him my designs and he ordered a certain number of each style. Typically, these buyers would order six to eight pieces from a selection of ten to twelve styles they liked to form a well-coordinated collection for the season. They would try them in one store first, and if they worked, they would expand to five stores, then more. Those first items purchased from me were all ivory pendants with semi-precious stones suspended on braided cording. The buyers would then mark up my wholesale cost by two or three times for the retail price. Later on, when I became well-known, the average retail price for my pieces at Neiman Marcus and at the exclusive Bergdorf Goodman was between US$400 and US$1,000. But I did not pursue Bloomingdale's very aggressively as they only operated stores in the New York region. It was Neiman Marcus, with stores throughout the country, that turned out to be my biggest client, and my lucky break arrived when I got into the chain in1978.

Neiman Marcus, headquartered in Dallas, Texas, and numbering 35 stores, was fabled in those days. It had stellar status as a store chain selling exclusive luxury merchandise. Its legendary director was Stanley Marcus who came to the Far East early on to buy Chinese antiques, taking them back to the U.S. where he set up a Chinese department in his stores. I first met Stanley at The Mandarin when he came to Hong Kong on one of his buying trips. And when I started to develop my jewelry and accessories, I showed him my designs; he liked them and introduced me to his buyer, who bought some of my selection and — hooray hooray! — I was in the number one department store chain in the United States!

Filled with excitement and expectation, I visited the main Neiman Marcus store in Dallas, expecting to see my name in lights, but found that not one piece was being shown. Asking why, I was told, 'We have no department for it. Jewelry is either costume or real. Yours doesn't fit into either category.'

Nine months later, and after much discussion, Neiman Marcus set up a semi-precious jewelry department, technically referred to as the 'bridge' department.

The same thing happened at Saks Fifth Avenue, and in the late 1980s, at Harrods in London. I was instrumental in helping to set up semi-precious jewelry departments in these stores. I suppose that's really my most significant contribution, the creation of a new category of jewelry that soon became a mainstay in jewelry design. I am proud of this achievement.

Without a presence in department stores, there was no effective way to display or to sell in quantity, so the category problem plagued me: semi-precious stones were a completely new concept for the stores, and effective

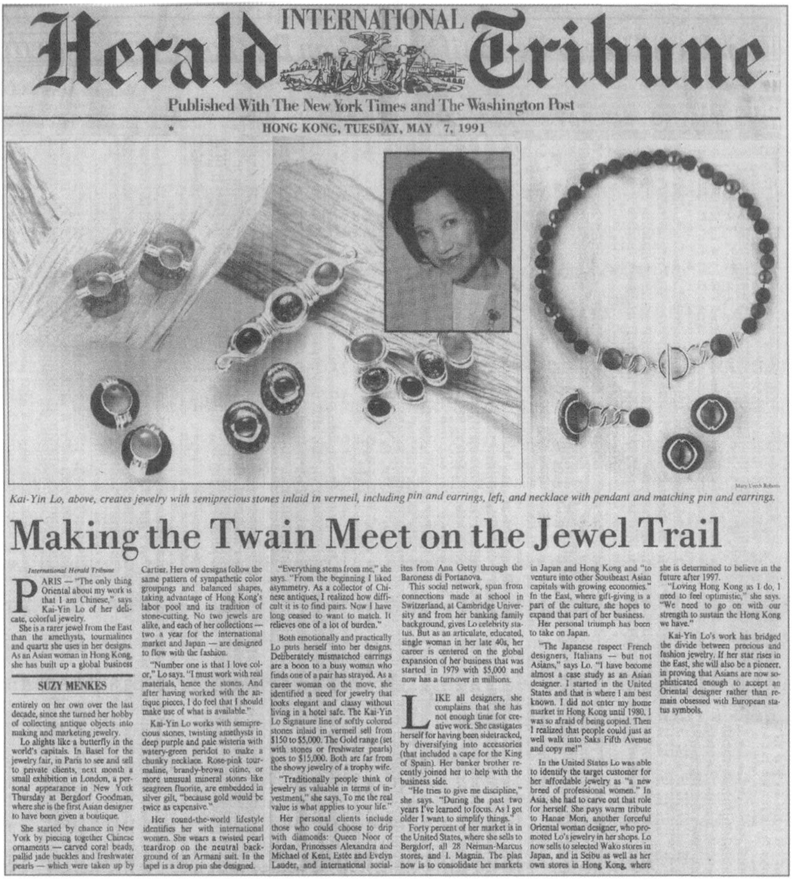

INTERNATIONAL Herald Tribune

Published With The New York Times and The Washington Post

HONG KONG, TUESDAY, MAY 7, 1991

Kai-Yin Lo, above, creates jewelry with semiprecious stones inlaid in vermeil, including pin and earrings, left, and necklace with pendant and matching pin and earrings.

Making the Twain Meet on the Jewel Trail

International Herald Tribune

SUZY MENKES

PARIS — "The only thing Oriental about my work is that I am Chinese," says Kai-Yin Lo of her delicate, colorful jewelry.

She is a rarer jewel from the East than the amethysts, tourmalines and quartz she uses in her designs. As an Asian woman in Hong Kong, she has built up a global business entirely on her own over the last decade, since she turned her hobby of collecting antique objects into making and marketing jewelry.

Lo alights like a butterfly in the world's capitals. In Basel for the jewelry fair, in Paris to see and sell to private clients, next month a small exhibition in London, a personal appearance in New York Thursday at Bergdorf Goodman, where she is the first Asian designer to have been given a boutique.

She started by chance in New York by piecing together Chinese ornaments — carved coral beads, pallid jade buckles and freshwater pearls — which were taken up by Cartier. Her own designs follow the same pattern of sympathetic color groupings and balanced shapes, taking advantage of Hong Kong's labor pool and its tradition of stone-cutting. No two jewels are alike, and each of her collections — two a year for the international market and Japan — are designed to flow with the fashion.

"Number one is that I love color," Lo says. "I must work with real materials, hence the stones. And after having worked with the antique pieces, I do feel that I should make use of what is available."

Kai-Yin Lo works with semiprecious stones, twisting amethysts in deep purple and pale wisteria with watery-green peridot to make a chunky necklace. Rose-pink tourmaline, brandy-brown citine, or more unusual mineral stones like seagreen fluorite, are embedded in silver gilt, "because gold would be twice as expensive."

Her round-the-world lifestyle identifies her with international women. She wears a twisted pearl teardrop on the neutral background of an Armani suit. In the lapel is a drop pin she designed.

"Everything stems from me," she says. "From the beginning I liked asymmetry. As a collector of Chinese antiques, I realized how difficult it is to find pairs. Now I have long ceased to want to match. It relieves one of a lot of burden."

Both emotionally and practically Lo puts herself into her designs. Deliberately mismatched earrings are a boon to a busy woman who finds one of a pair has strayed. As a career woman on the move, she identified a need for jewelry that looks elegant and classy without living in a hotel safe. The Kai-Yin Lo Signature line of softly colored stones inlaid in vermeil sell from $150 to $5,000. The Gold range (set with stones or freshwater pearls) goes to $15,000. Both are far from the showy jewelry of a trophy wife.

"Traditionally people think of jewelry as valuable in terms of investment," she says. To me the real value is what applies to your life."

Her personal clients include those who could choose to drip with diamonds: Queen Noor of Jordan, Princesses Alexandra and Michael of Kent, Estée and Evelyn Lauder, and international socialites from Ann Getty through the Baroness di Portanova.

This social network, spun from connections made at school in Switzerland, at Cambridge University and from her banking family background, gives Lo celebrity status. But as an articulate, educated, single woman in her late 40s, her career is centered on the global expansion of her business that was started in 1979 with $5,000 and now has a turnover in millions.

LIKE all designers, she complains that she has not enough time for creative work. She castigates herself for having been sidetracked, by diversifying into accessories (that included a cape for the King of Spain). Her banker brother recently joined her to help with the business side.

"He tries to give me discipline," she says. "During the past two years I've learned to focus. As I got older I want to simplify things."

Forty percent of her market is in the United States, where she sells to Bergdorf, all 28 Neiman-Marcus stores, and I. Magnin. The plan now is to consolidate her markets in Japan and Hong Kong and "to venture into other Southeast Asian capitals with growing economies." In the East, where gift-giving is a part of the culture, she hopes to expand that part of her business.

Her personal triumph has been to take on Japan.

"The Japanese respect French designers, Italians — but not Asians," says Lo. "I have become almost a case study as an Asian designer. I started in the United States and that is where I am best known. I did not enter my home market in Hong Kong until 1980. I was so afraid of being copied. Then I realized that people could just as well walk into Saks Fifth Avenue and copy me!"

In the United States Lo was able to identify the target customer for her affordable jewelry as "a new breed of professional women." In Asia, she had to carve out that role for herself. She pays warm tribute to Hanae Mori, another forceful Oriental woman designer, who promoted Lo's jewelry in her shops. Lo now sells to selected Wako stores in Japan, and in Seibu as well as her own stores in Hong Kong, where she is determined to believe in the future after 1997.

"Loving Hong Kong as I do, I need to feel optimistic," she says. "We need to go on with our strength to sustain the Hong Kong we have."

Kai-Yin Lo's work has bridged the divide between precious and fashion jewelry. If her star rises in the East, she will also be a pioneer, in proving that Asians are now sophisticated enough to accept an Oriental designer rather than remain obsessed with European status symbols.

An endorsement by influential journalist Suzy Menkes in the International Herald Tribune: "She bridged the gap between precious and fashion jewellery – she is a pioneer", 7 May 1992

introduction and promotion of this new category was highly necessary. But once introduced, they took off. It was in a way the birth of affordable luxury, which is now such an important retail category in a wide range of products. It's not a phrase that was used at the time, but I think 'affordable luxury' sums it up well. That is what I was aiming at. Something that had style and depth, value as art, and which was reasonably priced.

If you were to ask the most important thing I have done, that is probably it. I initiated the 'in-between' range of jewelry. Department stores realized that my re-purposed antique pieces were too rarefied for general taste, but the affordable semi-precious stone pieces commanded wide appeal and endured.

Suzy Menkes, at the time the most powerful fashion editor, wrote a feature story on my jewelry which appeared in the *International Herald Tribune* on May 7, 1992. It described me as a pioneer who ushered in 'a new direction in jewelry design' that had the potential to change the world.

Something real, colorful but also affordable. That is the market I saw and created for working women. It extended to other women, too. Estée Lauder could afford most things, but she was also a working woman and she said, 'When I travel, why do I have to lug around all this valuable jewelry that I have to pay attention to?'

The jewelry appealed to secretaries, executives and women who couldn't afford expensive jewelry but who appreciated good design. They would otherwise buy plastic or glass from Macy's or the like, and I provided them with an alternative, something real and affordable. It worked for a small group of executive women in many urban centers, especially New York, Houston and Los Angeles.

The look and concept took hold, and in 1983 I got into Bergdorf Goodman, a single-store luxury emporium, which is as elevated as you can achieve in the department store world. It was like being admitted into Valhalla — it was that difficult to get in. And to be the first Asian designer to be granted access in any category was a thrill. I was there for ten years occupying a stand-alone counter before leaving as a result of management changes at the store and the consignment system that most stores at that time adopted.

The key relationship is always with the buyers. The top managers, the merchandising managers can give an indication, but the buyers actually control what is selected — the business. Unless you are a very big name, the buyers are not so easy to deal with. They have their favorites. But Bergdorf Goodman offered the best exposure for my work. And it was also because of my presence there that I finally managed to get into the Japanese market.

The fifth floor of Bergdorf Goodman consisted of all the top fashion name brands, and whenever there was a fashion show they would use the accessories available in the store, unless the fashion house also produced their own accessories. Happily, they would often use my jewelry to accessorize at these shows. So, the designs obviously sat well with European and American fashion buyers.

I think it was important that there were no cultural connotations attached to the pieces, but that they were also obviously real. The cultural basis of my designs was different from traditional European-American design. It wasn't Chinese either, but it wasn't completely un-Chinese. What was it? Culturally speaking, it was a No Man's Land. It projected an international appeal. That was a very important aspect of it. People did not particularly like to wear ethnic Chinese-looking designs. It was easy to wear for work, lunch or dinner. Husbands also liked my style. There were very well-known costume jewelry brands like Kenneth J. Lane who mixed with the high and the mighty and produced costume jewelry. He represented the high point of popular costume jewelry, which was in a way my main competition, and his things sold for anything between US$50 to US$500. But they were costume, made of plastic or glass stones and set in base metal. Costume jewelry is basically reproducing luxury jewelry designs using cheaper materials — rhinestones, plastic and others. It is not in itself authentic, it is reproduction.

In terms of competing with costume jewelry, I had a problem with the size and weight of my pieces. Costume jewelry is light while semi-precious stones are heavier. Often I had to avoid the weightier stones such as hematite, which was limiting in terms of what I could do.

Dawn Mellow was then chief merchandiser at Bergdorf Goodman and it was she who gave me the opportunity to display my pieces in a stand-alone case and create my own department. She gave me a big chance and became a friend. She lived at 470 Park Avenue as well. We all need a guardian angel at some point, and she was mine at Bergdorf Goodman. She later became president of the store and then chief executive at Gucci where she innovated changes to revive that brand. After Dawn left Bergdorf Goodman, I lasted only for three more years. The business shifted to consignment terms, and I decided I couldn't support that. Merchandisers at Neiman Marcus also understood my concept and recognized the potential of my work. But getting into Bergdorf Goodman was the big break — no Asian designer had done that before, and in the end, what made it possible for me to get into Japan was my reputation as 'Kai-Yin Lo San from Bergdorf Goodman'. I could not be merely 'Kai-Yin Lo, a Chinese designer'. To add cachet to my line in Japan, I branded it 'Lumia', referencing the luminescence of the stones.

At the peak of the business, in the mid-1980s, Neiman Marcus would order two collections a year. Spring and Summer, and Autumn and Winter. One collection would be twenty styles and each style would be ten to fifteen pieces, depending on the price; more pieces if less expensive. It was the same for Saks Fifth Avenue, although volumes were somewhat smaller. Then I started selling into Singapore, Japan and London at Harrods and Harvey Nichols, adding to the production numbers. But the core market was always the United States.

To promote sales, personal appearances were necessary. I had to go and smile behind the counters. It's a must if a store buys your collection; they require your assistance in promotion. And you sell much more through friendly face-to-face contact and persuasion. The personal touch is crucial in launching a line, especially at the beginning of the season. First, you explain the concept and the highlights to the sales staff and then to the public. Who better than the designer to explain the special features? Each season, this was part of the game. The stores would commit to buying 'X' amount, and I would have to support it with 'Y', which included my time, presence and some contribution to advertising. I avoided agencies as the mark-up from the wholesale to the retail price was already 3 to 3.8 times. But of course, I was making my money off the wholesale price. Towards the end, Bergdorf Goodman tried to take it beyond 3.8 times, but the market would not support the collection at a higher price. And if the items became too expensive, it defeated my concept of designer accessories made of real stones that could be sold at affordable prices.

The trajectory of my business was that it started in the late 1970s with Bloomingdale's, and then it took off in the 1980s with stores like Neiman Marcus, Bergdorf Goodman, Saks Fifth Avenue, Nordstrom and many

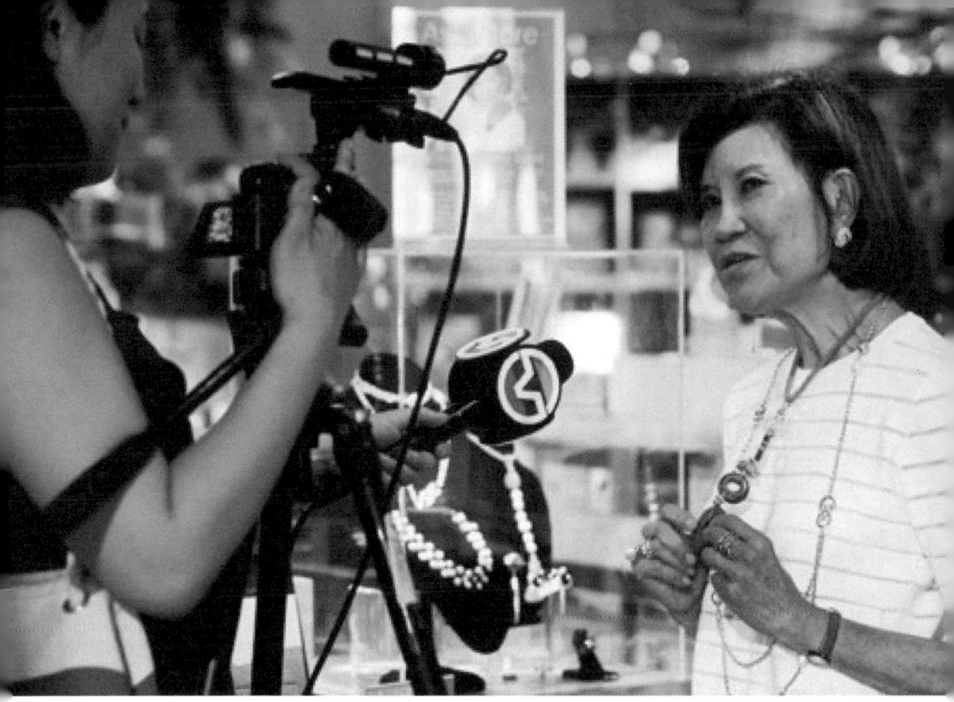

Regular personal appearances at the Asia Society Store, New York, since 2005 have been great exposure

other boutiques. At the high point of my sales into U.S. department stores in the mid-1980s, we were supplying in excess of fifteen Neiman Marcus stores, plus eight to ten Saks Fifth Avenue stores. The volumes were never huge, no more than hundreds of items a year, as we were a high boutique brand. But even so, the volume of sales we were getting could not be handled by the Hong Kong workshops and it called for moving our manufacturing to Guangdong Province to meet the demand.

Houston was a very important city for me. It turned out to be my second biggest market after New York. The Neiman Marcus store at Houston Galleria was a top draw. The Asia Society later chose to set up its first branch outside New York in Houston. Why? Because the Houstonians in the 1990s and the early 2000s were rich, expansive and giving, more than people in San Francisco and Los Angeles, for instance. The United States is king of consumption, but the expansiveness of consumption in those days was nowhere greater than in Texas. People liked to spend, and still do, although the mood now has changed. The Houstonians used to change into lovely couture outfits just to have lunch, and I had to adapt my thinking, to produce jewelry that was right for that market. The designs represented colorful jewelry that complemented clothes, which they appreciated. I have no idea what the younger people are buying today. I had better go and talk to the daughters and the granddaughters of my clients! Many value the handed-down pieces and I am in touch with the next generation.

The market for my jewelry remained small and given the taste and price levels, we could not sell to the less exclusive echelon of stores. Retail was robust, but my line was too expensive for the likes of Macy's and Marks & Spencer, which sold costume jewelry. The United States was the most open to my design concept, but even then it was a small segment of the American market.

I left Bergdorf Goodman because of the introduction of a consignment sales model where there was no agreement to purchase any pieces up front — you only got paid after a piece was sold. This was a model I could not sustain. I had caught the end of the era where the stores committed to purchases up-front. When I started, all designs were bought, and unsold pieces were marked down by 20 to 30 per cent until they moved. Having invested the money, stores had to promote the brand. Then the department store business model changed, and all goods were taken in on consignment. That is a game you cannot win.

During the 1980s, I spent many months each year in New York and other major cities in the USA. It was my main market for selling and promoting jewelry. The rest of the time I was in China, where the jewelry was mostly made, and in Hong Kong, where I opened shops dedicated to my jewelry. And from 1985, I was also running around in Japan. It took a long time, almost ten years, to break into that market.

An important reason for my success was that I gained support from significant individuals in the American establishment, in New York and also in Texas. My Hong Kong Chinese background was not a disadvantage and didn't matter them to them. They just liked the stuff.

One of my early patrons was Mrs William Randolph Hearst Jr, Austine, the wife of the press magnate and daughter-in-law of the man represented in the film *Citizen Kane*. She was a style icon, and her husband Will Hearst – the son of the man who built a newspaper empire and the mansion at San Simeon – was a most loving and generous person. A lot of people thought that he was feeble, but I suppose anyone who survived that father needed extra courage. He was always saying, 'Pa said this, Pa said that…' He was definitely in the shadow of his father, but he was such a loving and kind person. His wife Austine was a southern belle and had a lot of strength to support him. She was a style icon in the 1980s and her support and endorsement certainly helped in building my business in the U.S.A. I remained friends with them both until they died in the 1990s. Austine was herself a fashion authority, perennially earning a place on the 'Fashion Hall of Fame' and always on Eleanor Lambert's Best Dressed List. She used to wear my designs and gave me a wonderful compliment. 'Diamonds', she said, 'are not a girl's best friend, Kai-Yin is.'

Austine wore my jewelry with aplomb. She and Will lived on Fifth Avenue and always spent the summer in San Simeon, and I stayed with them at the castle and bathed in the Neptune pool where *Spartacus* was filmed. I slept in a 17th-century French bed that Papa Hearst had bought from some European castle. For Mrs William Randolph Hearst Jr. to endorse me was such an effective push. She did not have to do it. She once gave me a big party in an exclusive Park Avenue club and invited her friends to meet me.

She was a wonderful lady, and not just because she supported me. She supported a lot of artists. She patronized things that were different. She had an eye for the unusual, for instance in the way she dressed. She took to asymmetry very easily. She once wore one of my brooches and asked me to convert it into an earring. And she wore just the one because I couldn't match it for a pair. She was always lauded for her sense of fashion.

Evelyn Lauder, wife of Leonard Lauder and daughter-in-law of Estée, was another friend with style and individuality who supported me. 'We are working women and we need to bring the right things on our constant travels,' she said.

She wanted to buy three earrings of different colors so she could mix and match like me, a concept close to my heart. She lived on Park Avenue near one of my agents who told her she could not sell odd earrings; you have to buy the pair. So she came to me and asked me direct, and of course I made them for her.

Then there was Eleanor Lambert. She was the grand dame of fashion who started as a journalist and founded the powerful best-dressed list and became the arbiter of taste for some twenty years. Everybody who was anybody wanted to be on her list. Eleanor wore my designs, which was an affirmative promotion. And so did my friend Yue-sai Kan, a Hong Kong girl like me, who became famous with her program on cable TV in New York and launched a cosmetics line under her name. She interviewed me first in the 1990s on cable TV. Now based equally in Shanghai and New York, she is still as energetic and versatile as ever.

During those years, I started getting invitations to stay in stately houses, such as Cowdray Park in England, owned by Viscount Cowdray. I was not accustomed to having my messy suitcase unpacked by domestics. I also stayed at the house in San Francisco of Ann Getty, another client, where every piece of furniture was antique, mostly Louis XIV or XV from France, and where the only lighting was provided by candles. One had to be so careful not to turn on the wrong switch, or stumble into an expensive antique.

On many occasions, I have visited Oare House, the magnificent estate of Henry and Tessa Keswick, south of Marlborough in Wiltshire, England. Every time I have come away with renewed energy and respect for the love and dedication the owners have lavished on the flowers and vegetation in their 140-acre gardens designed by Clough Williams-Ellis, which they have preserved and cared for since 1975. As has been said of them, 'Rarely does one see such unity achieved as here where the gardens, an almost perfect blend of discipline and exuberance, perfectly complement one of the most handsome houses in Wiltshire.' *West Country Gardens: the Gardens of Gloucestershire, Avon, Somerset and Wiltshire* by John Sales, a catalog of the trees and shrubs on the estate, was published in 2016, recording approximately 2,000 species of historic trees and shrubs and existing vegetation, as well as more recent additions of species raised from seeds collected by the Royal Botanic Gardens in Kew and the Kunming Institute of Botany in China.

To add an up-to-date interpretation of the traditional folly, a contemporary pagoda was designed and erected in the garden by celebrated architect I. M. Pei and is perfectly positioned at the end of an avenue of lime trees. About this pagoda, the landscape historian Timothy Mowl has written, 'Tall as a three-story house, it is challenging modern… a geometric pagoda that asks the eye to unravel its logic. It is a great garden achievement….'

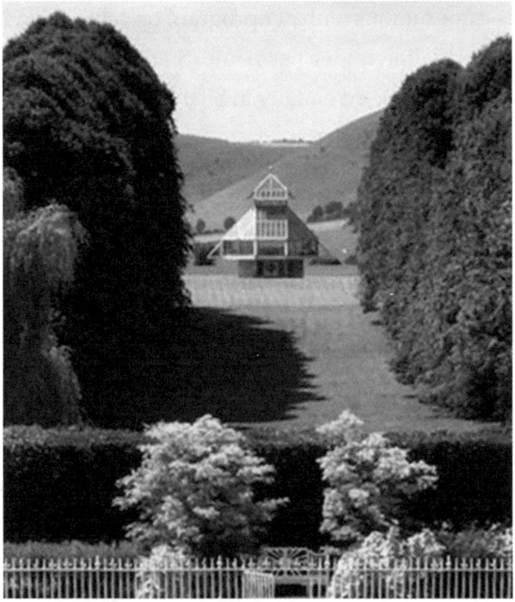

The "Folly" pagoda on the grounds of Oare House, England, on the only private commission undertaken by architect I.M. Pei

I have so enjoyed sitting by the Oare Kitchen Garden and the Magnolia Gardens and walking by the lawn and borders with so many species lovingly selected and groomed.

I was fortunate to be taken by Henry and Tessa to lunch at nearby Waddesdon Manor, home of Lord Jacob Rothschild, in the summer of 2015

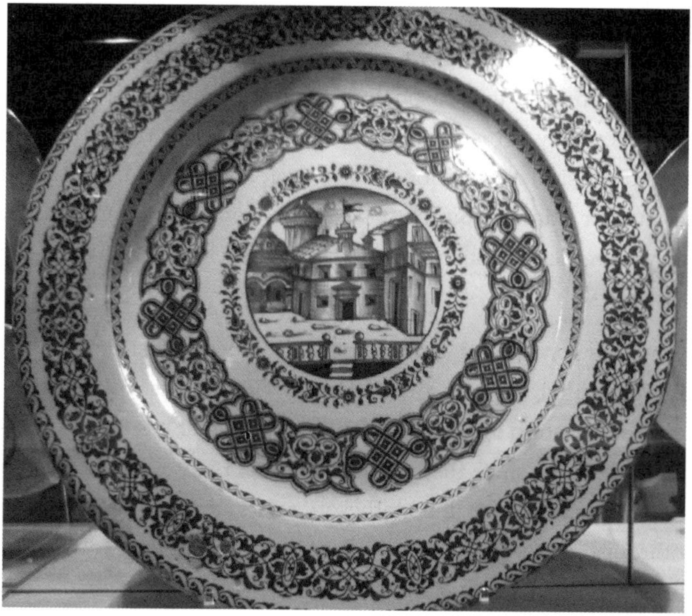

A large Majolica blue and white plate made in Urbino, Italy – from the Rothschild Collection housed in Waddesdon Manor, Oxfordshire, England – showing a border depicting the "Eternal Knot"

and was shown the Manor's magnificent gardens and nurseries. I cannot resist mentioning the highlight of that visit which has contributed so much to my knowledge of cross-culture, and which underscores the influence of my favorite 'Knot Without End'. As it turns out, I skipped dessert and ran to the Manor's exhibition hall to see the blue-and-white exhibition of Majolica plates featuring a border of the Endless Knot from the collection of the Duke of Mantua, whose duchy was located near Venice, confirming the influence of the Silk Road traffic! A year later, I found another plate with the knot design bearing the insignia of the same duke at the Hermitage Museum in St Petersburg.

I am a great fan of opera, and Salzburg is the music capital of that world. I have tried to go to the festival there as often as I can since the 1990s. I was lucky in that one of my clients during my San Francisco days was Ann Getty, who was married to Gordon Getty, the billionaire and composer. Gordon in those days used to buy jewelry for his wife. Each summer, he would take a house in Salzburg for the season and I would go and occupy a bed space there for a few days. It is the best opera in the world. We are all snobbish — but good classical music is one of my great loves. When I was a student in England, for a time I would buy tickets to opera performances at Covent Garden with a friend to share the cost, and we each occupied the seat every other act.

U.S. Congresswoman and House Speaker Nancy Pelosi bought a set of my earrings in San Francisco and Hillary Clinton also purchased from the Asia Society shop in New York, an outlet that that has been successfully selling my designs since the mid-1990s. Tessa, Lady Keswick, wife of the chairman emeritus of Jardine Matheson, and Lady Lipworth, the London philanthropist, are both long-time clients who take easily to wearing Kai-Yin Lo designs on their constant travels.

Carrie Lam, the Chief Executive of the Hong Kong SAR Government, has a quantity of my earrings, brooches and other accessories purchased over the past twenty years which she wears nearly every day. I am so delighted and flattered! She is a shining example of the important female executive who finds that wearing well-designed and affordable jewelry projects the right impact and allure.

The clear sense of identity of this group and the connection to my jewelry was fundamental to its success. Those buying my pieces are wealthy enough to buy anything that they want, but they see the practical side of my designs and also appreciate the fact that the jewelry is real.

Added to this group are the working executives who since the beginning of the launch of my semi-precious line have been loyal supporters, finding it both comfortable and becoming to wear. These women represent the biggest group of my supporters. I'm grateful to them all.

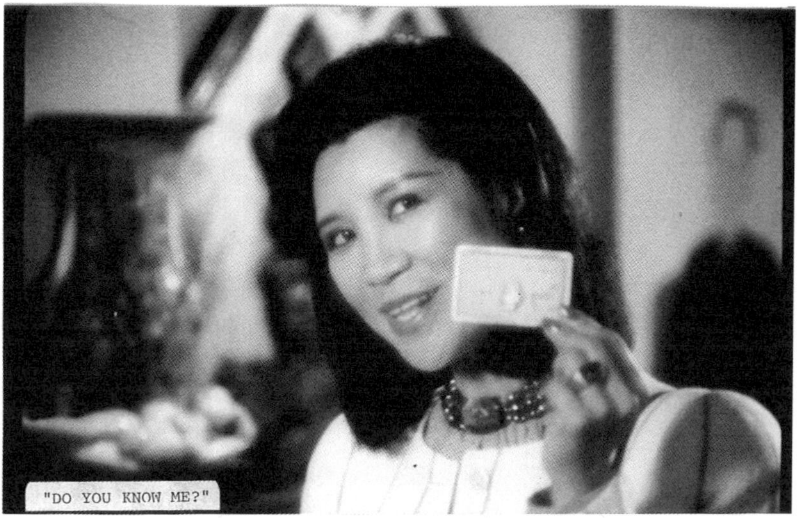

"Do you know me?" American Express ad from 1995

9

Harmony Through Asymmetry

I am known for wearing non-matching shoes, and for wearing trousers with each leg in a different fabric. For me, this mix of style has become a way of life. Just as with my designs, there is no need for an identical match. Asymmetry is a convenient way of doing things, and also of expressing personal style. It involves balancing but not matching, reflects an unconventional attitude, and in many ways is also a practical way of conducting life. This style of expression has become a core concept for me, projecting my taste, individualism and above all providing me with a great opportunity to expand aesthetic possibilities. Balancing with imbalance is my signature and has been central to much of what I do.

What led me originally to embrace asymmetry was practicalities: I did not have enough materials, and mixing what I had available became my solution. I soon realized that balance does not necessarily require matching and that you can create harmony and balance through other means. The originator oracle of Taoism, Lao Tzu, talks about how opposites can balance each other like male and female; opposites and non-matches can achieve harmony. Physically and metaphysically for me, I found this approach not only offered a convenient solution, but at the same time it created a visually pleasing appearance. In my design, in decorating and in dressing, my principal aesthetic expression, 'harmony with asymmetry' or 'balancing with imbalance', is a defining principle. I create harmony and equilibrium out of disparity, and to provoke. This approach encourages creativity, and the expression of self and individualism, and opens up more possibilities.

Traditional Chinese gardens were often asymmetrically designed, different from the prescribed symmetry of European gardens, although actually very often the Chinese reproduction of the randomness of nature was 'borrowed asymmetry'. Chinese calligraphy is also mostly asymmetrical, and its personality comes from individual interpretation and expression. But I was not directly inspired by this cultural tradition of asymmetry. For me asymmetry first and foremost is only a necessity, and the balance and harmonious effect achieved is a satisfying by-product.

A classic example of my work is a *bi*, a jade circle I found that was broken into equal sections with one piece missing. Standard collectors would ignore it, but I made use of it with an ingenious treatment.

It is one of my favorite designs. I linked the existing parts of two curved pieces of jade together using knotted cording, creating two curves facing in different directions. Then I balanced the crescent-shaped pieces with a circle at the bottom in coordinating colors, which fortunately is still in my collection. (The design is illustrated on page 1 of this book).

I began to fashion necklaces and pendants secured by cording and knots, inspired by traditional techniques. Many of the shapes I created and continued to feature, such as the circular *bi*, signifying the cosmos, were clean and strong. Knots in many configurations are favorite cultural symbols from China to India to the Middle East, having traveled along the age-old Silk Road. For me, the knot projects a striking look that is at the same time traditional and contemporary. The cording system I devised, adapted from traditional Chinese cording, is key to the 'Kai-Yin Lo' look in jewelry, especially the pieces that make use of antique stones and artifacts. Cording with knots became a crucial way of incorporating and securing loose and disparate elements — larger and smaller carvings and beads in jade, semi-precious stones and small metal ornaments — into an attractive, wearable whole.

I use stones and materials from different periods: carved jade animals and round *bi* circles from the Western Han dynasty (206BC-9AD), and agate with striking markings and clear crystal beads from the Liao era

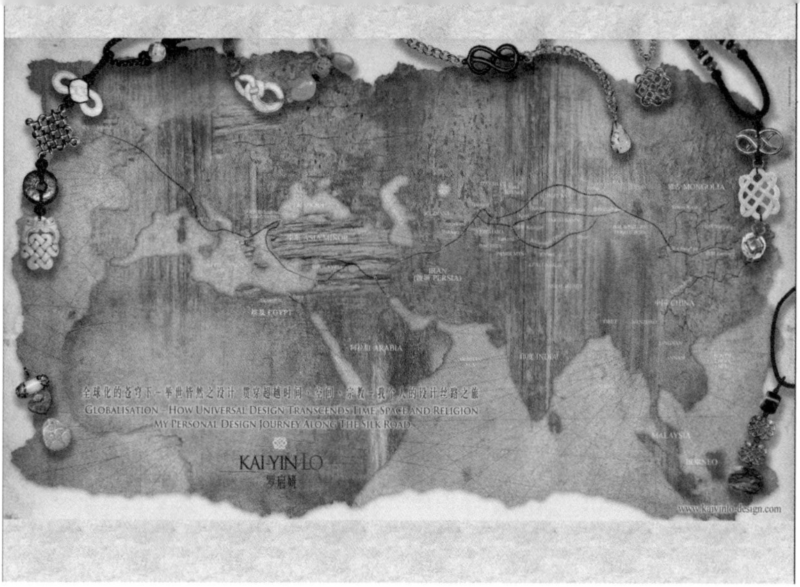

The Silk Road was my theme presented at the Hong Kong Pavilion, Shanghai World Expo, in 2010

(907-1125AD). We learned glassmaking from Central Asia and innovated new styles during the Han dynasty (206BC-220AD). Some jade and stone carvings date as far back as the Hemudu era (5000-3000BC). Some are from the Tang dynasty (7th-8th century) and came from beyond China's borders. And that is just one necklace looking stylish and asymmetrically contemporary.

I was a novice, with no experience nor formal training in design or what was regarded as *de rigueur*. But I had good aesthetic judgement, a sense of history and an innate appreciation for artifacts, precious and semi-precious stones that could be arranged as beautiful adornments.

So, I was able to act with a certain daring in developing my own style. After all, I wear mismatched clothing and socks and shoes. Using this 'balancing without matching' approach may only be possible because I am not married. Husbands climbing the corporate ladder would not tolerate a wife who did not conform. I have been in Japan enough to see how wives there are required to observe unwritten but nevertheless constraining rules applied to behavior, etiquette and mode of dressing. Now, happily, things are changing. But I remember the days when wearing a string of perfectly matched cultured pearls was *de rigueur*. Now women buy the more affordable and casual irregular-shaped freshwater pearls, or a necklace or earrings from my range of semi-precious jewelry.

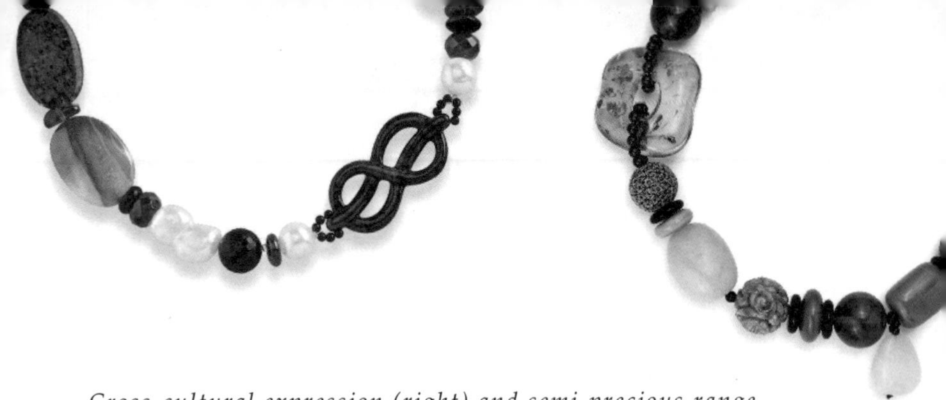

Cross-cultural expression (right) and semi-precious range of jewellery (left) have made Kai-Yin Lo design a cherished name synonymous with wearability and style

I do not consider myself a professional designer, especially if the word is used to describe those involved in creating product lines such as furniture or fashion. A client does not usually commission me. I create or invent from scratch. I would rather give disparate elements an unusual order or arrangement and create a new look and impression.

While my design sense is inspired by Chinese culture, it is also influenced by Central Asian and Western cultures. I was not groomed in the traditional Chinese arts but I did grow up in a Chinese cultural environment — southern Chinese or Cantonese — and that is my cultural anchor. Having studied Medieval and Early Modern European history, I was also exposed to the design sensibilities of the West via an effective mix of Eastern and Central Asian materials, with European sensibilities as an ongoing inspiration.

My knack for aesthetics was expanded, I think, all those years ago working for a short spell at the well-known interior decoration firm, Trollope & Sons in London. Even though I was doing little more than some sourcing and shadowing the decorators, the exposure provided me with some hands-on practical experience.

Working in the Reading Room of the British Museum and regularly visiting the Long Gallery to see the wonderful objects there — Chinese, Japanese and Korean ceramics from early dynasties and other artifacts — in the end liberated me. The collections reflected randomness, and a breadth of historical coverage that allowed me the freedom to seek connections, linkages and also variances. I was exposed to several worlds. Art, design and culture are part of an interconnected and borderless enterprise and I was ever-conscious that history and heritage blend past and present to become an entity for the future. I have tried to interpret that spirit in my designs, and in all I do, ever since.

I am forever fumbling for things which link East and West as our knowledge of these areas increases in a more interconnected and networked world. What draws me is the visual aspect and style differences, and being a historian, the embodiment as well. I suppose that is my strongest asset. I have to rely on my own judgment. And my historical knowledge backs me up. My mind is always open to possibilities, and with the perspective that comes from time and the passing of the years, I see that history is a great choice for learning about present life and past heritage. Studying history led to insights that nourished me and helped me understand and appreciate my own culture and exposed me to the connectivity of East and West, launching a life-long interest in artifacts and human development which I have interpreted in my designs and writings.

My pieces are hard to slot into existing categories for this reason and this has created some problems for me. In 2008, for example, I was asked to present a collection of jewelry designs to the Victoria & Albert Museum in London. It so happened that jewelry with metalwork belonged to the museum's department of metallurgy (imagine!). And the feedback I received was that my work was rejected because the materials I used differed markedly from what was displayed in the museum's jewelry department. So the capsule retrospective exhibition of my jewelry mounted as part of the exhibition 'China Chic' at the Kennedy Center in Washington, D.C. in October 2008, and the retrospective of my designs as well as my books, staged at Tokyo's up-market Wako department store in 2009, were all the more special to me. The former was a validation of my design, and the latter was the conservative, up-market store's first such exhibition for a non-Japanese brand.

Most sales in my main markets — North America, London, Paris, Japan and Southeast Asia — have been made up of jewelry designed not with

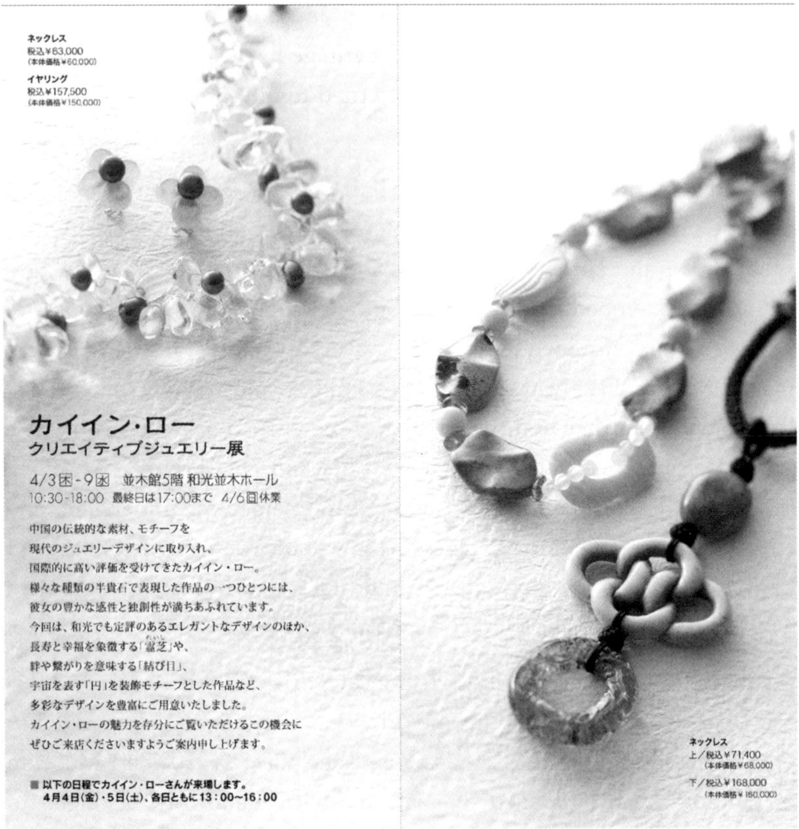

As seen in a Wako catalogue, 2008

antique beads and artifacts, but with the more affordable and easier-to-wear semi-precious stones. Color is important to me. I use natural stones, so choices are circumscribed. I work to coordinate colors and also to contrast them in the same piece of design. The spring and summer fashion scene in America and Europe used to pose a particular problem for me because these seasons usually feature a distinct signature color that dominates fashion of the season. One season it could be pink, another bright blue, then on to orange. For me, these stronger summer colors obliterate the effect of the accessories you wear. Using plastic or fabricated stones, you can create any color, but with semi-precious stones you are limited to the colors that come naturally. The main stones I use are agate, aquamarine, turquoise, onyx and lapis lazuli. I match or contrast, because there are only so many colors in the semi-precious range.

I pay close attention to fashion, but before a collection was designed for presentation in the ready-to-wear season, say in Paris, Milan or New York, I needed to know the colors or else I would not have enough time to create the appropriate accessories. Agate is the stone I work with the most because it is plentiful and affordable. It exists in quite a range of colors and shapes, and has the hardness of quartz. Agate stones have been used for millennia — by nomads of the Euro-Asian steppes from Central Europe to Siberia. Its rich browns and reds go with most things. Another stone I tend to count on is lapis lazuli and similar quartz stones which exist in shades of blue, usually considered to be a spring color. I am always happy to find a new semi-precious stone, such as the recent discovery of dumortierite, a blue crystal quartz found near water.

My design process starts with determining colors and I work generally in tandem with the trends in fashion. Some stones are more fragile than others and cannot be carved, and some stones only exist in small sizes. Therefore, instead of coordinating, I need to contrast as well. I had to start work really early — far in advance of when the clothes would be reviewed, and orders placed. The fashion people would work with fabrics and I needed to know what the colors of these fabrics would be because colors determine so much with me. I would be eager to get feedback when the fabrics were being presented, before the collections were made. But it still involved a lot of guesswork. Then the buyer would come and say: 'We are featuring blue.' But until recently, I only had one blue stone, lapis lazuli. It was always quite demanding. When pieces and colors superficially did not fit, I worked to create the effect that they would fit!

Spring was always more difficult for me because the season is associated with vivid colors. One finds a greater range of semi-precious stones in autumnal colors, or neutral colors — white and black, and brown and gray. In spring, I tended to work with white and black background colors. Natural materials, however, do not have a wide enough range of hues and varieties. Japan particularly has fixed preferences. In spring, they would wear white, especially crystal and mother of pearl. Blue, as in lapis lazuli, thankfully, is a year-round preferred color.

To handle a certain volume and to conform to a certain price level, it was too expensive to work in gold, so from early on I worked mostly in silver. I had my own process for making a silver base, which was not easy to do. Some pieces were plated in 18-carat gold with a three-micron seal to ensure longevity — the essence of the Kai-Yin Lo semi-precious range of jewelry.

The semi-precious range never made much headway in China because semi-precious stones have little perceived value there. Jewelry in China connotes value and status, and decorative accessories without intrinsic value are of little interest. My semi-precious range has only recently caught on in the bigger cities like Beijing, Shanghai and Chengdu, while my antique range of jewelry appeals to those who appreciate the value of the antique components, which is a smaller market. But ultimately, design and color are not the most important factors for the Chinese. Things are measured in perceived value and status. But things are changing — I now count amongst my clients ladies of discernment who appreciate my designs that 'make history wearable'. Also, mainlanders do respect that I was the first Chinese brand to be accepted in the United States, Europe and Japan, and have embraced my jewelry for that reason.

What is good taste and bad taste? That is a serious question. It has nothing to do with money. And how to value jewelry? Is value just in the eye of the beholder? No, it is more than that. Jewelry is a good way to store wealth. I know a man who used to run a shop on Hong Kong's Hollywood Road and has now moved to Shenzhen, dealing in diamonds. His customers come to him with satchels of cash to buy diamonds that have a clear and recognized resale value, and besides they are highly portable! Diamonds, you can say, are taken as an absolute guarantee of value. Is that the ultimate worth of jewelry? Who is to say?

Jade, on the other hand, is more subjective. If I put a necklace containing Warring States-period jade up for auction, is it worth $50,000 or $150,000? Or more? Whoever buys my jewelry usually has sufficient knowledge of antiques to be able to establish its worth and needs an understanding of provenance and history — and hopefully also has an appreciation for my designs and for the taste and ingenuity of the assembled piece. As with all art and good design, the subjective element plays a significant role. Not so with diamonds, which require no great demand for interpretation or design. With my pieces, while some of the materials used have an intrinsic value, ultimately it is the design that elevates the piece as a work of art. That is its true essence and value — taking materials, rearranging and redesigning them to enhance their appeal and increase their worth.

A friend of mine is a dealer, and I asked him why the prices of jade and other items traditionally cherished by the Chinese have gone up so much. He said that there are many families with a child now graduated from a good university and with a good job, a good salary. There is for them a perception of value in these things because they signify a new social status, and the family would like to own one or more antique pieces. There are so many families in China like that. The rise in the value of antiques generally is also a form of hedging. Chinese people appreciate the history, but they are also preserving the value of their assets too. To make money off my semi-precious stones requires volume and markets. Ultimately the range seems to have decorative rather than investment value, but with the antique pieces, there are more and more Chinese who appreciate their historical and monetary significance.

The question of value relates to the concept of 'affordable luxury', which is a trend now found everywhere. We see it in terms of hotels, clothing and a wide range of items where there is a sense of luxury in a price range that is affordable to a much wider group of people. For me, a lifestyle can be enhanced by superb materials, but it is more wonderful to have materials put into well-designed and well-constructed forms. While many considerations factor into value, it is certainly true that the ability to realize good design helps to cultivate good taste and enhance value.

I used to save up to buy rather expensive new clothes, but then I became a fan of Uniqlo in Japan in the 1990s and used to buy items there for myself and for presents. The quality was superb, all made in Japan at that time. Now Uniqlo is everywhere — made in Vietnam, China and elsewhere — but the quality is still good enough. And quality is essential, a pre-condition for any item. In London, I would go to Harrods and Harvey Nichols to look at the styles, then go to Uniqlo to buy basics. I went to two rather fancy weekend house parties in stately homes, and Uniqlo was what I wore with my accessories, and the brand more than held its own. The look today is casual, and so diverse. I used to be able to tell who had designed an outfit someone was wearing by just looking at it. That no longer matters.

In many ways, it is now much more difficult to design, as constant changes are called for. The ready-to-wear range also needs to have something new to go with ever-changing fashions, which is why I more and more frequently return to my first preference — assembling antique-related items for China and other discerning markets.

Trends cannot be ignored, but if you decide to set yourself apart from them, then you have to build up your entire personality and image of 'persona' much more strongly. I do not follow trends, but you could say that I initiated a few. Even then, you still have to make things wearable, make them serviceable and convenient. To what extent did Chanel follow trends or initiate them? Alexander McQueen initiated trends, but many of his creations were showpieces and were not easy to wear. And how long can the legacy of such a brand name last with evolution and adaptation without the guiding hand of the creator, and still maintain its core spirit?

MAKING A NAME IN JAPAN

10

Making a Name in Japan

By 1985, I had made a name for myself in the United States and was making progress building a clientele in the international market, selling my jewelry in department stores including Harrods and Harvey Nichols in London, and Galeries Lafayette in Paris. I felt the need to explore another market, and there was only one that met my requirement for a wealthy and sophisticated consumer base — and that was Japan.

I went to Japan ambitious and vain enough to expect that I could easily repeat the success I'd had in America. The choice of Japan had nothing to do with the fact that it is an Asian country adjacent to China, with which it shares a long history. And my being Chinese was in no way an advantage in Japan; indeed, it was a huge liability. From the mid-19th century the Japanese have projected a military and cultural superiority over the rest of Asia (with individual exceptions, of course). This attitude had to do in part with how things developed for Japan and China after the Europeans appeared and blew open the doors. The Japanese admired the military and institutional accomplishments of the West, and immediately worked to absorb and incorporate them into their own system. The Meiji Restoration reshaped Japan and led to tremendous changes. By the end of the 19th century, Japan had been accepted by the Western powers as more or less an equal. China under the Manchus, meanwhile, suffered successive humiliating defeats at the hands of the Western powers, and from the Japanese after a decisive battle fought in Chinese territorial waters in 1905. But after the defeat of Japan's militarists in World War II, the Japanese embraced American-style consumerism, while keeping to their preferences and tastes. My being a name in America was something I needed to make work to my advantage if I was to establish a foothold in Japan.

When I went to Tokyo and Osaka in the late 1980s, Japan was at the height of its economic boom. I immediately saw that the Japanese had refined taste. It would be a good market for me, once I found a way around the problem of being Chinese and the challenges in establishing my brand in this market historically closed to foreigners. In art and culture, the Japanese have always shown great sensibility and refinement. The nation has guarded its heritage with care and pride, as evidenced by the well-preserved ancient buildings inspired by Chinese Tang and Song architecture next to their own carefully kept shrines in Nara, Kyoto, around Lake Biwa and in other parts of the country. With the newfound affluence of the 1980s, Japan was in what seemed a mad rush to acquire luxury products from Europe; the French commanded the most cachet, then the Italians. In the 1980s it appeared that every Japanese working girl's ambition was to save up to buy a Louis Vuitton handbag. Japanese consumers reportedly accounted at the time for 20 to 30 per cent of the luxury brand's worldwide turnover. Nowadays, Japan is a tiny market compared to China, but in the 1980s, Japan dominated. Outside the United States it was the single most valued market and source of revenue for many luxury houses and jewelers.

Hanae Mori, the premier fashion brand in Japan in the 1980s, facilitated my breakthrough in the country

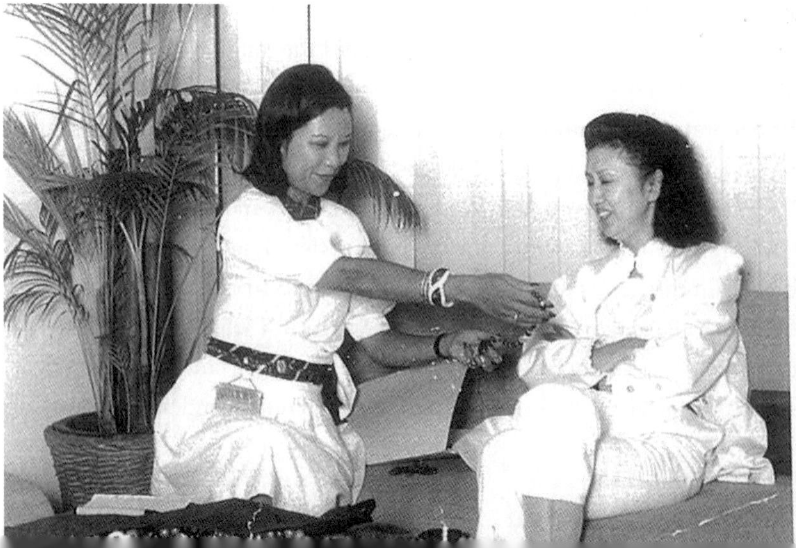

While in New York, I had met the celebrated Japanese couturier Hanae Mori, a forerunner in fashion design who commanded national attention as one of the most high-profile designers of her day, dressing the Imperial family and the wives of the industrialist elite. Fortunately for me, she liked my jewelry and my cashmere shawls which I had fabricated in China.

She asked me to design and produce some jewelry for her haute couture collections shown in Paris. The Japanese had suddenly become so internationally ambitious, and she was the first Asian couturier to establish a fashion house in Paris selling both haute couture and ready-to-wear. Her *maison* was on posh Avenue Montaigne, not too far from the house of Givenchy. With our Paris collaboration underway, Hanae Mori asked me to go to Japan to create accessories for her collections. Those were the golden days of Japanese affluence and expansiveness, but at that time Chinese people, in fact Asians of any kind other than Japanese, were considered not good enough to market their wares in Japan. Even with the help of the Hong Kong Trade Development Council, there was no way I was able to rent shop space in top Tokyo retail areas like Ginza, Akasaka or Roppongi. When she kindly offered me space for a small shop in her own Hanae Mori building on fashionable Omote Sando, I gratefully accepted with alacrity.

Having established a foothold, I started to look at the market, trying to sort out how I might be able to repeat my American success selling through department stores. My first contact was a director of the Seibu chain, Mr Kei Egashira, the former international chief of the Japanese financial house Nomura until he was recruited by Mr Seiji Tsutsumi, the powerful *supremo* of the Seibu conglomerate, which included department stores and real estate businesses. Seibu was my preferred choice because it was a more progressive retailer than Mitsukoshi and the other more traditional stores. But being an unknown in Japan, I was too much of a risk for Egashira. He ultimately decided against taking a chance on a brand created by a Chinese, even though I was already an established U.S. brand that he was familiar with. It was a disappointment.

The owner of the Isetan department store chain, Mr Kasuge, had seen my designs in Paris, liked them and sent a buyer to Hong Kong to purchase some. I cannot emphasize enough how different my pieces looked among the jewelry of the day. The buyer bought a small selection and I was given a counter in the middle of the ground floor of Isetan's main Tokyo store in Shinjuku. Wow, was I pleased! Until that moment, a Chinese brand hadn't been represented with a stand-alone case in any Japanese store. It just didn't happen.

We set up a counter in Isetan but sales of course were disappointing. I had no sales agent servicing the sales counter I was given, and only one sales girl had to cover two to three counters. I just didn't have anyone to advocate for me in the store, or to help market and merchandise my collection. At the time, I had no experience with merchandising in Japan, where the norm was to employ a sales agent approved by the store who would service your business operations including representation in the department stores, then the main channel for exposure and distribution. The agent would also assist with promotion and handle all money matters. But I did not have an agent or a commitment from the store to invest in promoting my line, so the launch was not a success. I lasted for one season, which is all that retailers will usually give you to prove yourself. If after one season sales are not robust, you are branded as unsuccessful — you are marked, essentially, which makes it very difficult to find an agent to represent you. On top of that, I was Chinese.

But I later found a way into Japan, through the only route that could have worked for a Chinese person. I entered Japan via New York.

Sometime after the Isetan debacle, I met the North American head of the Mitsukoshi department store, a nice man named Mr Shigoshi. He liked my designs and he introduced me to a contact at Mitsukoshi headquarters in Tokyo as — and this was decidedly crucial — 'Kai-Yin Lo-san from Bergdorf Goodman.' That proved to be the magic formula — linking me with an internationally-known luxury brand. With the Bergdorf Goodman association, I was less of a risk.

So Mr Shigoshi 'discovered' me and also found me an agent (and this was essential) who was approved by the department store on the basis of their proven ability to generate a certain amount of business. I was installed in Mitsukoshi. They first test your collection in three stores, then in more branches. This time, it worked well. The name I chose for my line, 'Lumia', accented the luminosity of the semi-precious stones.

Lumia, the Kai-Yin Lo semi-precious jewelry line for Japan in 2002

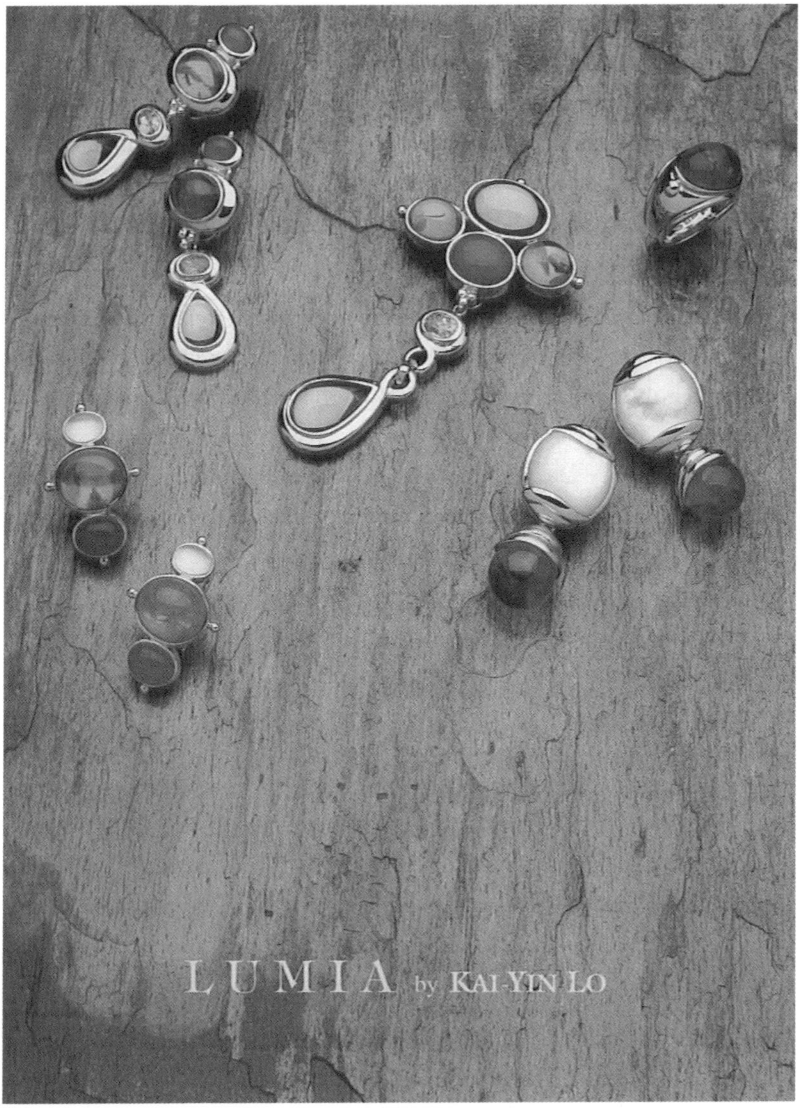

The jewelry pieces that sold well in Japan were the same semi-precious stone designs that had been successful in the U.S. market, except that sizes were smaller. Heavyweight stones were avoided as Japanese preferred lighter adornment.

Size of stones had to be reduced and the colors were more prescribed. Japanese prefer to wear certain stones and colors in particular seasons. I used light green aventurine, which looked like more costly jade, lapis lazuli and blue topaz, and pearls galore in necklaces and brooches, the latter a favorite accessory. The Japanese were not adventurous with styles or color in those days. However, every season I introduced a new palette and above all an exciting selection of new shapes.

Then in about 1995, Wako, the most exclusive store in Tokyo, located on the corner of Ginza-dori, installed me in a stand-alone area on its fifth floor, which also housed international brands such as Buccellati. Founded by Kintaro Hattori in 1891, the Wako building is distinguished by a clock tower completed in 1932. The Hattori family also founded Seiko watches.

Everybody who wanted special and quality merchandise would shop at Wako, including the Japanese Imperial family and the families of the top industrialists. Without their belief in my designs and the installation of a stand-alone department, I would not have gained such high-profile exposure. I am grateful for the support given by Mr Reijiro Hattori (who was chairman) and his kind and charming wife Etsuko, and the other family members including the vivacious Kumiko for their belief in my designs. These people became good friends, proudly introducing me to their exclusive circles.

Even with a connection that opened the door, performance was important. It was *de rigueur* to conduct seasonal promotions at Wako and Mitsukoshi. In Japan, it was a social occasion — clients and friends came to look at the designs, and to chat. I felt that I was more than a marketer of jewelry, I was being received with respect and friendliness as a designer who introduced a new point of view and dimension in Japanese consumer culture.

No wonder they classify artisans, designers and artists, these important cultural properties, into varying grades of excellence, the highest being 'national treasure,' a telling term of respect for quality and creativity.

The Japanese nation has mass discernment – they are punctilious about quality in material, fabrication and design. Shopping and acquisition is not a casual habit – it involves judgement, taste, a passion for the pleasures of collecting and possessing – all rolled into one experience that enriches life. All these were traits I found in my clients at Wako, Mitsukoshi and at my shop in the Hanae Mori building. Understanding the concept and background of the design was important to these clients and they cherished design and the purchases they picked. I still get requests by Japanese clients who ask for an update on my designs.

One unforgettable event for me was the retrospective that Wako mounted for my designs in June 2009 after a successful twelve-year cooperation. It occupied two floors, and my major clients, friends and other distinguished guests attended, including the important industrial designer, Kenji Ekuan, president of GK Design, whose work including models of the 'shinkansen'

Manning my counter at Wako Department Store in Tokyo's Ginza

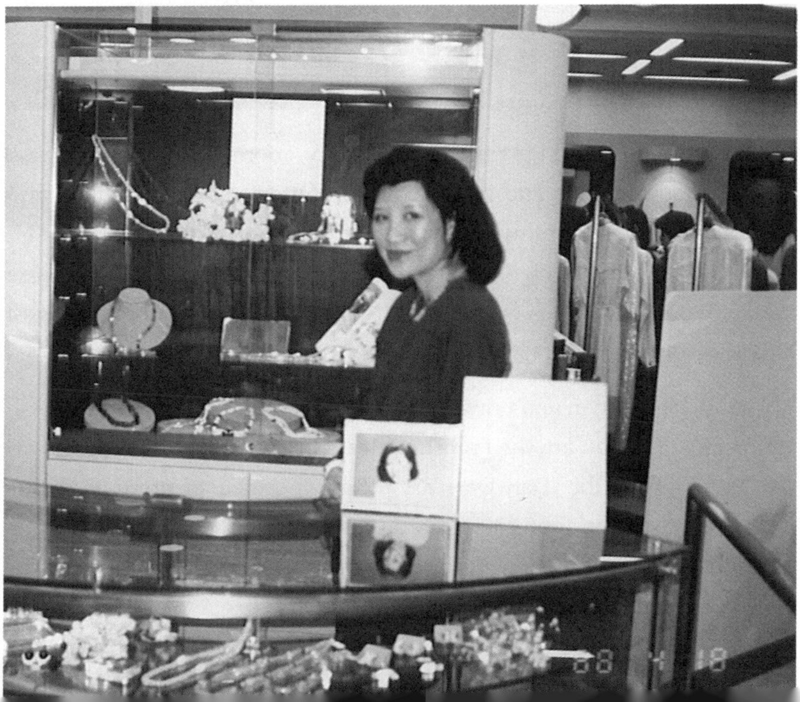

bullet train I greatly admire. To have been given this recognition by the foremost store in Tokyo moved me to tears.

With Kazuko Aso, who helped me to cross cultural and democratic barriers to establish myself in Japan as an Asian brand

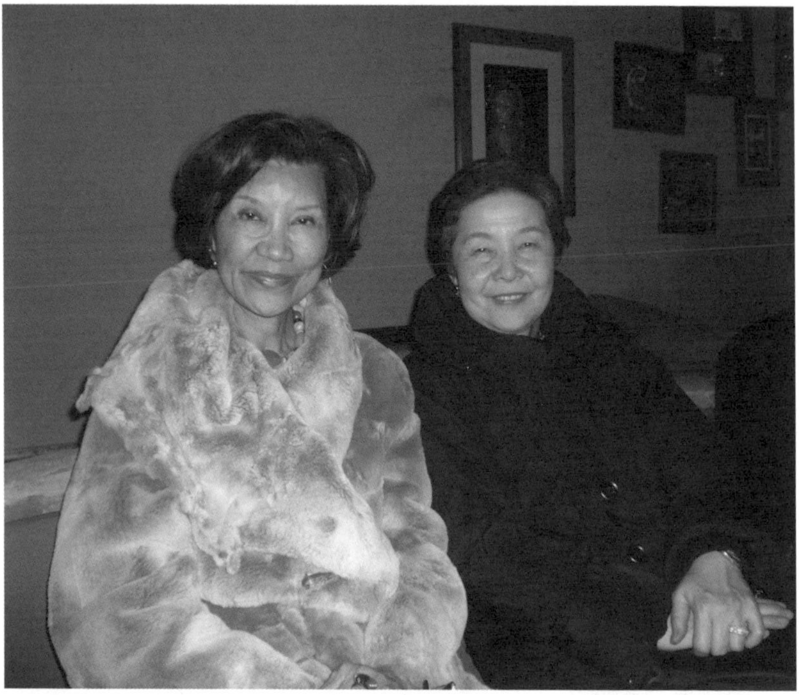

I am fortunate to be friends with the Aso family, another respected Japanese clan. Without the help and support of the Hattori and Aso families, and those who kindly introduced me to their circles of interesting and well-connected friends and creative practitioners, my pathway to the Japanese market would have been even more strenuous, and my understanding of Japanese society would have been much more restricted.

My good friend, then and now, is Kazuko Aso, married to the second Aso son, Binky. Keen on art, the French-educated Kazuko for many years was the force behind the 'Dan Dan' art project founded to promote young Japanese artists. She appreciated my designs and was helpful in organizing exhibitions and introducing me to her friends, amongst whom was Mrs Abe, wife of the present prime minister. They were all polite and kind, but I still needed to prove myself with my designs, despite the fact that I came with certain credentials. Brother-in-law, Taro Aso, has been a politician holding different cabinet posts for as long as anyone can remember. Known as the kingmaker of his party, he was prime minister for a short spell and is at present once again the deputy prime minister since Mr Shinzo Abe came to power. His maternal grandfather was Prime Minister Shigeru Yoshida, the first prime minister in post-World War II Japan, and his daughter Dame Kazuko Aso, who spoke with a clipped British accent, was a delightful grand dame. I was in awe when I first met her, but she had a humorous way of putting one at ease and I liked her immediately.

I cite these people because without them, it would have been even more difficult for a Chinese to be accepted by Japanese society and to make headway in the Japanese retail arena. These particular people supported me because they were open-minded and had an international perspective – and they liked my designs. I am grateful for their friendship and appreciation of my work.

My business in Japan continued until the year 2010, and then began to ebb as the department stores went through a crisis, mirroring the trend in the United States. Many of them closed, and the jewelry business became consignment-based, just as it had in the U.S., so I pulled out. But it was both enormously challenging and satisfying to have succeeded in what had been a market hitherto closed to Asian designers, and I am proud of what I managed, and grateful for the experience gained and the friendships I made in the process.

My parents, Lo Hing Kwong and Lucy Lo Thom Lai Ming, with Robert, Anthony, Marina and myself, 1950s

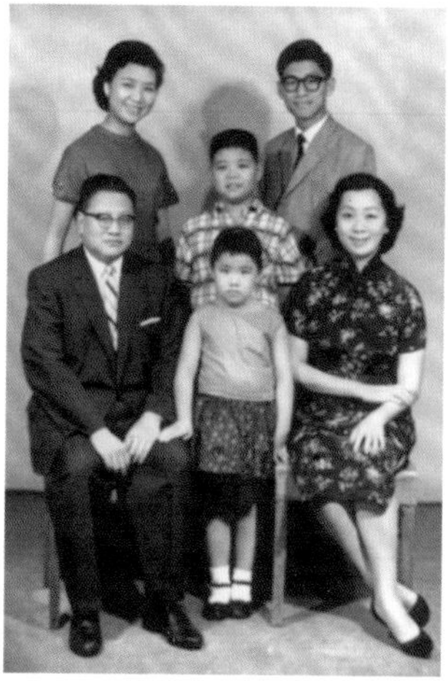

Benjamin and Jonathan, sons of Anthony and Audrey, with family and mother—her last portrait, 2010

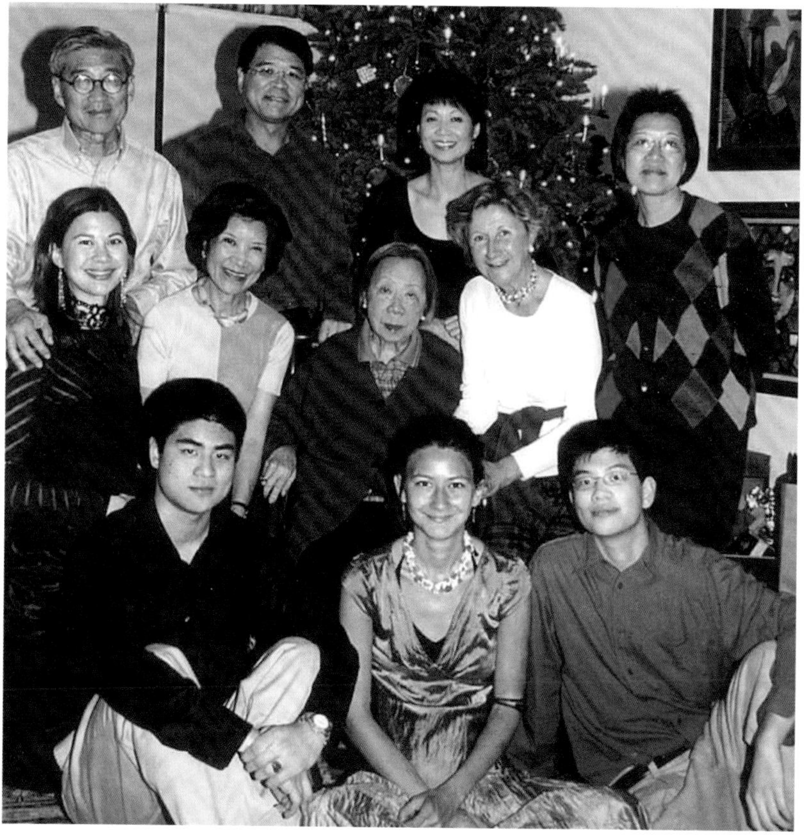

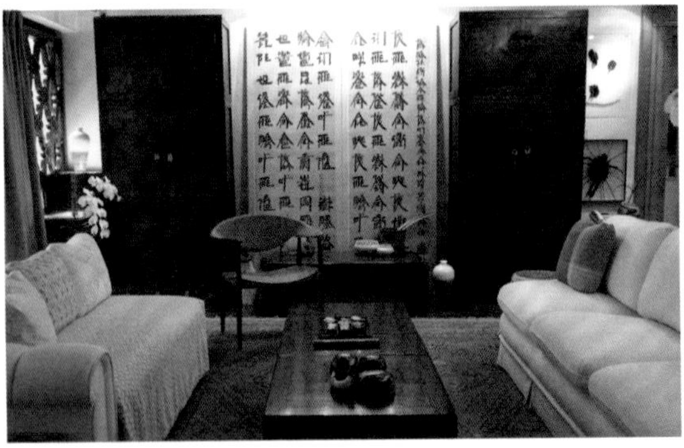

My spacious flat 2003-2016 where I could hoard too many things!

Dinner at home hosting guests from government, education, art, cultural institutions and business, 2017

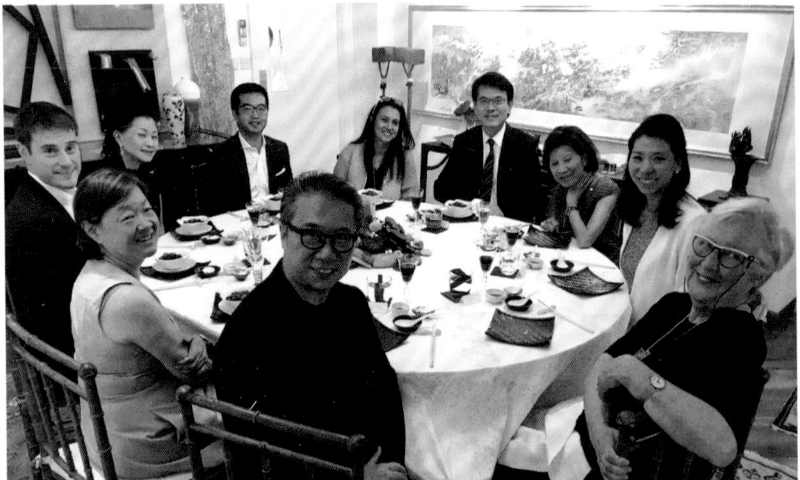

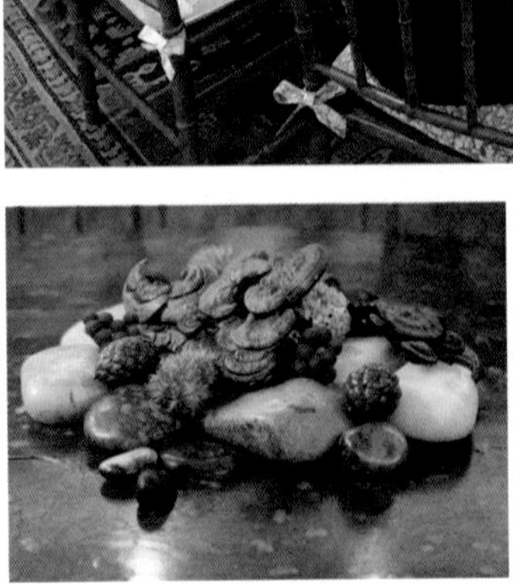

Table decoration to chart memories—jade pebbles from Hetian and Three Gorges Yanzhi River and *lingzhi* mushrooms from Yellow Mountain Anhui

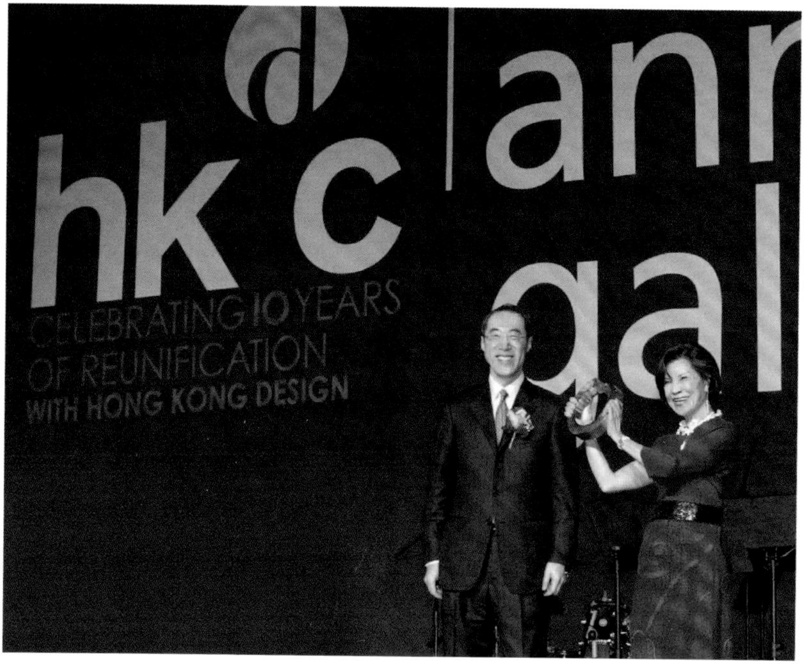

Receiving "World's Leading Chinese Designer" award, 2007

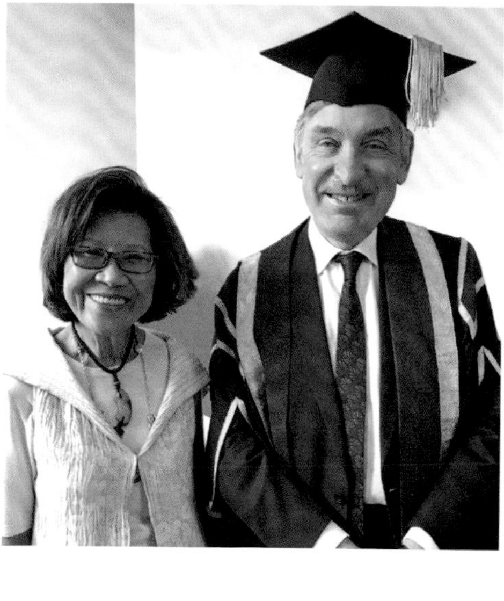

With Nigel Carrington, Vice Chancellor, University of the Arts London—I cannot believe that a historian with little training in design is installed as the first Visiting Professor, Cross Culture at Central Saint Martins, University of the Arts London!

CURATING AND EXHIBITIONS

I learned a lot curating *Hong Kong: Creative Ecologies—the Shaping of Design Culture* exhibition at Shanghai Expo, 2010

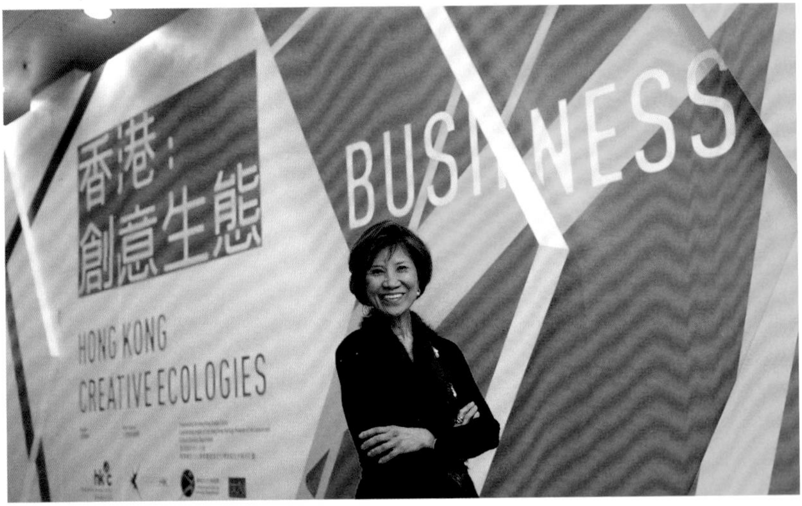

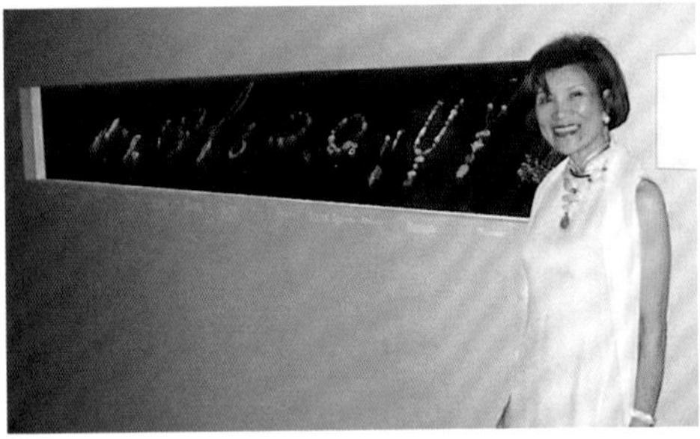

So encouraged my jewelry design occupied the only individual vitrine at *China Chic* showcasing contemporary Chinese design at the Kennedy Center, Washington, DC, 2006

Inscription from my book, *Classical and Vernacular Chinese Furniture in the Living Environment*, with endorsement by Wang Shixiong—it meant a great deal! 1998

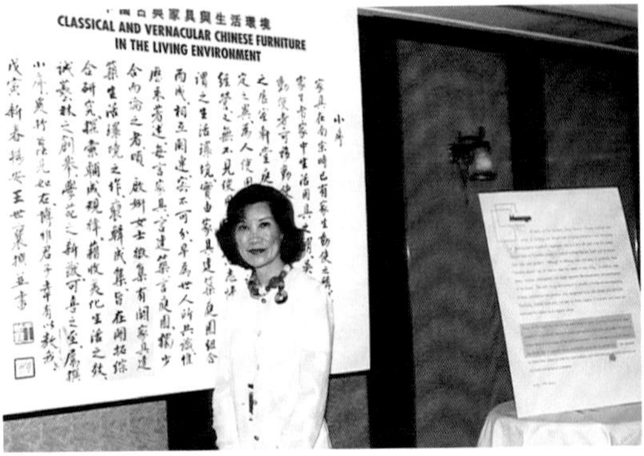

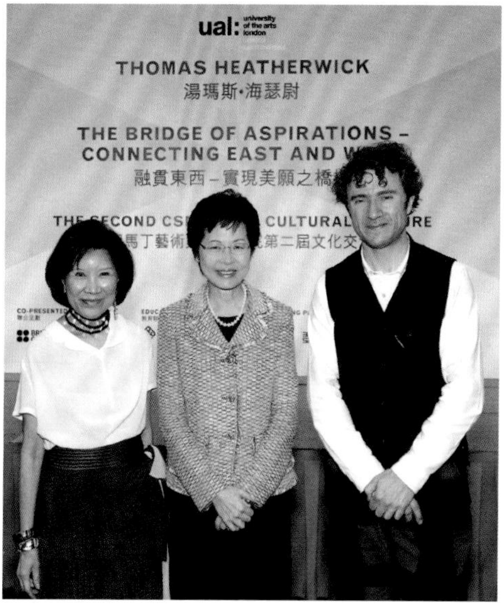

Thomas Heatherwick, maverick all-rounder, was speaker at the Central St. Martins Cross-Cultural Lecture, opened by Carrie Lam, 2014

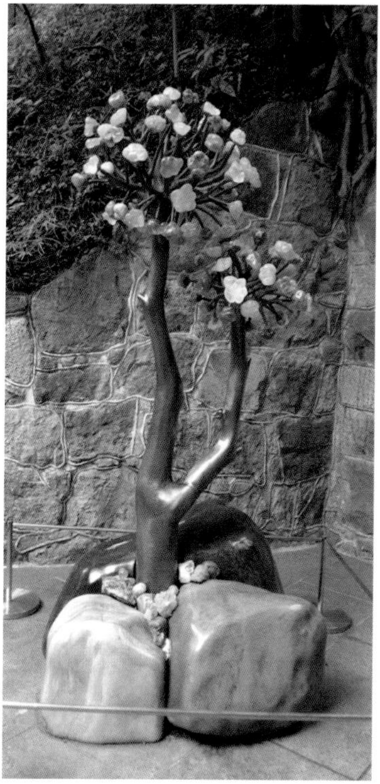

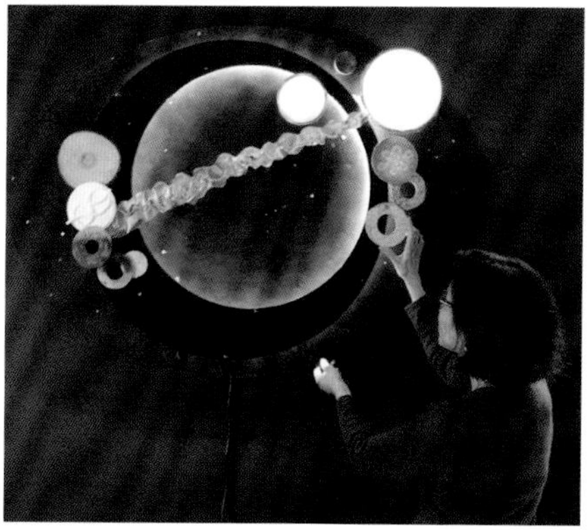

Cosmos linking East and West, which I curated, brought a new concept of art/design exhibition, Asia Society Hong Kong, 2013

As pioneer of semi-precious stones jewelry, herewith *Tree of Life* with everlasting bloom, 2015

CHINESE VERNACULAR ARCHITECTURE

Researching at center pond
of Hongcun, Anhui, 1999

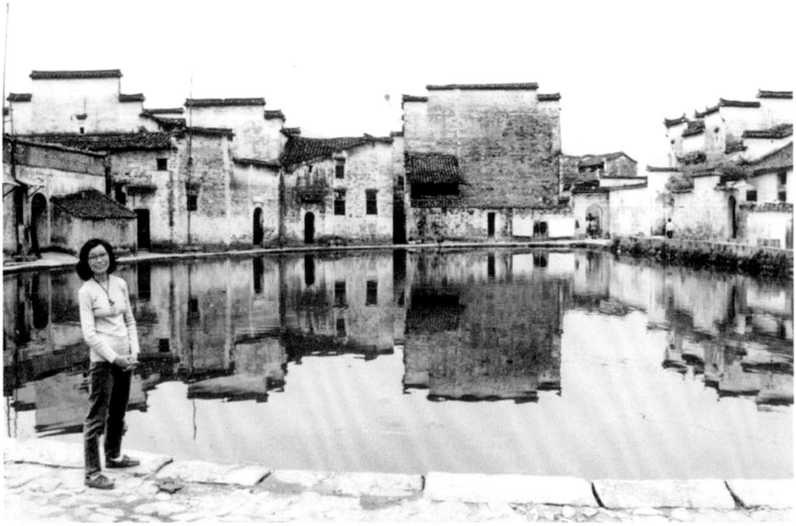

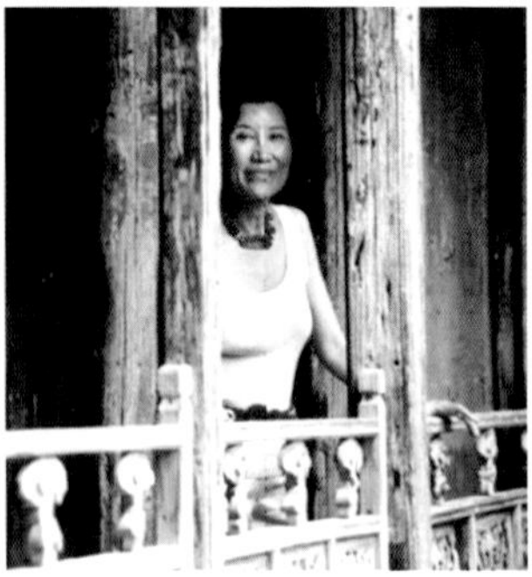

Laowujiao, a fine example
of a 16th-century house
located in Huangshan district,
South Anhui, China

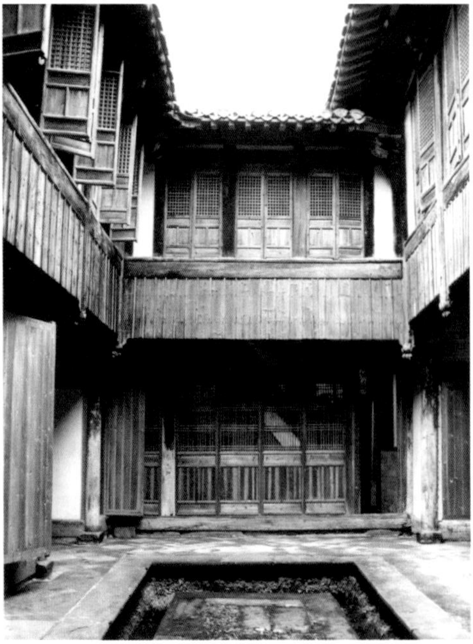

Wood-carved window
partitions, a characteristic of
Huizhou house architecture.
I bought many house parts to
save them from destruction.

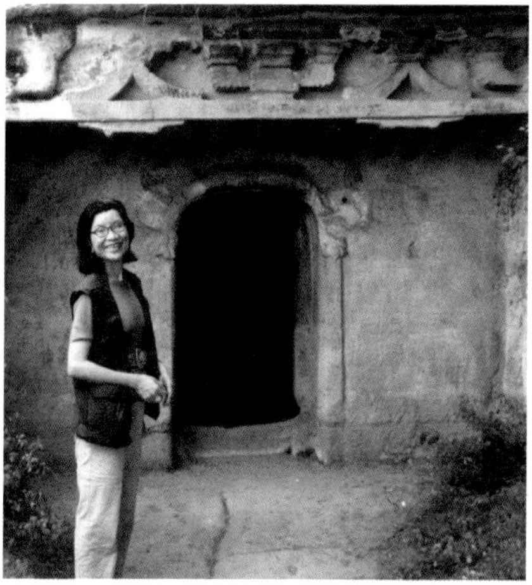

Very rare depiction of 'dougong' in stone in a 9th-century tomb in Henan, 1955

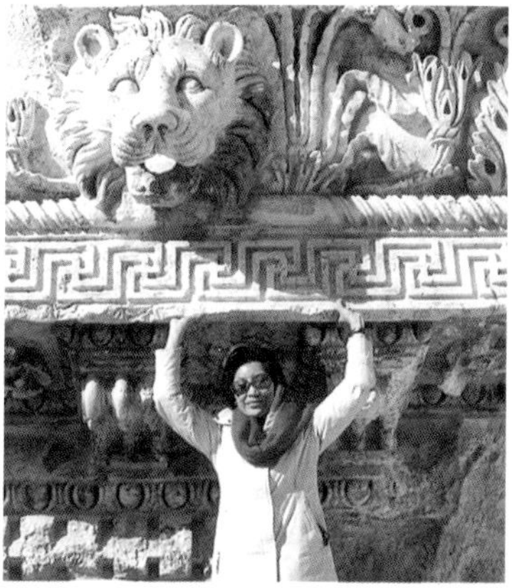

East and West connecting—3rd-century key pattern on stone frieze in South Syria, 2008

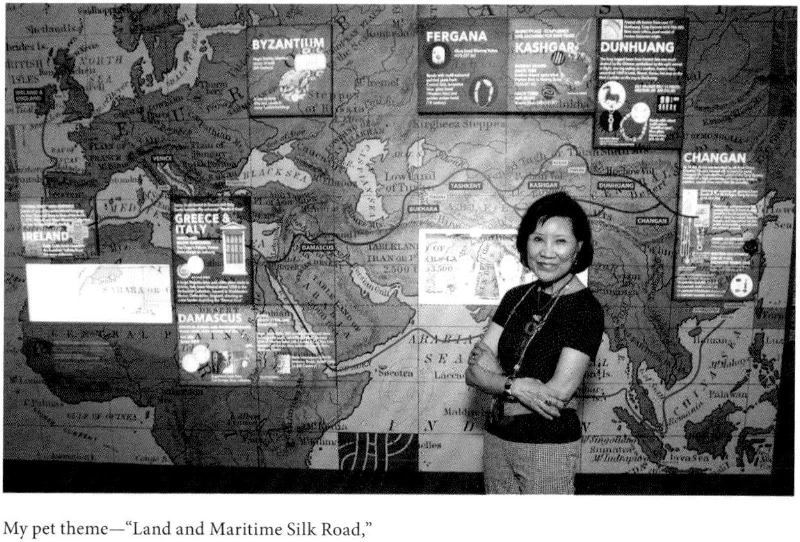

My pet theme—"Land and Maritime Silk Road," confluence of cultural and commercial exchanges for over 3,000 years as depicted in the traveling exhibition to mark the 20th anniversary of Hong Kong's return to China, 2017

SEMI-PRECIOUS JEWELRY

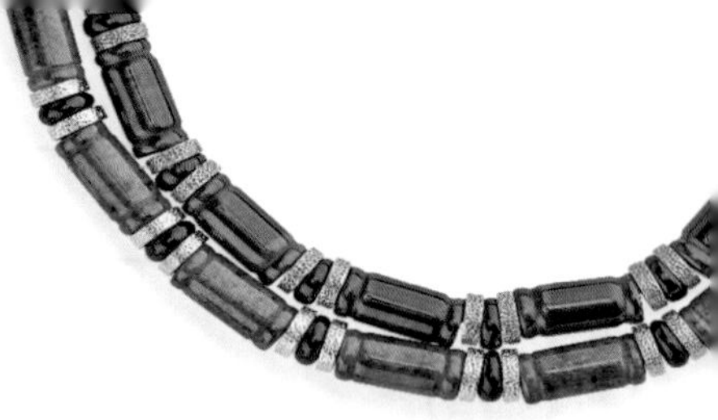

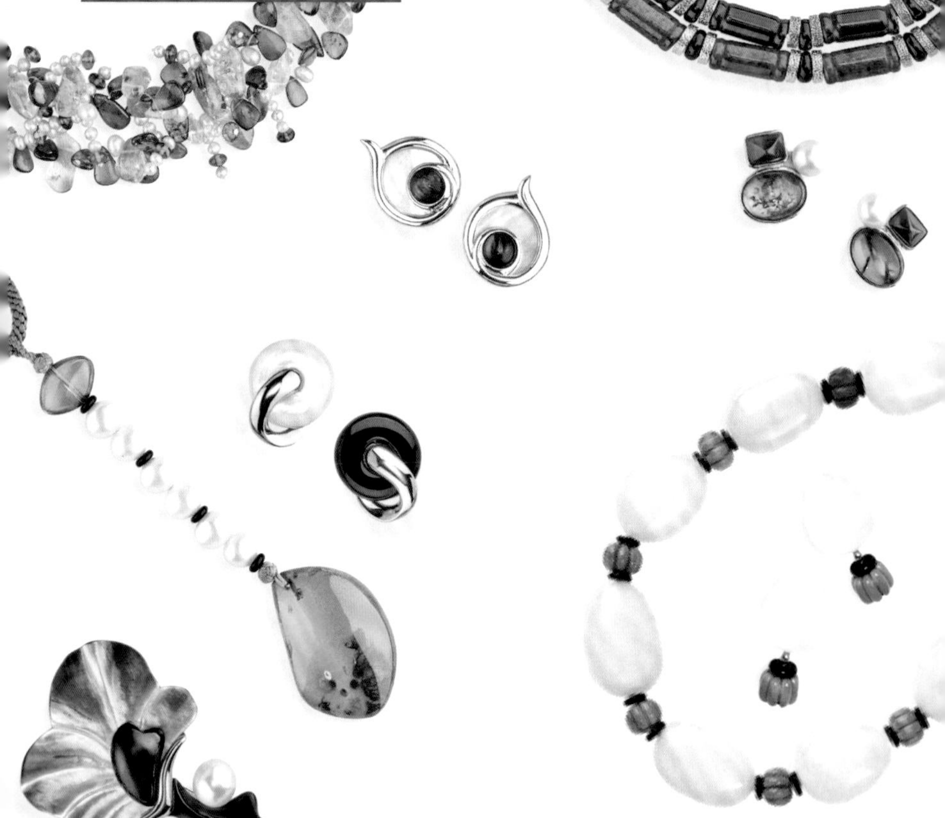

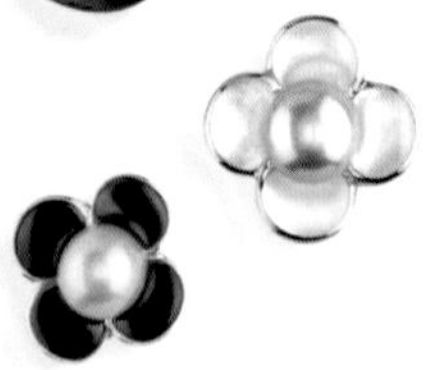

"KAI-YIN LO WAS PROBABLY THE FIRST HONGKONGER TO SUCCESSFULLY TURN HER OWN NAME INTO A LUXURY BRAND IN THE 1980S."

Enid Tsui,
South China Morning Post,
Hong Kong

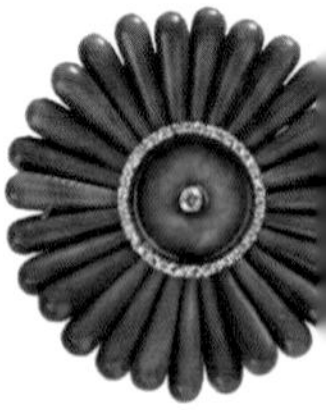

"SHE BRIDGED THE GAP BETWEEN PRECIOUS AND FASHION JEWELRY– AND SET A NEW DIRECTION. SHE IS A PIONEER."

Suzy Menkes,
Current International Editor, *Vogue*,
Former Fashion Editor,
International Herald Tribune

"HER AESTHETIC CONCEPT AND TREATMENT 'BALANCING WITH IMBALANCE' HAS MADE HER WORLD-RENOWNED. EAST AND WEST CONVERGENCE IN HER STYLE OF DESIGN ALSO REPRESENTS A WAY OF LIFE"

Vogue China

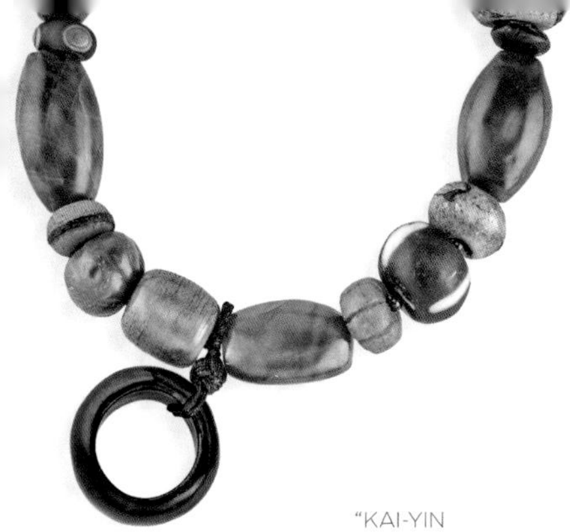

MAKING HISTORY WEARABLE

"KAI-YIN IS THE FIRST TO INTERPRET THE CULTURAL PAST IN A CONTEMPORARY SENSE."

David Pillings,
Former Asia Editor,
Financial Times

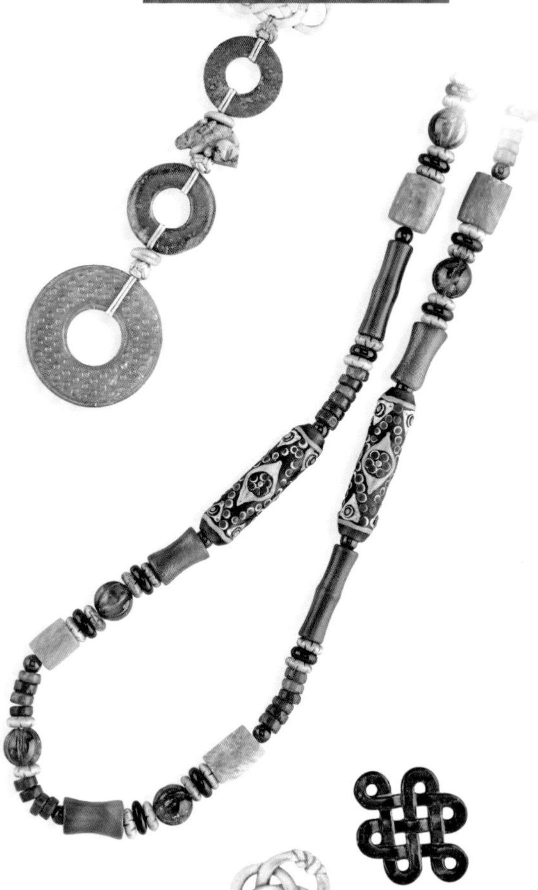

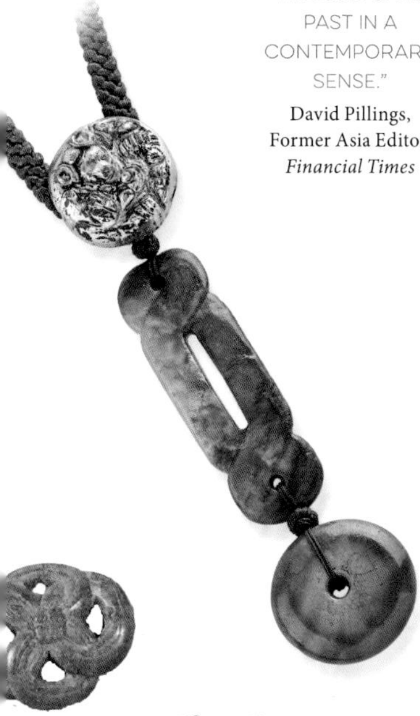

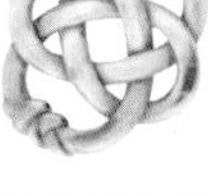

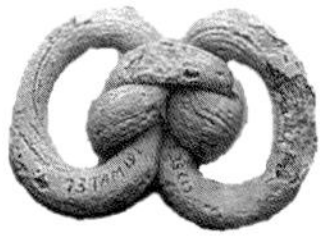

"HER UNDERSTANDING OF CHINA'S RICH LEGACY AVOIDS IMITATION AND SHE CONSTANTLY REINTERPRETS CHINA'S HERITAGE IN ENTIRELY CONTEMPORARY TERMS."

Citation for awarding Kai-Yin Lo as
"World's Best Chinese Designer"
Hong Kong Design Centre

"SHE INTERPRETS CULTURE AND HERITAGE INTO ORIGINAL AND HIGHLY WEARABLE ART THAT REFLECTS CHINA AND ASIA'S PAST AND PRESENT, AND HERALDS THE FUTURE."

Asia Society New York

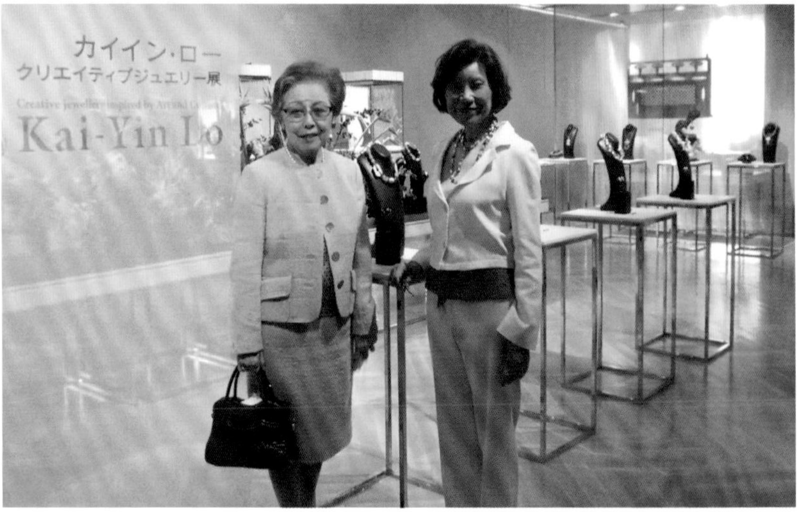

A memorable retrospective of my design at Wako Tokyo Store shared with Etsuko Hattori, wife of Wako Chairman, 2008

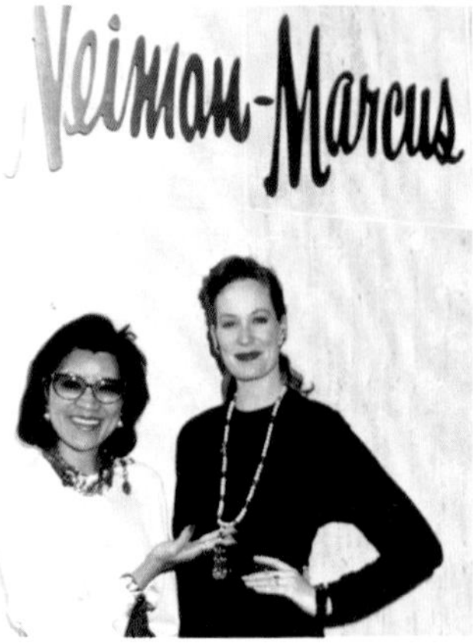

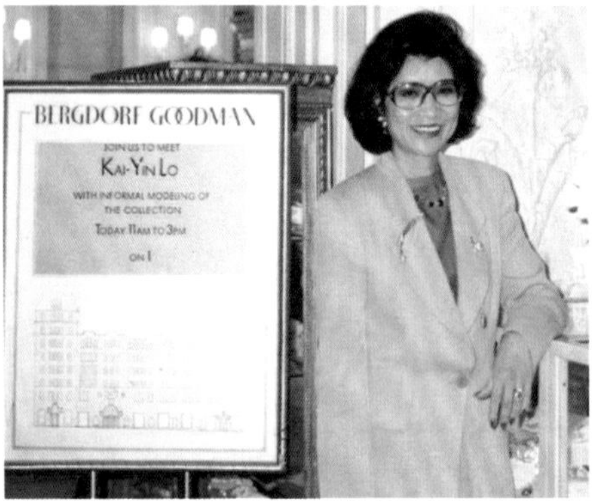

Bergdorf Goodman was the highest platform of luxury retail in the USA—to get there and remain there was a thrill, 1988

It took such effort to be represented in more than 25 Neiman Marcus stores in 1985—my advice to budding designers—don't give up!

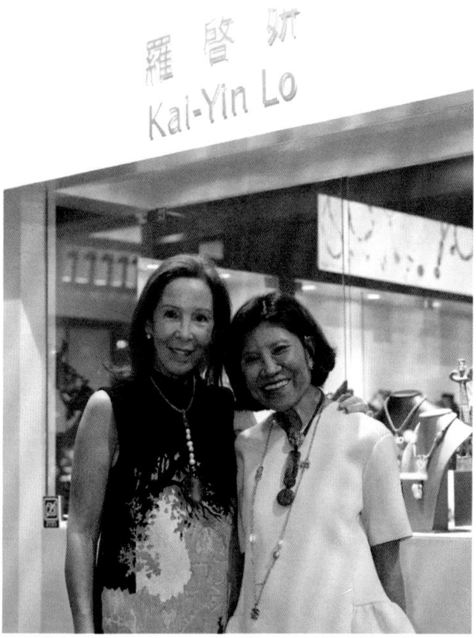

My design patronized by Betty, Lady Kadoorie—an encouragement! 2018

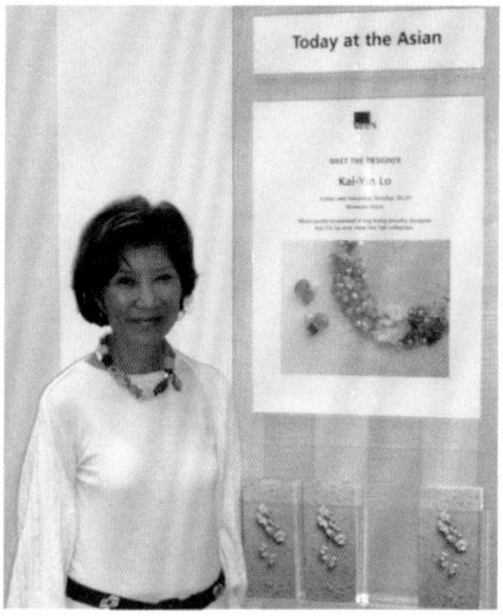

Exhibition at Asian Art Museum, San Francisco—very touched that a lot of Chinese came to support me, 2006

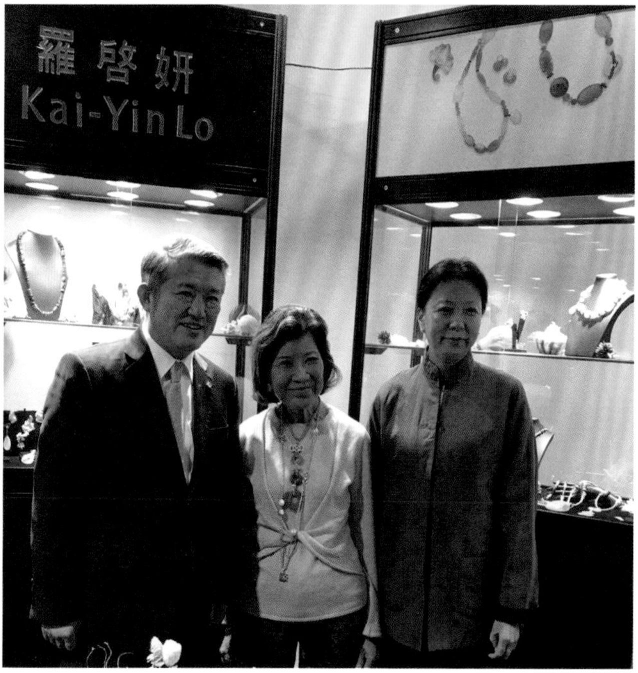

Chairman Chen Dong Sheng and Founder Wang Yannan visited my booth at Guardian Fine Art Asia Beijing, 2017

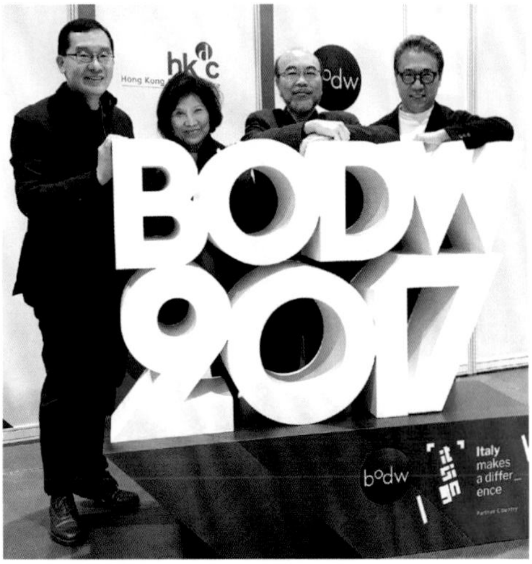

I worked with leaders of Hong Kong Design Centre for over ten years. *(r to l)* Chairman Eric Yim, Former Chairman Victor Lo, Executive Director Edmund Lee—all active drivers making Hong Kong a center of design and creativity, 2017

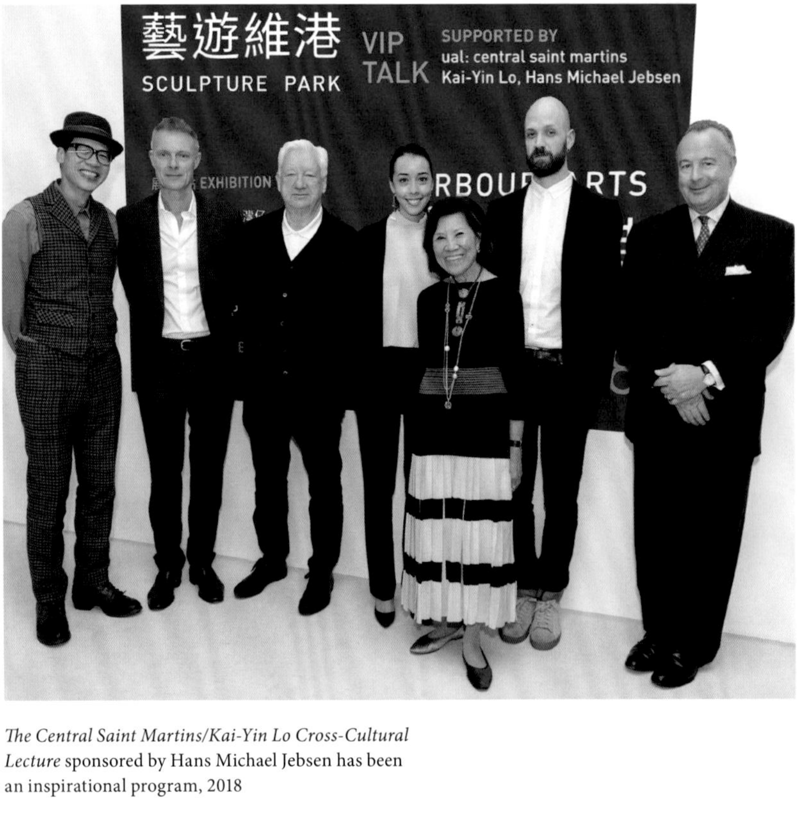

The Central Saint Martins/Kai-Yin Lo Cross-Cultural Lecture sponsored by Hans Michael Jebsen has been an inspirational program, 2018

Historic meeting with painter Zhao Wuji and teacher Lin Fengmian, 2002

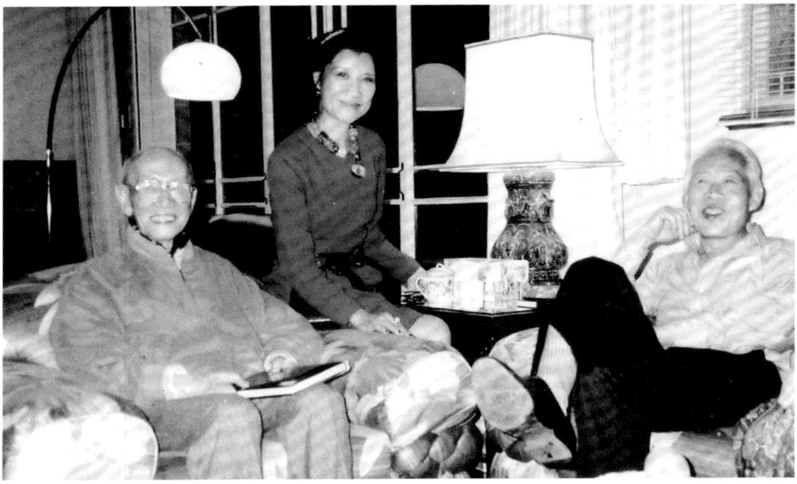

Embedded in Antony Gormley's famous sculptures is a deep appreciation of East and West philosophies, 2014

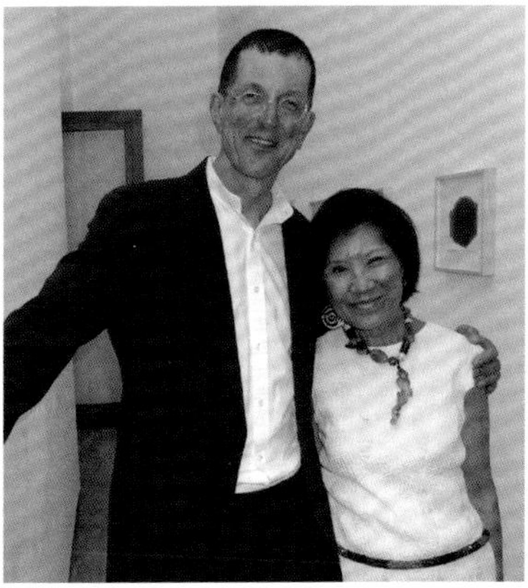

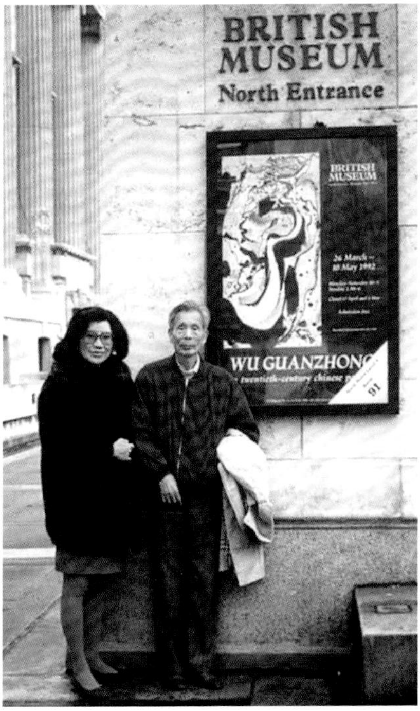

I organized the historic retrospective of Wu Guanzhong, the first exhibition of a living artist at the British Museum. It was a highlight for both of our lives, 1993

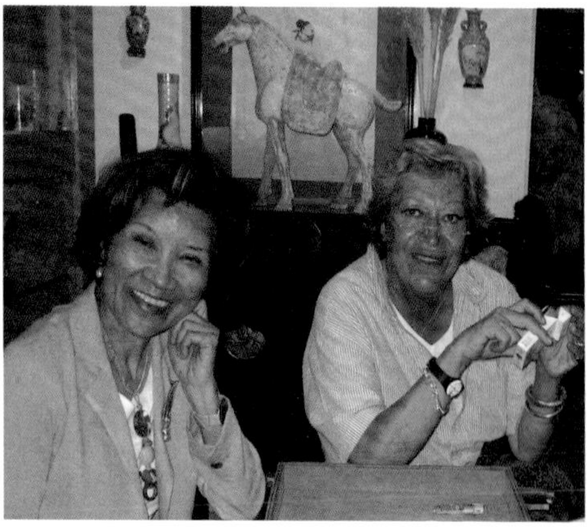

Famous jewelry and ceramic designer Elsa Peretti came to visit, 2012

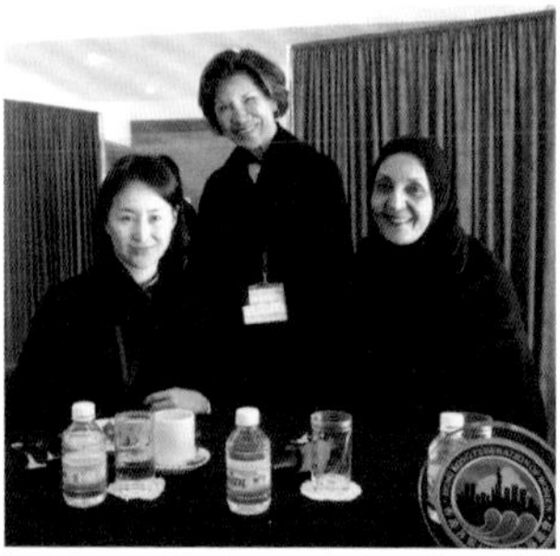

Accompanied by Pansy Ho, I made my second visit to Saudi Arabia with Hong Kong Federation of Women. Met Princess Loulwah Al-Faisal, 2007

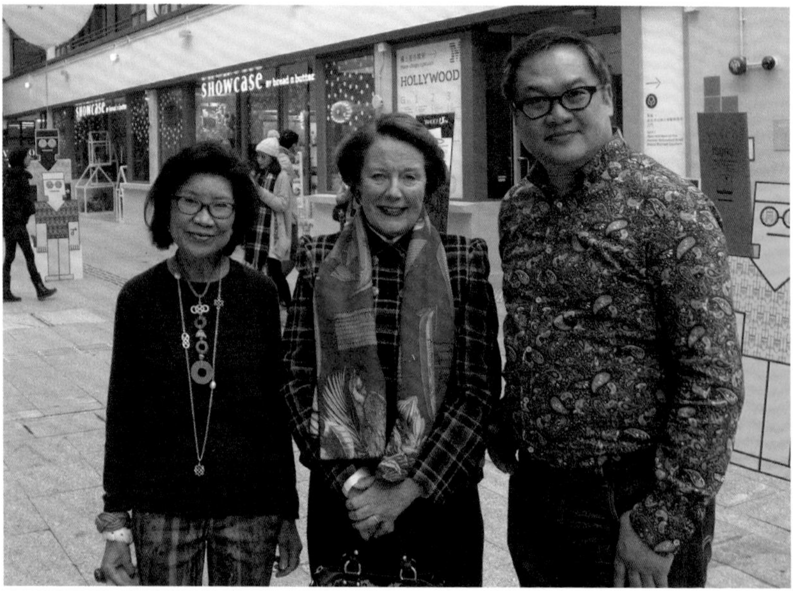

Victor Tsang showed Lady Tessa Keswick how Police Married Quarters, built in 1951, was revitalized as PMQ, to be a base for Hong Kong's creative industries, 2014

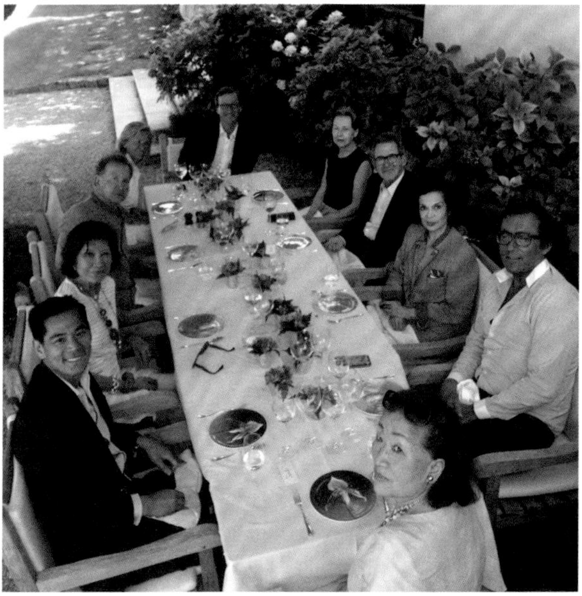

Lunch at Thaddaeus Ropac's garden, Salzburg, where the world meets, 2016

I love this Paradise on earth—sunset from brother Robert's villa in North Phuket, Thailand, 2014

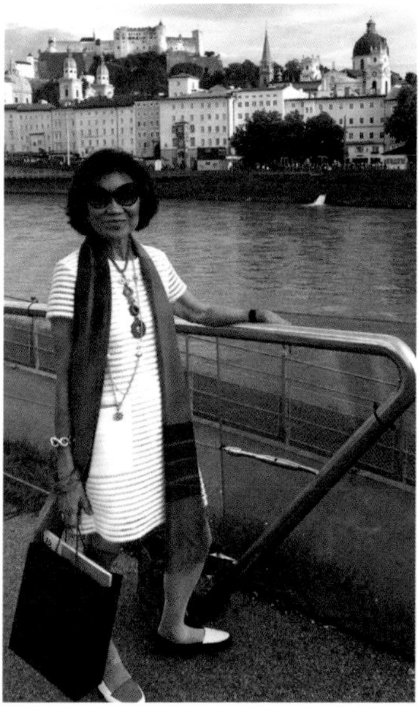

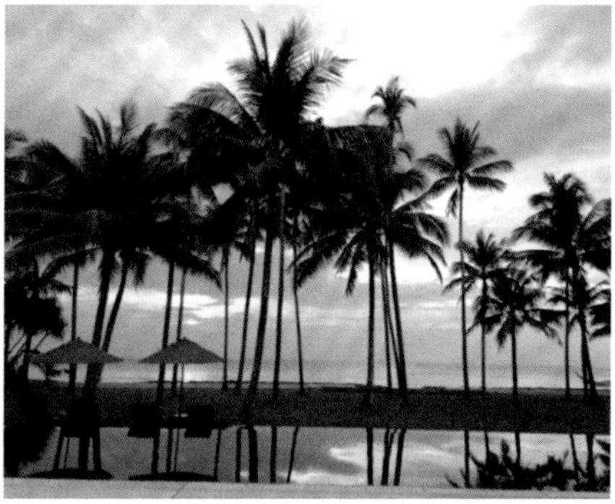

One of my greatest pleasures—Salzburg's Summer Festival

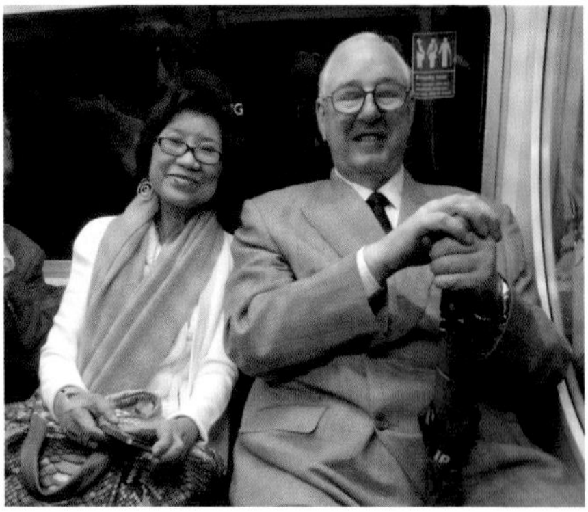

Took Sir Henry Keswick on his first ride on London Underground in 30 years—to catch the Queen's Jubilee procession, 2012

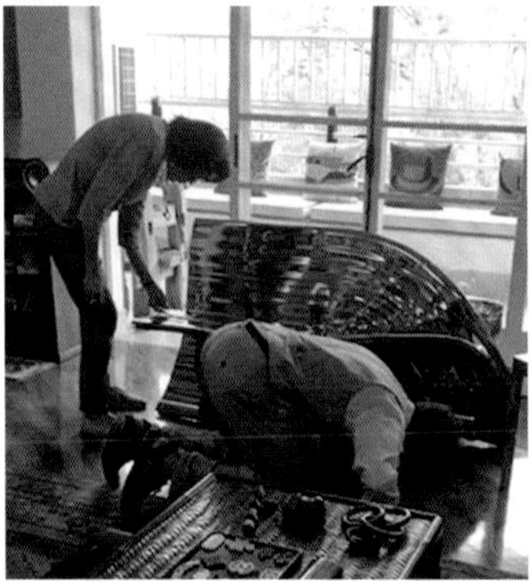

When we sat, he felt it not perfect enough. Thomas Heatherwick fixing his extrusion steel chair at my home—3cm higher! 2018

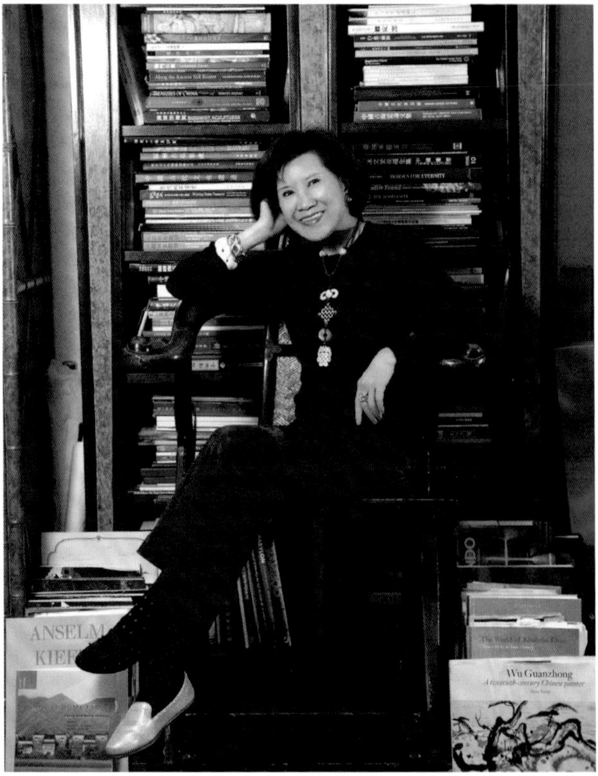

My favorite memorial portrait—after the photo was taken, the 18th-century Japanese monk's chair collapsed… 2013

THE 1990S & BEYOND

11

The 1990s & Beyond

The early 1990s were the peak of my jewelry business. The time called for new design interpretations and fabricating techniques and I found myself working as hard as I could. By 1994, the U.S. department store business was cresting. I had approximately fifty outlets across the country and I was making progress penetrating the Japanese market. My brand was resonating in Hong Kong as well as in some other cities in the region including Singapore and Bangkok. I was also collecting Chinese antique furniture and ceramics on a personal quest to document and preserve China's cultural and historical development, traveling widely, helping to promote the works of artists and cultural historians who shared my fundamental beliefs in the links between West and East, the universality and influence of art and design, and the importance of understanding Chinese culture.

I was ambitious. I wanted to grow the business even further, and particularly wanted to succeed in the third great economy of the world at the time after the United States and Japan: Germany.

I had by then established a factory in Dongguan in Guangdong Province, not far from Hong Kong, as the base for my jewelry production. The craftsmen in Hong Kong were skilled, but they could not handle the volume that the business now required, and I had to cut costs by moving the seat of fabrication to a less costly base. Running the factory in Dongguan was challenging and time consuming, and training the workers to construct my intricate designs was demanding and required that new manufacturing

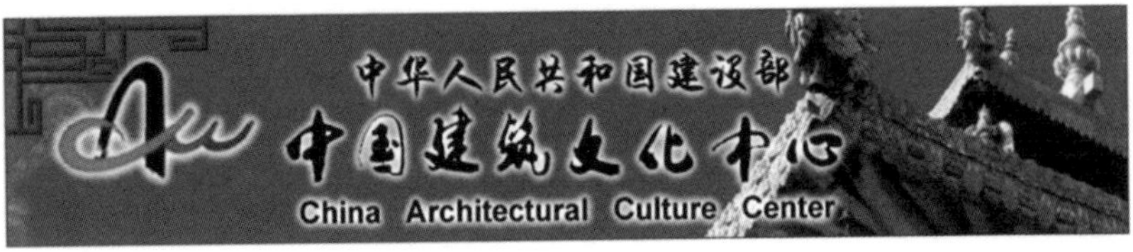

Honoring **Kai-Yin Lo** for

- Creative Interpretation
- Harmonious Fusion of East and West
- Constructive Development and Promotion of Chinese Culture

Lo is recognized as a pioneer for bringing a contemporary and easy-to-wear style to traditional Chinese jewelry and for elevating semi-precious stones into the mainstream of jewelry design.

Lo was honored alongside Cartier as one of three jewelers lauded for their "influence, style and excellence" by the Kennedy Center, Washington DC, in a groundbreaking exhibition, "The New China Chic"(Oct., 2005) showcasing the best Chinese fashion and jewelry brands in the world.

BBC World will air a 30-minute profile of Lo in January, 2007, in a series to mark the Tenth's Anniversary of Hong Kong's Return to China.

An advocate and consultant on issues related to the interaction between culture, heritage, design and business, Lo is a frequent speaker on these subjects at international forums.

建设名家 羅啟妍

罗氏的成就，将中华创意及建设文化传播至全世界，为国家做出了突出的贡献。

罗氏为是次展示中国建设艺术成就活动中，唯一获选的珠宝饰物设计师。其独特的设计，融合了东西方文化，为传统中国饰物注入了新生命，广为世界认同。

罗氏曾于二零零五年十月获邀参加了华盛顿肯尼迪中心（Kennedy Center）举行的『新中国时尚』大型展览，与卡地亚等共三个杰出、成功的珠宝品牌联袂展示具影响力的设计，被誉为殿堂级。

为庆祝香港回归中国十周年，英国BBC国际台将于二零零七年一月全球播放三十分钟的『罗启妍专访』。

罗氏长期以来不遗馀力地推广文化产业及创意经济，以此推动企业的认知度以及中国建设事业的发展。

The Ministry of Development and China Post honored me with stamps bearing my designs

techniques be adapted for the local conditions. Further complicating things, every Chinese New Year, ninety percent of the workers would take a break to return to their homes, usually in Sichuan and Yunnan, and would not return. We would then need to train an entirely new production crew. I grew tired of it. I have to thank my accountant Raymond Chan who exerted special efforts in setting up and supervising the factory.

I ran the factory for five years and then sold it as part of the business to a German company, Egana, based on their assurances that they would help establish my brand in the German market, and help expand the jewelry business in Japan where they had an office and network for watch distribution. At the time, I did not fully appreciate that the company handled a lower grade of merchandise and that they were not really interested in my jewelry line at all. It was the gold manufacturing license I had secured with the Dongguan factory that they were after.

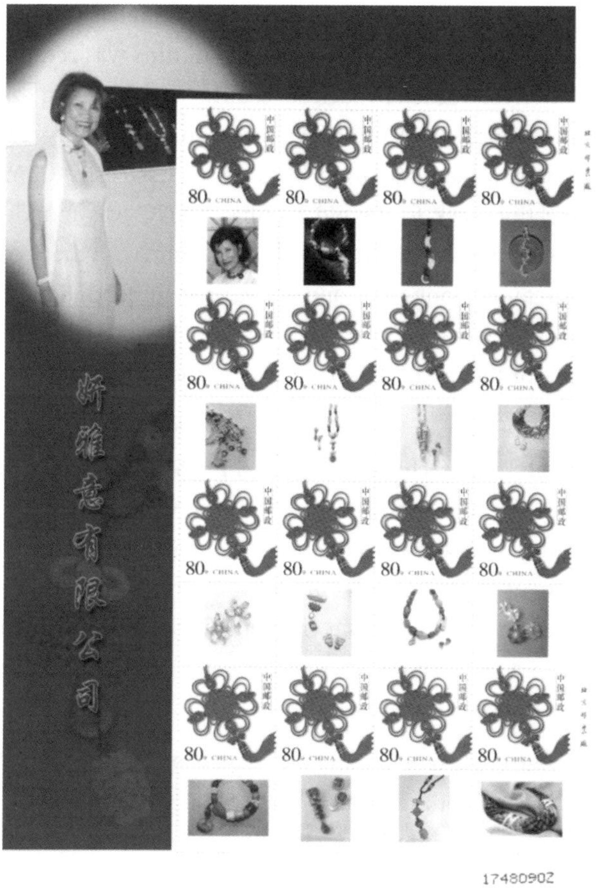

If you manufacture any kind of jewelry using precious metals in China, you have to have a gold or precious metal license. Precious metals included silver, which was the main base ingredient for my jewelry, and gold. This license was not easy to obtain, and you could not just create one. The holders of the licenses were mostly long-established, state-owned enterprises. Finding a company with a license to sell precious metals — gold or silver — was possible, but it was difficult, and these businesses were usually found in remote parts of China. King Fook, for instance, which is a sizable Hong Kong jeweler, ended up cooperating with a company in remote Gansu Province in the northwest.

I obtained my license to manufacture in precious metals or gold through a referral by the conglomerate CITIC, which in turn was receptive to the recommendation forwarded by Jack So, chairman of the Hong Kong Trade Development Council. The Council was eager to help a well-known Hong Kong brand start a manufacturing business in less-costly China. It was again a connection back to the old families. CITIC was founded by the Yung family of Shanghai, and they had a connection with the Second Light Industries Bureau in Dongguan, and at their recommendation I linked up with this entity. It worked because at the time, I was a significant brand. We paid them for the use of their facility, and the bureau also had a small stake in our operation.

Precious metal manufacturing was highly regulated, and whatever materials went in and out, both gold and silver, were closely monitored. I was also dealing with semi-precious stones, some of which were available in the Pearl River Delta, and others that were imported into China from South America, or South East Asia via Hong Kong. I went to the factory at least three days a week to review the work and to assure that we were in compliance with all regulations.

The designs were created by me and my small team of designers. We would buy large batches of stones cut into smaller blocks for easier transportation. Everything brought into the factory was meticulously recorded and had to be accounted for. The workers then sorted, arranged and cut the stones into required shapes, with some set with silver, often gold-plated. Beads were threaded, strictly in line with the designs that I had created, and according to our rigorous specifications. I am not that skilled technically and I could not set stones, but I knew the process, which in the case of my designs was very often established through trial and error because they required both special settings and unique production techniques. I had learned a long time ago that successful designers have to know the process of making jewelry and not just be able to conceptualize design. It is not boastful to say that our semi-precious line of jewelry, set in sterling silver and often plated in 18 carat gold, introduced new manufacturing techniques.

We had a staff of a hundred at the factory, who we had to house and feed, and training them was crucial and arduous. I provided the required specifications and insisted on workmanship of the highest quality. The casting of the settings and the fitting of the stones had to be executed precisely and each piece was required to be created for longevity. Quality control was a massive problem as a result of the annual changeover of staff following every Chinese New Year, which resulted in the need for constant and vigilant training.

It was during one of these periods that an arrangement was proposed with Egana, a company founded in Hong Kong in 1972 by a German businessman named Hans-Joerg Seeberger. Their core business was selling inexpensive watches like Pierre Cardin and Carrera in the German market where they had a good retail network, and the license to sell some popular brands. They wanted to add the Kai-Yin Lo brand to their portfolio and I had hopes that they would get me into the European market through their retail channels in Germany. They were planning to merge it into their network and also sell their watches through more Kai-Yin Lo shops in Hong Kong. I handed the entire business over to the Germans, holding back only the U.S. market. But it proved to be an ill-matched arrangement.

Egana's original idea was to take over production in China and then sell my semi-precious jewelry at higher volumes in Germany and in Japan. They did take my products to Germany, but they did not sell well as German taste was conservative, and my designs did not appeal. In Japan at the time Egana took over, my jewelry was represented in the Wako and Mitsukoshi department stores. Egana expanded the sales to other stores for a while, but it didn't last. They also took over the Guangdong factory, and brought in a German manager to oversee production. Their main interest in acquiring my business turned out to be obtaining that precious metals license, not taking over my China production operation.

I ultimately came to realize that I had made an error in judgment by getting involved with them. But the future was looming. Hong Kong was soon to be handed over to China and the market for my jewelry was softening.

Egana didn't add anything to the business, and the arrangement ended. The basic problem was a mismatch of taste levels.

My business in the United States also changed. In 1993, Neiman Marcus, my most important client in the United States, cautioned me, 'We are entering hard times.' Psychologically, the 1990s were also overshadowed by the impending handover of Hong Kong back to China. We all were thinking of moving out of the city. I thought I would maybe park myself in London, or Singapore or Thailand. All of us in Hong Kong considered such options very seriously. My brother Robert lived for a long time in Thailand and my brother Anthony was thinking of going to Vancouver. In the end, all of us decided not to move. But the early 1990s was a time of anxiety and the property market was in flux and provided some opportunities. I bought a lovely flat at 39 Kennedy Road in 1990 (I was sentimental about having an address ending with #9 as our ancestral house was located at 19 Kennedy Road.) It was my most luxurious and glamorous flat, and it was featured in *Architectural Digest* and all sorts of places. I sold it in 1996, because I got the handover jitters.

Then the Bergdorf Goodman business softened and that was a big chunk out of my revenues. Neiman Marcus continued for a while, but under threat of a takeover. I was by then selling at Harrods and Harvey Nichols in London, but sales were not comparable to those in the American market. Jewelry is a complicated business, and not just a matter of sales. In retail, with this kind of product, you have to support the outlets with constant promotions and personal appearances. My designs appealed to the French and Italians, but I never made headway in France mostly because of the distribution system, and because the French had their own style. Having worked so hard to build the American market and seeing the business there eroding, I wrongly believed that Germany with its strong economy was the answer, which was what led me to Egana.

But Germany did not have the same robust retail environment as the U.S. and consumer tastes and market trends were different, too. Or to put it another way, German taste was conservative and my style was too flamboyant for them. The Japanese business lasted longer, until around 2010. The Japanese took a long time to come around to appreciating my jewelry, but once they did, they were committed. Then Seibu and a number of other department stores either went belly-up or drastically curtailed their business. Even Mitsukoshi was not doing well. Wako, the premier department store in Japan — not in turnover but in prestige — struggled on, but eventually, that relationship ended as well. By that time, I had anyway grown quite weary of maintaining and expanding markets. It was time for a change.

My first shop in Hong Kong was opened in 1986 at the Peninsula Hotel in Kowloon. I chose the Peninsula because of the Japanese — at that time they were the most valued group of purchasers in many markets including Hong Kong, and I was in the depths of my Japanese period. It went well, and I opened another shop at The Mandarin.

I recently went to see the chief executive of Hong Kong Land with a friend, on an introduction from Henry Keswick, then the Jardine Taipan. Robert Wong spent quite a long time discussing a proposed land deal with my friend, but for me, the key moment in the meeting was when he turned to me and said, 'You have no idea! When I joined Hong Kong Land, you had a shop at The Mandarin and I used to go and gaze at your beautiful designs which were trailblazers.' That was nice. The Mandarin store did very well. There is no question about it, when you have a shop in an international hotel, people notice you.

In 1989, I also opened a shop at Hong Kong's big shopping mall, Pacific Place. I was one of their first tenants. Then came the Tiananmen incident in Beijing and we didn't see a client for over a year. But in the end, it turned out to be my most successful shop. A lot of local Hong Kongers still remember my designs from that outlet. It was well positioned at the entrance from the Marriott Hotel into Pacific Place. And for a while, I also had a small place in Sogo in Causeway Bay.

But by the mid-2000s, I had cut all the major business channels. It was not possible to do business with the department stores anymore because of the consignment sales model adopted. In the jewelry business nowadays, no one buys non-returnable upfront. By the late 1980s, the consignment model had been adopted by Neiman Marcus, Bergdorf Goodman and Saks Fifth Avenue. Today the entire U.S. market is consignment. I decided it was not worth doing business with these retailers, except for the odd personal appearance to ramp up sales and to cultivate new customers.

Today I have some pieces on display at a store at The Mandarin, and at the museum store at the Asia Society on 725 Park Avenue in New York, where I have maintained a counter since the year 2000 and where I hold 'personal appearances' once a year or so. I am always pleased to see my loyal customers and friends, many of whom bring their families to greet me.

Houston, Texas, had long been a major market for my jewelry and I made many good friends there, as the Texans are always so expansive and open. In August 2017, I was touched to be called upon to set up a small exhibition at the Asia Society Hong Kong Center at the request of the Rice University Board of Trustees and a visiting alumni delegation from Houston. It was touching to see some of the delegates still wearing my earrings purchased two decades ago. It conjured up fond memories of my many personal appearances at Neiman Marcus at Houston's Galleria mall in the mid-1980s and early 1990s. At the inauguration of the Asia Society Texas Center, built by famed Japanese architect Yoshio Taniguchi (who also renovated MOMA in New York) in 2012, it was wonderful to reconnect with my dear friends Judy Allen, Nanette Finger, Anne Symonds and Nancy Allen. The latter was the chief fundraiser responsible for building the impressive center. Imagine my joy seeing her at the press conference launching the new center, wearing a necklace I had designed in the 1990s!

There had been a long-standing invitation to visit my Cambridge chum Abdullah Alireza in Jeddah, Saudi Arabia, and in 1995 I finally took the plunge. It coincided with an invitation from Queen Noor of Jordan (who had been purchasing my jewelry at the Asia Society Shop in New York), and I visited Amman as Her Majesty's guest, staying at the guest house with a view of the Gulf of Aqaba which reminded me of *Lawrence of Arabia*!

I flew from Amman to Jeddah without an entry visa and fortunately an aide sent by Abdullah was there to whisk me through. In Jeddah I was accompanied by a small entourage of ladies wherever I went. Daughter Sara and her husband Faisel were very good hosts, and fortunately old friend David Salzburger, who dealt in artifacts from Central Asia, was also visiting.

I returned to Jeddah in 2007 as member of a tour organized by the Hong Kong Federation of Women, invited by the former Consul General of Saudi Arabia who was promoted to a post at the Foreign Ministry. Led by Chairman Peggy Lam and Vice Chairman Pansy Ho, we were cordially received. Sara Alireza organized a successful and well-attended jewelry exhibition and sale for me. I found that the well- traveled invitees

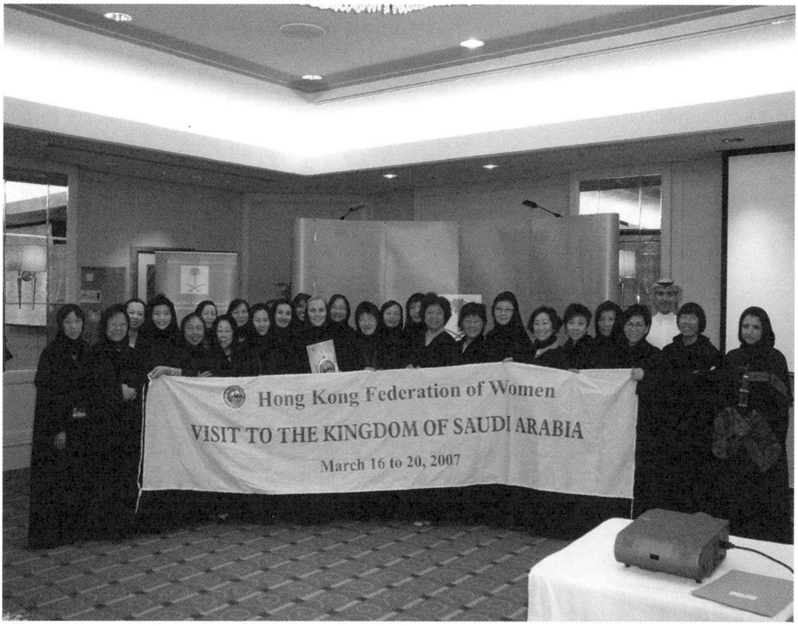

My second trip to Saudi Arabia was with the Hong Kong Federation of Women in 2007

displayed good judgement and taste. I recall the elegant presence of HRH Princess Loulwah Al-Faisal Bin Abdulaziz who headed a good number of educational causes.

In 2006, I experienced a memorable encounter at an event hosted by Louis Vuitton at the Rosewood Hotel in Beijing to launch artist Xu Bing's creation of special travel luggage for the house that had taken the artist three years to design and realize. I was greeted by Jeffrey Hang, CEO of Louis Vuitton China, and his opening words were, 'I know you via the bracelet you designed for the 1993 Neiman Marcus Christmas catalog, which I saved up to buy for my mother as a present. She still wears it!'

What a joy to be reminded of my successful times by a leader of the luxury trade. Indeed Neiman Marcus, headquartered in Dallas, Texas (where Jeffrey comes from) was my best account, and their prestigious Christmas catalog enjoyed wide popularity. I recall that bracelet well — it was set with black agate, white mother of pearl and accented with cabochon sapphires

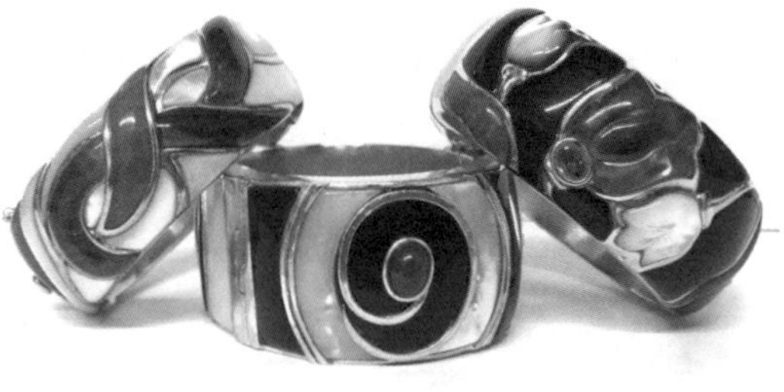

Jeffrey Hang, CEO of Louis Vuitton China, saved up to buy his mother the middle bracelet, inlaid with semi-precious and precious stones, set in silver vermeil from the Neiman Marcus Christmas catalog, 1994

and rubies, mounted in sterling silver and plated in 18 karat gold vermeil. It was daring to set precious color stones in sterling silver, then plate in 18k gold. But if well made, it would endure, and that was my signature. Fifty pieces were sold, and I was thrilled to learn that this bracelet had worn very well after all these years!

While I still have private clients and hold private events, and cooperate with several local and international associations, I have mostly moved on. I love jewelry design, but it is not my main focus any more. For the last few years, I have taken a booth in late September at Fine Art Asia in Hong Kong, a leading international fair steered by Andy and Susannah Hei, featuring jewelry, objets d'art, Asian and European antiques and contemporary art. In addition, I have taken part in the Guardian Auction Fair in Beijing in October. At the Hong Kong Fair, I have also staged focused exhibitions on European modern furniture created by Hans Wegner, Alvar Aalto and other masters, to contemporary Japanese and Chinese designers including Nendo, Shao Fan and Tian Jiaqing. I mounted an exhibition depicting the influence of the Chinese round-backed chair on the designs of Hans Wegner and other 20th-century European designers.

I have conducted lectures and symposia in New York, London, Beijing and Shanghai. To celebrate the 20th anniversary of the return of Hong Kong to China, I was one of 20 designers selected to represent Hong Kong in showcasing design at exhibitions that debuted in Milan (in April 2016) followed by Hong Kong, Seoul and Chicago.

Life remains hectic, diverse and satisfying. I have been on a rousing roller-coaster ride with recognition and success in jewelry and accessories design, and have been recognized for contributions to history and culture, both endeavors close to my heart, reaffirming values and beliefs which I have always held dear.

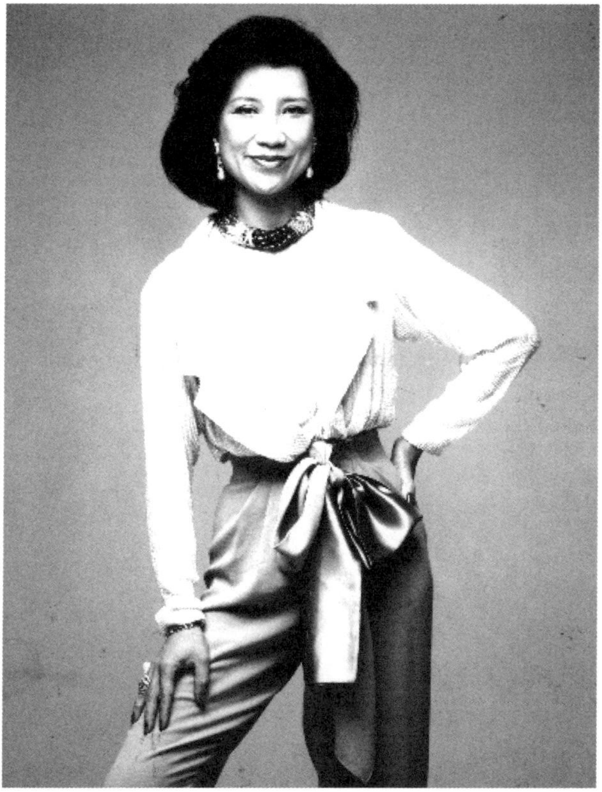

I encourage the empowerment of women
to achieve at work, run a happy home
and focus on self-development

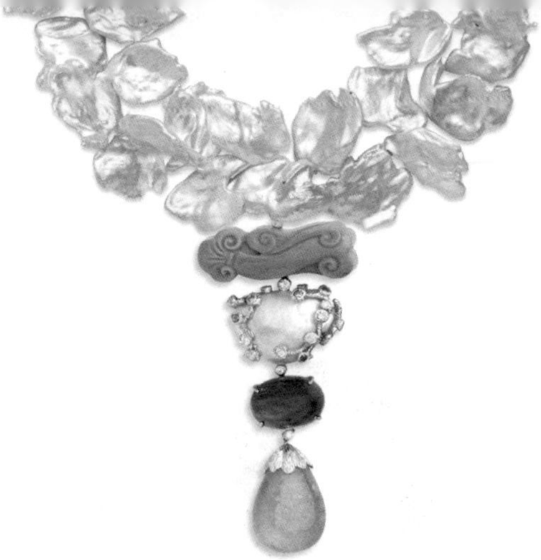

PART II

'Art speaks for itself; Design needs to show process.'

—Deyan Sudjic

Director, Design Museum, London

12

Furniture in the Living Environment

In 1996, a great number of people were leaving our city. We had no idea what would become of Hong Kong the following year when Britain was obliged to hand over the territory to Beijing. People feared the worst. While most of the valuable old Chinese paintings and ceramics had already been shipped out of Hong Kong, the bulky classic and valuable Chinese furniture was not as easily moved. I had developed a keen interest in Chinese furniture, more from a design, sociological and cultural perspective than as an investment. I had also compiled a book about classic furniture that accompanied an exhibition that year at the Asian Civilization Museum in Singapore. One of the reasons for my participation in that project was to get my collection out of Hong Kong.

I wanted to understand furniture's role in traditional Chinese family culture. I realize that furniture and its de rigueur placement, especially in the main hall (*tingtang*) where guests were received and important decisions were made, signifies the symbolic order of the Chinese domestic universe, whether in rich or poor households. The arrangement of furniture was formal and was clearly prescribed.

I have been collecting both hardwood and softwood Chinese furniture since the late 1980s. Chinese buyers today only value hardwood pieces, but the point for me was that 99.9 percent of the population had softwood furniture, and this was the aspect that fascinated me. The book I produced, *Classical and Vernacular Chinese Furniture in the Living Environment*, was eventually published in 1998, in a bilingual English/Chinese edition edited by Catherine Maudsley and myself. It was endorsed by the erudite pioneer of classical Chinese furniture scholarship Professor Wang Shixiang. His endorsement validated my interest and the direction of inquiry. In fact, he wrote an edifying introduction to the book in his beautiful calligraphic hand.

Wang Shixiang is a remarkable person, a giant of a man, metaphorically. He spent forty years studying Chinese furniture and Chinese wood, and in 1985 he published his great work, *Chinese Classic Furniture*, with the Hong Kong publishing house Joint Publishing, which fundamentally changed our conception of Chinese furniture. I gave my book the title I did because I wanted it to reflect most of the furniture styles we came across and also the uses of furniture in the real world, the world in which most Chinese lived, not just the rarefied world of the aristocracy. In Professor Wang's Foreword to my book, he pointed out my interest and mission — that I provided an

Written in his distinguished handwriting, furniture authority Wang Shixiang's wonderful endorsement of my view on the role of furniture in the house

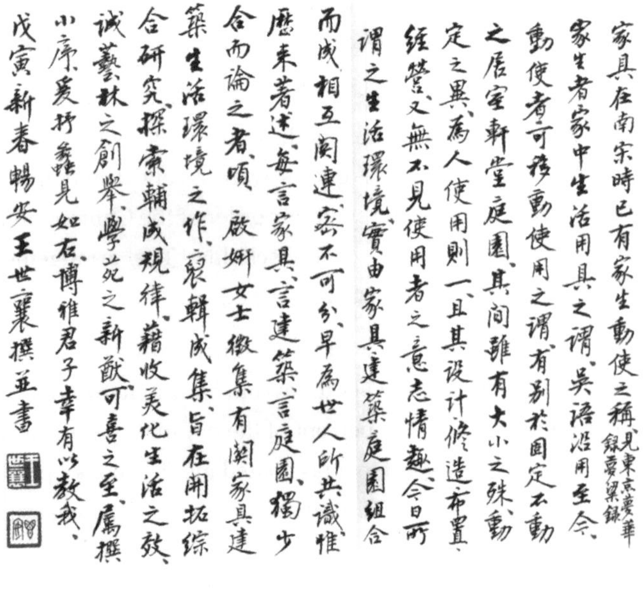
小序
家具在南宋時已有家生動使之稱、見東京夢華錄、夢粱錄
家生者家中生活用具之謂、吳語沿用至今、
動使者可移動使用之謂、有別於固定不動
之居室軒堂庭園、其間雖有大小之殊、動
定之異、為人使用則一、且其設計、修造、布置、
經營、又無不見使用者之意志情趣、今日所
謂之生活環境、實由家具、建築、庭園組合
而成、相互關連、密不可分、早為世人所共識、惟
歷來著述、每言家具、言建築、言庭園、獨少
合而論之者、頃啟娟女士徵集有關家具建
築生活環境之作、裒輯成集、旨在開拓綜
合研究、探索輔成規律、藉收美化生活之效、
誠藝林之創舉、學苑之新猷、可喜之至、屬撰
小序、爰抒蠡見如右、博雅君子幸有以教我、
戊寅新春暢安王世襄撰並書

overview of the house and the role furniture served as necessary "portable tools" in the rooms, which was a key perspective examining the role of furniture in the living environment. Wang Shixiang's own consequential tome on hardwood furniture did not provide social or economic context, but only identified and discussed the genre of the pieces. Nevertheless, his book was a landmark, an authoritative classification and analysis that led me to collect Chinese furniture and to seek a better understanding and appreciation of Chinese ways of housing, living and organization of the family, community relationships, tastes and social practices. A rich area indeed.

Professor Wang was the first person to describe and analyze how classic Chinese furniture developed in the late Yuan era and had its heyday in the Ming. Fine pieces of furniture were crafted from precious and expensive hardwoods with beautiful grains and rich colors, imported from Hainan and Indochina. In Ming times (1368-1644), zitan, huanghuali and top-grade jichimu (all precious woods) were available to only a small number of people — officials and the literate class. Furniture made from softwoods indigenous to China, often coated with a lacquer veneer, was widely used in lesser households. But the expert employment of wood, constructed in finely decorated well- proportioned forms and supported by an ingenious system of joinery, elevated Chinese furniture above the level of craft.

One could say that the global market for classic Chinese furniture was created in the 1940s, and then went into the doldrums for decades, only to emerge again in the 1980s. Prior to that, the Drummond brothers took antique Chinese furniture to New York in the late 1940s and C.T. Loo started selling items in his fancy antique shop in Paris. But the most important figure in giving definition and recognition to Chinese hardwood furniture was Professor Gustave Ecke, who was much influenced by the Bauhaus viewpoint. He published his pathfinding book on Chinese hardwood furniture in 1940 with a small print run of only 100 copies, yet ignited new awareness of, and insight on, this important type of furniture.

I knew Professor Ecke's wife, Betty, who was a joy to be with. It was she who invited me to visit Wang Shixiang in his distinguished house built in the early Ming period, located in a Beijing *hutong*. I went, and found that it was so dirty, with dust everywhere. Professor Wang and his wife explained the state of their house by saying that 'we prefer to spend the limited time we have reading and writing rather than dusting.' Of course, the house was full of the most wonderful Ming furniture, most of it covered with dust.

All too often, familiar terms are taken for granted and their precise meaning is overlooked. One example is the term used in Chinese to denote family, or the domicile of a family — *jiating* (家庭). It literally means a 'domestic household with a courtyard.' The 'family in a house' is a fundamental component of Chinese society, and the 'household with a courtyard' is the archetypal form on which domestic dwellings, whether simple or grand, small or large, are based.

Another familiar term is *jiaju* (家具) for furniture. In Chinese, *jia* stands for both home, the dwelling and the family, and *ju* means tools. Hence the phrase means 'implements of the household'. What were the functions of furniture? How were they used? What was the cosmological and social significance behind the prescribed arrangement of furniture in the house? What were the circumstances and rationale for which they were created and used, and what was the relation of the house with architecture? These were a few of my queries, and exploring these topics proved to be a fascinating introduction to life in old China. Furniture, life in the household and architecture, primarily of the literati and official classes, have been much explored, researched and published. But my book examined them as an organic whole and as an expression of the 'living environment.'

The next book I edited was *Living Heritage — Vernacular Environment in China*, also published in 1998, with input from Professor Puay Peng ("P.P.") Ho and fine photography provided by Li Yuxiang. The book identified common elements in the structure, form and spatial layout of the traditional Chinese house, while focusing on living patterns in different geographic and ethnic regions of China. It also explored variations of home structures and the functional, social and symbolic meanings of the Chinese house,

Financial Times, dated 4 May 2003,
on my lifestyle and preference for asymmetry

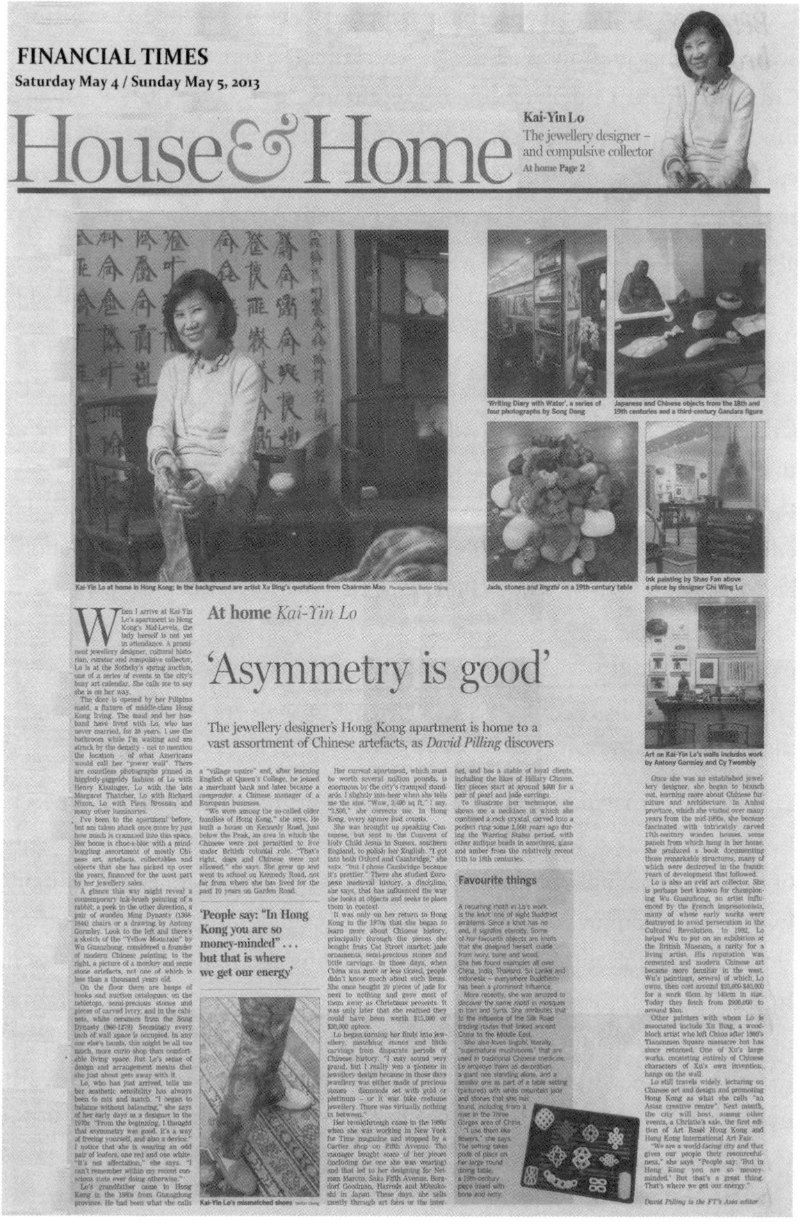

FINANCIAL TIMES
Saturday May 4 / Sunday May 5, 2013

House & Home

Kai-Yin Lo
The jewellery designer – and compulsive collector
At home Page 2

Kai-Yin Lo at home in Hong Kong; in the background are artist Xu Bing's quotations from Chairman Mao

'Writing Diary with Water', a series of four photographs by Song Dong

Japanese and Chinese objects from the 18th and 19th centuries and a third-century Gandara figure

Jade, stones and *lingzhi* on a 19th-century table

Ink painting by Shao Fan above a piece by designer Chi Wing Lo

Art on Kai-Yin Lo's walls includes work by Antony Gormley and Cy Twombly

At home *Kai-Yin Lo*

'Asymmetry is good'

The jewellery designer's Hong Kong apartment is home to a vast assortment of Chinese artefacts, as *David Pilling* discovers

When I arrive at Kai-Yin Lo's apartment in Hong Kong's Mid-Levels, the lady herself is not yet in attendance. A prominent jewellery designer, cultural historian, curator and compulsive collector, Lo is at the Sotheby's spring auction, one of a series of events in the city's busy art calendar. She calls me to say she is on her way.

The door is opened by her Filipina maid, a fixture of middle-class Hong Kong living. The maid and her husband have lived with Lo, who has never married, for 28 years. I use the bathroom while I'm waiting and am struck by the density – not to mention the location – of what Americans would call her "power wall". There are countless photographs pinned in higgledy-piggeldy fashion of Lo with Henry Kissinger, Lo with the late Margaret Thatcher, Lo with Richard Nixon, Lo with Piers Brosnan and many other luminaries.

I've been to the apartment before, but am taken aback once more by just how much is crammed into this space. Her home is choc-a-bloc with a mind-boggling assortment of mostly Chinese art, artefacts, collectables and objects that she has picked up over the years, financed for the most part by her jewellery sales.

A glance this way might reveal a contemporary ink-brush painting of a rabbit; a peek in the other direction, a pair of wooden Ming Dynasty (1368-1644) chairs or a drawing by Antony Gormley. Look to the left and there's a sketch of the "Yellow Mountain" by Wu Guanzhong, considered a founder of modern Chinese painting; to the right, a picture of a monkey and some stone artefacts, not one of which is less than a thousand years old.

On the floor there are heaps of books and auction catalogues; on the tabletops, semi-precious stones and pieces of carved ivory; and in the cabinets, white ceramics from the Song Dynasty (960-1279). Seemingly every inch of wall space is occupied. In anyone else's hands, this might be all too much, more curio shop than comfortable living space. But Lo's sense of design and arrangement means that she just about gets away with it.

Lo, who has just arrived, tells me her aesthetic sensibility has always been to mix and match. "I began to balance without balancing," she says of her early days as a designer in the 1970s. "From the beginning, I thought that asymmetry was good. It's a way of freeing yourself, and also a device." I notice that she is wearing an odd pair of loafers, one red and one white. "It's not affectation," she says. "I can't remember within my recent conscious state ever doing otherwise."

Lo's grandfather came to Hong Kong in the 1880s from Guangdong province. He had been what she calls a "village squire" and, after learning English at Queen's College, he joined a merchant bank and later became a *comprador*, a Chinese manager of a European business.

"We were among the so-called older families of Hong Kong," she says. He built a house on Kennedy Road, just below the Peak, an area in which the Chinese were not permitted to live under British colonial rule. "That's right, dogs and Chinese were not allowed," she says. She grew up and went to school on Kennedy Road, not far from where she has lived for the past 10 years on Garden Road.

'People say: "In Hong Kong you are so money-minded"... but that is where we get our energy'

Kai-Yin Lo's mismatched shoes

Her current apartment, which must be worth several million pounds, is enormous by the city's cramped standards. I slightly mis-hear when she tells me the size. "Wow, 3,400 sq ft," I say. "3,500," she corrects me. In Hong Kong, every square foot counts.

She was brought up speaking Cantonese, but sent to the Convent of Holy Child Jesus in Sussex, southern England, to polish her English. "I got into both Oxford and Cambridge," she says, "but I chose Cambridge because it's prettier." There she studied European medieval history, a discipline, she says, that has influenced the way she looks at objects and seeks to place them in context.

It was only on her return to Hong Kong in the 1970s that she began to learn more about Chinese history, principally through the pieces she bought from Cat Street market: jade ornaments, semi-precious stones and little carvings. In those days, when China was more or less closed, people didn't know much about such items. She once bought 20 pieces of jade for next to nothing and gave most of them away as Christmas presents. It was only later that she realised they could have been worth $15,000 or $20,000 apiece.

Lo began turning her finds into jewellery, matching stones and little carvings from disparate periods of Chinese history. "I may sound very grand, but I really was a pioneer in jewellery design because in those days jewellery was either made of precious stones – diamonds set with gold or platinum – or it was fake costume jewellery. There was virtually nothing in between."

Her breakthrough came in the 1980s when she was working in New York for Time magazine and stopped by a Cartier shop on Fifth Avenue. The manager bought some of her pieces (including the one she was wearing) and that led to her designing for Neiman Marcus, Saks Fifth Avenue, Bergdorf Goodman, Harrods and Mitsukoshi in Japan. These days, she sells mostly through art fairs or the internet, and has a stable of loyal clients, including the likes of Hillary Clinton. Her pieces start at around $490 for a pair of pearl and jade earrings.

To illustrate her technique, she shows me a necklace in which she combined a rock crystal, carved into a perfect ring some 2,500 years ago during the Warring States period, with other antique beads in amethyst, glass and amber from the relatively recent 11th to 18th centuries.

Favourite things

A recurring motif in Lo's work is the knot, one of eight Buddhist emblems. Since a knot has no end, it signifies eternity. Some of her favourite objects are knots that she designed herself, made from ivory, bone and wood. She has found examples all over China, India, Thailand, Sri Lanka and Indonesia – everywhere Buddhism has been a prominent influence.

More recently, she was amazed to discover the same motif in mosques in Iran and Syria. She attributes that to the influence of the Silk Road trading routes that linked ancient China to the Middle East.

She also loves lingzhi, literally "supernatural mushrooms" that are used in traditional Chinese medicine. Lo employs them as decoration, a giant one standing alone, and a smaller one as part of a table setting (pictured) with white mountain jade and stones that she has found, including from a river in the Three Gorges area of China.

"I use them like flowers," she says. The setting takes pride of place on her large round dining table.

a 19th-century piece inlaid with bone and ivory

Once she was an established jewellery designer, she began to branch out, learning more about Chinese furniture and architecture. In Anhui province, which she visited over many years from the mid-1980s, she became fascinated with intricately carved 17th-century wooden houses, some panels from which hang in her home. She produced a book documenting those remarkable structures, many of which were destroyed in the frantic years of development that followed.

Lo is also an avid art collector. She is perhaps best known for championing Wu Guanzhong, an artist influenced by the French impressionists, many of whose early works were destroyed to avoid persecution in the Cultural Revolution. In 1992, Lo helped Wu to put on an exhibition at the British Museum, a rarity for a living artist. His reputation was cemented and modern Chinese art became more familiar in the west. Wu's paintings, several of which Lo owns, then cost around $20,000-$40,000 for a work 65cm by 140cm in size. Today they fetch from $600,000 to around $3m.

Other painters with whom Lo is associated include Xu Bing, a woodblock artist who left China after 1989's Tiananmen Square massacre but has since returned. One of Xu's large works, consisting entirely of Chinese characters of Xu's own invention, hangs on the wall.

Lo still travels widely, lecturing on Chinese art and design and promoting Hong Kong as what she calls "an Asian creative centre". Next month, the city will host, among other events, a Christie's sale, the first edition of Art Basel Hong Kong and Hong Kong International Art Fair.

"We are a world-facing city and that gives our people their resourcefulness," she says. "People say: 'But in Hong Kong you are so money-minded.' But that's a great thing. That's where we get our energy."

David Pilling is the FT's Asia editor

which is 'structured to shape family organization and to weave the web of social and ethical norms that linked the household to the world beyond.'

It was a fascinating and absorbing exercise which appealed to the history scholar in me, and allowed me to learn more about my own culture – Chinese culture. Understanding the world inside and outside of the house involves many factors: socio-political, socio-economic, historical and cultural. In the book, we focused on the vernacular environment of five regions of China – Shanxi, Wannan (southern Anhui), Jiangnan (Jiangsu and Zhejiang), Minxi (west Fujian) and Hong Kong – and included a discussion of common and variant house forms, construction methods and materials used, along with a survey of distinctive regional styles and their characteristics in decoration.

China's long and continuous culture suggested a homogeneous society of unvarying form, but it turned out that this notion was not accurate. Since the 1980s, excavated artifacts and records, and increased communication and travel opportunities to remote areas, have led to new observations, and a new view; that while Chinese society was governed by prescribed disciplines, there also existed a marked regional diversity of creativity and exuberance. And while there was a profound conservatism and revered and shared cultural traditions, there were also localized expressions disregarding conformity.

The word 'vernacular' usually means local or informal modes of speech. But it also connotes places that are lived in, and by extension the items of furniture that are not just for show, but which are used as part of daily living. It also conjures up different associations geographically, places away from the capital and central control, allowing for freer local expression. In recent years, there has been a growth of interest in vernacular forms of furniture and living spaces, and the book included everything from modest one-room structures belonging to peasants to multi-courtyard dwellings of officials and the literati, and the extensive mansions of the wealthy merchants.

It is important to note that local traditions in China's arts and crafts have been sustained and interpreted through the centuries by anonymous artisans who constructed the houses, and embellished their exteriors and interiors. These underestimated master craftsmen of extraordinary versatility and skill were the same ones who created panels, doors and partitions for domestic interiors as well as furniture and small objects. These craftsmen were the unsung heroes who unknowingly contributed to the vivacity of vernacular expressions and diversity of China's artistic legacy.

Age-old customs, reinforced by Confucian tenets on the proper ordering of space to guide relationships in the house, led to a quest for harmony and good fortune. *Fengshui* is of course essential to this process, as are decoration and ornamentation.

The purpose of *fengshui* in this context is to identify auspicious and inauspicious siting and placement issues in the home, while decoration helps to usher in good fortune and ward off evil.The portrayal of auspicious images in the decorative arts — porcelain, textiles, enamels, furniture and carvings — was an essential reference and inspiration for the local artisans. Communicating the promise of good fortune via auspicious symbols is a direct and powerful channel which was universally understood, for until relatively recently the majority of Chinese people in the countryside were illiterate. These symbols, embedding visual metaphors and punning language, invoke hope and aspirations for the betterment of life. Folk beliefs and traditional customs remain a potent bond for Chinese people today all over the world. Whatever the level of understanding of the past and whatever the regard for the present, this consciousness and bond that we loosely label as 'Chineseness' is embodied in traditional beliefs, practices and patterns. These fundamental aspects of Chinese culture have been reflected vigorously and visibly in vernacular Chinese architecture and furniture.

After decades of the Communist regime, vestiges of age-old family, house and home, and social observations fortunately remain. I feel my book opened up a new interpretation of the relationship between the two elements of Chinese furniture and architecture. The two were part and parcel of one another, but people traditionally did not look at them together. That is one of the reasons why architecture in traditional China did not change. Craftsmen practiced their skills, passing them from father to son, working by hand and guided by tradition. It is also one of the reasons Chinese furniture-making traditions endured for so long. But things are changing.

Armed with enormous enthusiasm for the project, I produced a book that for the first time illustrated and discussed classical and vernacular furniture together. My guiding focus was not only differences and similarities in furniture styles and types of wood used, but also the proportions, flow of line and clarity of form of the two styles. And in this regard many 'vernacular' pieces hold their own in look, appeal and interest next to the revered and vastly more expensive Ming-style hardwood furniture.

Probing behind the facade of appearance to understand the differences and common features of these two categories of furniture requires an understanding of the social milieu and patterns of pre-modern China, with its rigidity of hierarchy, disciplines and traditions on the one hand, and the diversity, distinctive cultures and characteristics of the different regions on the other. Classical furniture was made for the social elite and the prosperous classes, entailing prescribed refinement in construction, finishing and decoration, using expensive hardwoods often imported from Southeast Asia, and conforming to aristocratic standards of elegance and craftsmanship. But vernacular furniture, while observing the outlines of traditional forms and styles, was not subject to the strict creeds of literati taste, and therefore could afford greater flamboyance, vigor and a freedom that led to variations on classic lines or adherence to earlier forms.

Collecting is an ongoing learning process of self-improvement. At the same time, it is humbling and stimulating as one discovers new information, and gains insight and new vision. The lack of records on vernacular dwellings account for the deficiency in textual information. The relaxation of restrictions on travel to China since the 1980s has facilitated greater possibilities of on-site visits for researchers and enthusiasts, as well as a more open atmosphere for the exchange of ideas. This has resulted in new studies of the village, the rural household and architecture, revealing glimpses of domestic lifestyle.

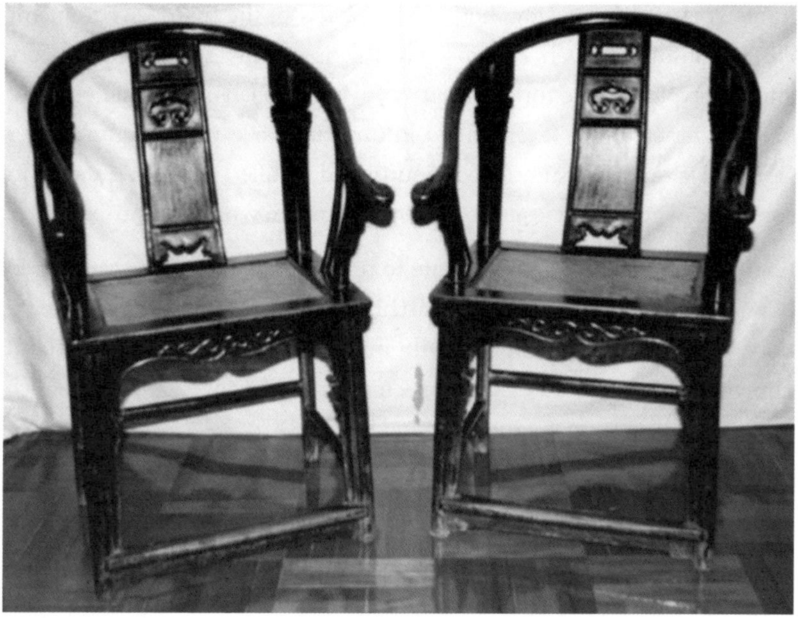

Chinese fine vernacular furniture – roundback chairs, lacquer over yumu, circa 18th century

The increasing availability of regional types of furniture brought to the antique market since 1990 unveiled styles, forms and carvings in miscellaneous woods hitherto unseen, or available only in isolated examples. This enabled dealers, collectors and the interested to study, compare and come to new conclusions. A relatively unexplored topic is the wide range of woods native to China whose classifications have, so far, relied not so much on botanical knowledge but on local or traditional references. The notion that the only worthwhile woods were zitan, huanghuali, and to a lesser extent jichimu, persists. Examining the common links and differences between classical and vernacular furniture, as well as the types of woods employed, reveals artistic and cultural aspects of each region, thus throwing light on the social and economic development of Chinese history and society.

I consider furniture to be very much a part of living. As Professor Wang observed in his introduction, furniture provides the portable tools in the framework of life, and the house is the basis of the living environment. His beautifully written and insightful script in my book sums up my journey exploring the fundamentals of what it means to be Chinese, and how Chinese culture (exemplified in furniture, silk, porcelain and other genres) for centuries stimulated inquiry and instilled taste and interest in commercial goods to mesmerize the other known world — Europe.

I have always aspired to contribute to open up greater understanding in new areas — Chinese furniture, architecture, ways of living and being, none of which has much to do with my jewelry-making. It is just about knowing China and understanding China and the way people live, which in turn will reflect on my thinking and being.

Chinese Furniture Vis–a–Vis European Furniture

Furniture in old China was designed not only to be functional, but also to add charm and enjoyment to the house and garden in the scheme of the living environment. In marked contrast, here is a European interpretation of the role of furniture from Finn Juhl (1912-1989), the prominent Danish designer: "The craftsman's ability to form is probably the same as that of the sculptor. A chair is not a product of decorative art in space. It is a form and space in itself." These lines confirm the creator's belief in the value of his art, and also point to the difference between art and functional objects — the latter usually commands only a lower price and also carries the burden of function, which art does not. As a collector of both Chinese and modern Scandinavian furniture, it is equally challenging and pleasurable to weigh the similarities and differences in physical structures and meaning between the two styles of furniture. The former is part of a 'mature and wise system' — balanced, simple, unchanging, having reached maturity long ago, observed Gustave Ecke. There were no architects in traditional China and the buildings, majestic or simple, were usually erected by master builders engaged in 'major carpentry' while the interiors and furniture were executed by expert craftsmen employed in 'minor carpentry.' Woodwork was connected and constructed using an ancient 'mortise and tenon' joinery system. Furniture in the house was part of the scheme of living.

My interest in Nordic modern furniture was ignited by Danish designer Hans Wegner's interpretation of what he called the 'China Chair' which he created in 1943. Wegner was very taken by a version of a Chinese round back 'crestrail' chair he obtained through the East Asiatic Company (founded in 1897) that conducted trade between Denmark and the Far East — Thailand, Vietnam and China — and then to other territories.

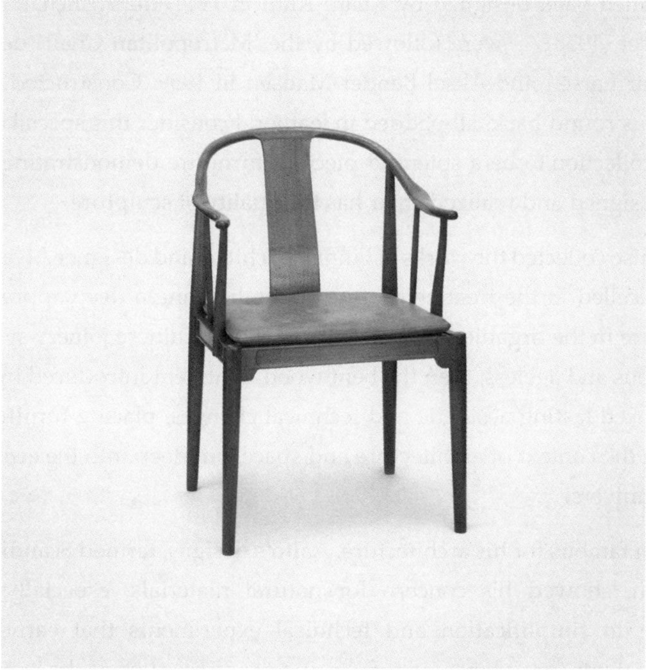

"China Chair" circa 1942 designed by Hans Wegner

Unlike the standard European chair with its rigid frame, Wegner (1914-2004) was aware of ergonomics. His 'China Chair' provided a curved form to allow for flexibility of body movement and created an 'experience' for the sitter. Then followed the famous version respectfully referred to as 'The Chair' (1949) with the 'continuous purification of wood cut down to the simplest possible elements with the back and side railings made of 11 pieces of wood joined by 12 mortise and tenon and two large finger joints,' as he wrote.

Ergonomics was even more evident in the swivel/desk chair he later designed for office use. In Chinese furniture, comfort was not a consideration — a seat was allocated its proper place to denote a certain purpose, and to a great extent, desirability was determined by the kind of wood it was made of. In the West, in contrast, furniture tends to combine form and function.

Notable early examples of the round back chairs — the Faaborg chair with caned back designed by Kaare Klint in 1914, the Armchair by Ole Wanscher (1958) — were followed by the 'Metropolitan Chair' designed by Ejnar Larsen and Aksel Bender Madsen in 1959. Constructed with a generous round back, all padded in leather, I consider this special edition in my collection to be a splendid piece of furniture demonstrating that a well-designed and realized chair has the quality of sculpture.

I have also collected the works of Finnish architect and designer Alvar Aalto who excelled in the treatment of wood, embodying a deep appreciation of nature in the organic forms he created. If the Chinese joinery system is ingenious and ageless, then the bent wood treatment introduced by Aalto has caused lasting aesthetic and technical changes, placing furniture not only in the context of architecture and space, but deep into the ecosystem of the universe.

Though famous for his architecture, Aalto's designs, termed Scandinavian Modern, showed his concern for natural materials, especially wood, leading to simplification and technical experiments that earned him many patents for various manufacturing processes such as the bent wood treatment applied to plywood.

In Chinese furniture, value and worth, to a very great extent (and in my opinion a concept that needs to be redefined) is determined by the type and quality of wood used, the most prized being zitan, huanghuali, jichimu and nanmu. Thus, the usually lowly-ranked plywood, even though made of rare curly birch indigenous to Finland, as used in Aalto's celebrated Paimio chair, should not be a determining factor of distinction. The chair in this instance is rightly prized for the innovative cantilever joinery technique, producing seamless graceful lines, establishing that great design can combine different types of aspirations, know-how and innovation.

Just as with jewelry and ornaments.

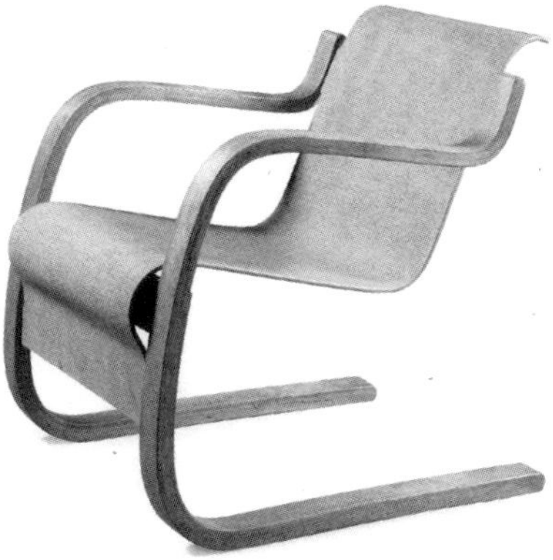

Curly Birch armchair with bent wood arms by Alvar Aalto, 1936

HOUSE, HOME, FAMILY

13

House, Home, Family

From the early 1990s, I also traveled extensively in Central and Northern China, and edited four well-regarded books on Chinese furniture, ceramics, heritage and the vernacular living pattern. My goal, I suppose, was to understand the Chinese DNA and way of life — old and new — and to attempt to know China and its culture better.

I started with university trips accompanied by Professor Puay Peng Ho, then Professor of Architecture at Chinese University of Hong Kong, with whom I collaborated in 1990 on a fine book, *Living Heritage — Vernacular Environment in China,* covering five regions of the country, each with its own vernacular culture and regional characteristics. In the Huang Shan (Yellow Mountain) area of Anhui province, in particular, the traditional culture has been preserved more than in most other places in China — owing to the fact that it is isolated, has less industry and therefore has experienced less change.

In 2001, we developed a photographic exhibition from the book and staged it first at City Hall, Hong Kong, then at the China Institute in New York where it created quite a sensation. As a Hong Kong Chinese traveling around China in those years, absorbing the culture and social practices, I very much felt the connection, and enrichment of cultural understanding. The China Institute organized many school groups to visit the exhibition and it cast a deep impression on children of many nationalities, especially people of Chinese ancestry born in the United States who had not seen these aspects of rural China.

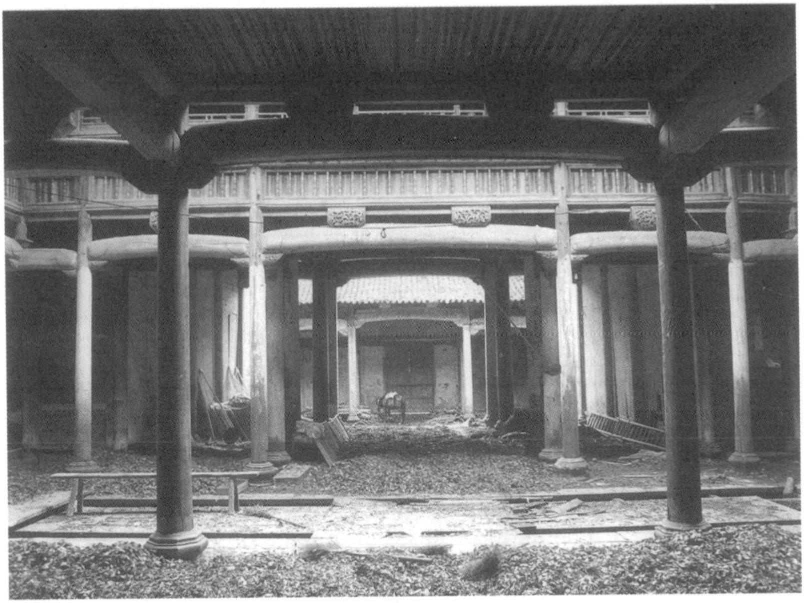

Vernacular architecture, Yixian, Anhui: an abandoned ancestral hall used for storage of hay

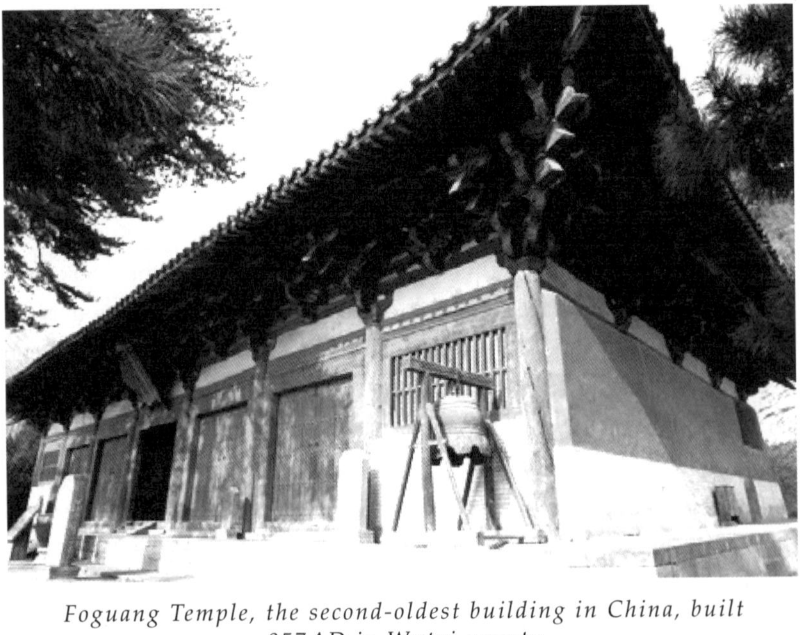

Foguang Temple, the second-oldest building in China, built 857AD in Wutai county

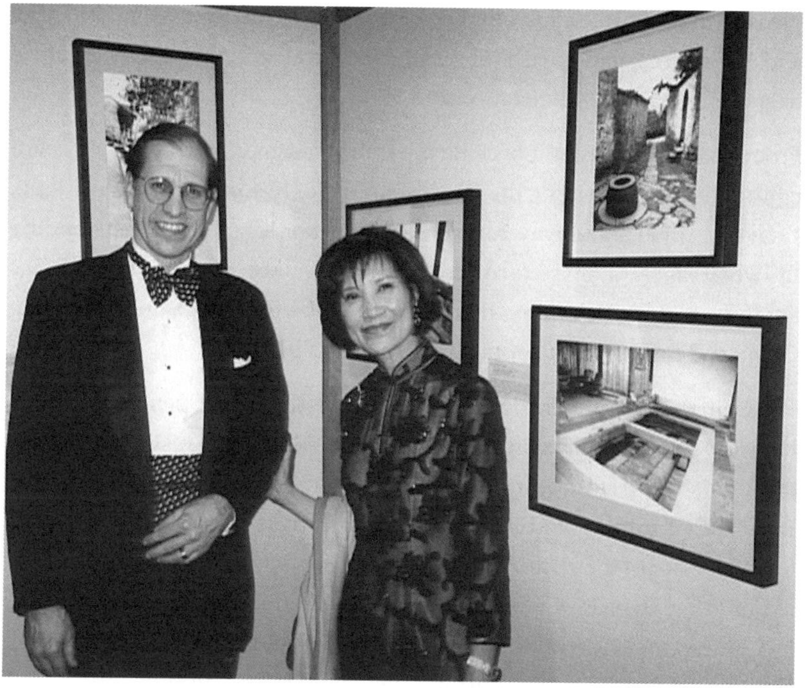

Maxwell Hearn, at that time Senior Curator of the Metropolitan Museum, New York, with me at the opening of a photographic exhibition of vernacular China at the China Institute, New York, in 2001

I owe a lot of my knowledge on architecture and religion in China and Japan to Professor Ho. He is now Head of the Department of Architecture, Design and Environment at Nanyang University, Singapore, which is a new and significant combination of disciplines. Also, I owe a lot to Ron Knapp, who is likely the world's most eminent cultural geographer on China. He and I produced a book called *House Home Family – Living and Being Chinese*, published in English in 2005 and translated into Chinese in 2011. It featured important essays from respected cultural and social historians, and contributed to our understanding of what constitutes 'Chineseness'. To have impact and influence in cross-disciplinary study, one needs to be an interpretive scholar, which a lot of the experts in China are not. This is my aim. I am a cross-discipline person. I fuse things. I am pleased that I studied history, because it allows me to evaluate linkages and differences, and have a long and concentrated focus on diverse areas of survey — culture, civilization and life.

From being a historian, I became a jewelry designer, but my designs are culturally based, melding the two disciplines of history and design. I think I have in some small way contributed to better scholarly understanding in two areas — Chinese furniture and architecture, neither of which has anything to do with jewelry. It is just about knowing China, understanding China and the way that people live, think and behave.

The China scholar that I admire a great deal is Jonathan Spence. His books have a depth of understanding of Chinese culture and history that truly distinguish him. I also admire Craig Clunas, an art historian specializing in the material culture of Ming Dynasty, who has just retired after being the first Professor of the History of Art at the University of Oxford. The topic of Art of Ming Dynasty China, and new social and economic developments in Chinese society with the rise of the merchant class, will never be the same again thanks to his contributions. His research into the artists and literati of that era is stimulating and groundbreaking.

Jan Stuart, the former Keeper for Asia at the British Museum and now with the Freer Gallery of Art, Smithsonian Institution in Washington D.C., once told me "... your books are so very impressive — the way you look at art, design, and life in a holistic fashion is very special, and that you do it with a historical understanding and true connoisseurship makes you rare indeed." She was referring in particular to my books on Chinese society and vernacular culture and also a book I edited on recent design culture called *Hong Kong, Creative Ecologies — the Shaping of a Design Culture*, published in 2010. Jan is an art historian on Chinese culture, and I regard her comment as a great validation of my scholarship and aspirations.

Foreign architects and art historians conducted much of the study of Chinese architecture and furniture in the early 20th century. There was little available information and interest in Chinese architecture until the publication in 1925 of a Song dynasty manual about construction methods including layout and materials specifications, first produced in 1103. Entitled *Yingzao Fashi* (Building Standards), it was compiled by the scholar-official Zhu Qiqian. That, and the *Gongcheng Zuofa* (Engineering Manual of the Board of Works) printed in 1734, were the only books that appear to have been compiled about Chinese construction and related matters during a period of a thousand years. By the late 1950s, the study of traditional Chinese architecture had become widespread, but it was not until 1981 that researchers published findings that deciphered a key puzzle in *Yingzao Fashi* relating to measurements and building standards.

There is one more important work that related to the construction of the living environment, and that was *Lu Ban Jing*, written in the late Yuan or early Ming dynasty. It is an illustrated carpenter's manual eventually published during the Wanli period (1573-1619) in the late Ming, and is partially devoted to the construction of furniture, implements and the house.

Apart from these compilations, knowledge of construction in wood and timber units was confined to builders and carpenters, and simply handed on by word-of-mouth. The artisans of functional or decorative crafts were considered to be no more than 'tools' in the process of execution. The term 'architect', as it is generally understood today, did not exist in old China. Rather, traditional buildings in China were constructed by craftsmen according to specified forms and dimensions. These were craftsmen involved with major carpentry, that is, building the structure.

At the heart of the creation of the living environment in old China was wood. Wood was almost always used for the construction of buildings and furniture because of its availability, versatility and flexibility. It is easily fashioned into different forms and sizes but is not too hard nor dense for carving and decoration. Above all, it is a suitable material for executing an intricate and ingenious system of joinery, and its pliability helps structures to withstand earthquakes — although the destruction of China's old buildings has been due more to fire, rot and neglect than to natural disasters. The oldest timber structure in China today is Nanchan

Monastery in Wutaishan, Shanxi Province, which dates back to 782AD. It is a small structure, being part of a formerly larger complex. The second oldest timber structure, the eastern main hall of a larger complex nearby, Foguang Monastery (Temple of Buddha's Life), was built in 857AD. Softwoods were used for most parts in the construction of palaces, temples, mansions and small dwellings, but hardwoods were used for pillars. Compared to the extent of wooden edifices in Japan, derived from these Chinese models, one must ask why China has not better maintained its built heritage.

Woodwork in old China was divided into 'major carpentry' (*damuzuo*) or 'minor carpentry' (*xiaomuzuo*). The builders who erected both buildings were not architects; they were the anonymous craftsmen whose knowledge and skill were passed down from father to son or from craftsman to apprentice. Their comprehensive knowledge of their craft was the main contribution to the development of Chinese architecture, and also the reason for its slow and conservative advance.

Craftsmen of 'minor carpentry' were responsible for the construction of the interiors of houses, including partitions, lattice panels, windows, doors and ceilings, all of which would be intricately carved in wealthy households. They also produced a whole range of furniture and small articles including chairs, bed railings, racks, shelves, screens and boxes. There are many similarities between the decorative styles and motifs of buildings and furniture. The carpenters were as adroit as they were inventive. The elaboration, simplification and continuance of the complex yet workable mechanism of joinery that led to new forms and possibilities were amongst theirlasting contributions. A note of kudos must be extended to the architects Liang Sicheng and Lin Heiyin, a husband and wife team, who surveyed and recorded China's overlooked ancient buildings. The most notable was the rediscovery of Foguang Monastery in Wutai County, Shanxi province.

14

Bright as Silver, White as Snow

As a newcomer to collecting Chinese artifacts in the 1970s and 1980s, I began by focusing on ancient jades, colored stones, small carvings and bronze ornaments, partly because they were affordable and suited my purpose, which was turning antique objects into stunning wearable adornments to add interest and color to everyday life. My collecting attitude was dedicated but relaxed — partly due to the fact that such pieces were much less sought-after in those days.

Collection of white and qingbai ceramics from 7th to 14th centuries displayed in two 19th-century cabinets

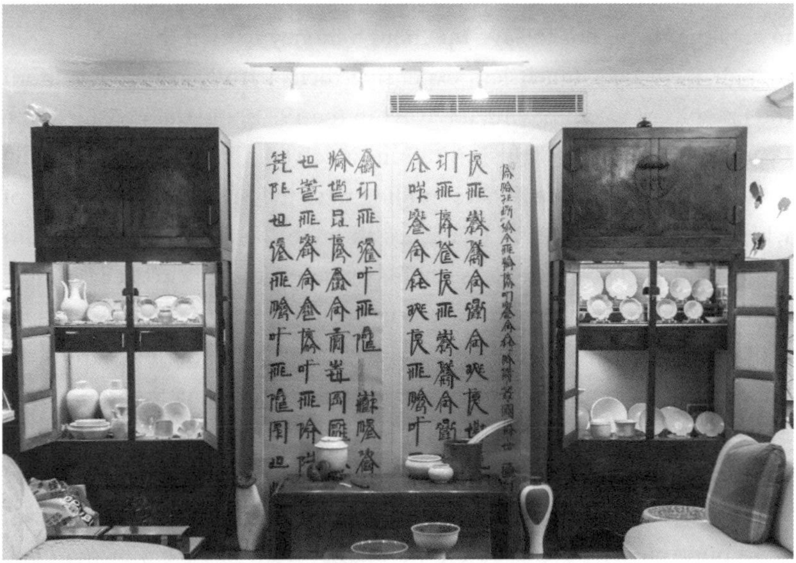

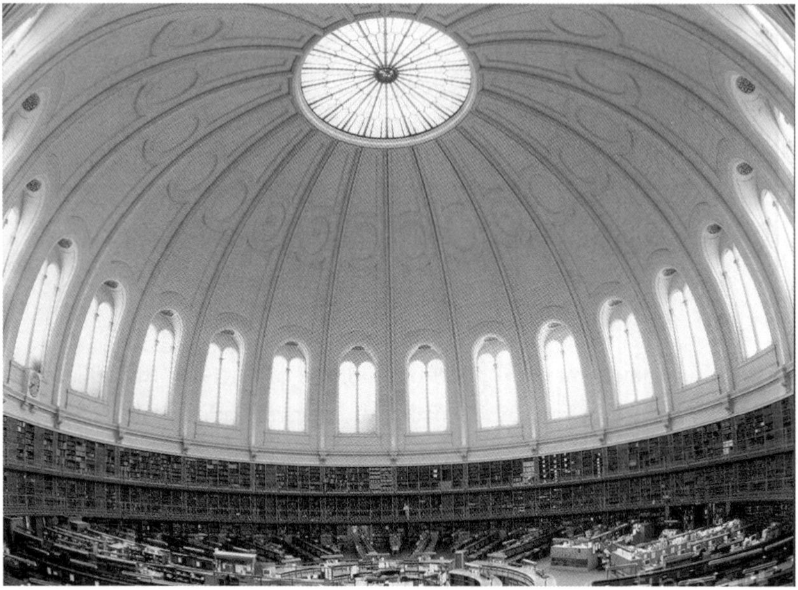

The Reading Room of the British Museum, a library that for years I called home

I admired the refinement of Ming and Qing porcelain, but they never moved me sufficiently to want to study the skill and technique involved in creating them, nor to save up enough money to own them. And even though they were much less expensive then, I really could not afford the fine pieces worth having anyway! In the 1970s, my daily visits to the Reading Room of the British Museum involved a stopover at the Long Gallery one floor above, where mulling over the Museum's collection of white wares from the Five Dynasties through the late Song period (6th-12th centuries) became a pleasurable pastime. Nearby, a corner building on Gordon Square housed a selection of the famous Percival David Collection, regarded as the best private collection of ceramics from the Song, Ming and Qing dynasties outside the holdings at the two Palace Museums in Beijing and Taipei. Out of some 1,700 pieces in the collection, the forty or so white ceramics on display at that venue, dating from the Five Dynasties (907-960) period to the end of the Jin Dynasty (1115-1234), were purportedly purchased on the market from members of the Qing

Dynasty's Imperial household, who offered them for sale, it is said, in 1900 during the chaotic days following the lifting of the Boxer siege of the Peking Legation Quarter. Between 1880 and 1895, the Empress Cixi is said to have used many antique items as collateral for loans from Chinese banks. The Percival David collection, formed at that time, always had educating the public as its mission. It was first donated to the Courtauld Institute, part of the University of London, and was later established as a foundation attached to the School of Oriental and African Studies (SOAS), University of London.

Due to funding problems, the Gordon Square building housing the collection closed at the end of 2007. As of April that year, thanks to funds once again provided by Sir Joseph Hotung (who also funded the two renovations of the Long Gallery at the British Museum in 1993 and in 2018), the David Collection has been moved on a long-term basis to the British Museum and is now housed in a wonderful special gallery (Room 95) for all to enjoy.

Being in close proximity to the massed treasures of the British Museum, often I would spend my lunch hour ogling the wonderful ceramics, particularly my preferred white and *Qingbai* (literal translation: shadowy green white) wares from the David collection. Certainly it did not occur to me that one day I would have the opportunity to have my own collection of these types of ceramics when collectible pieces gradually began appearing on the Hong Kong market in the late 1980s and early 1990s. The best-known collectors of these ceramics from the 1970s onwards included the King of Sweden and his friend, the Swedish industrialist Karl Kempe, along with a host of Japanese collectors, including members of the Sumitomo Group.

The pristine forms of the white monochrome ceramics from the late Tang (9th century) to the end of the Song Dynasty (13th century) greatly appealed to Japanese aesthetics. The directors of the Sumitomo Corporation in Japan decided to assemble a representative collection of 144 pieces of Chinese ceramics, many of which were white or *Qingbai* wares dating from the 7th to the 13th century. The collection, which boasts several pieces classified as 'national treasures', was donated to the Museum of Oriental Ceramics in Osaka. This collection shares honors as the finest in the world with the Percival David Collection and to some extent with the great examples at the National Palace Museum in Taipei.

In the late 1980s and early 1990s when I was actively promoting my designs in Japan, I would often treat myself with a visit to this museum in Osaka, drooling over the collection of Chinese white, *Qingbai* and celadon ceramics along with other treasures, including an excellent collection of Korean celadon wares. The Museum offered a comprehensive display and opportunity to study the best of Chinese and Korean ceramics and added much to my education and enjoyment of white and *Qingbai* wares.

An additional bonus was that one could also buy very fine copies of well-known prototypes or 'interpreted versions' especially of white ware from the Museum's 'commissioned' collection, which even to this day I take great pleasure in using for special dinner parties. I recall vividly when in about 2002 Julian Thompson, Head of the Chinese Department at Sotheby's London and a well-known expert on ceramics, upon seeing my 'Song' dishes laid on the dinner table, exclaimed, 'Welcome to Kaifeng!' (Kaifeng was the capital of the Northern Song Dynasty.)

From modest beginnings in the early 1990s, I began to form a collection of about 70 pieces of white and *Qingbai* wares dating from the Five Dynasties (907-960AD), the Northern Song (960-1126AD) and also including examples from the Southern Song (1127-1279). The prices of these pieces were far lower than the polychrome porcelain of the Ming and early Qing, and that was the main factor that enabled me to pursue my collecting. The elegant clean lines and subtle hues of the ceramics greatly appealed to my sensibilities. These ceramics have, in fact, long been viewed as the ultimate expression of high taste in the development of Chinese culture, representing the cultural maturity and connoisseurship of that era, and were championed by scholars and by the Emperor. This beginning of connoisseurship in ceramic culture gave rise to patronage in collecting, and stimulated the search for perfection by both the patron and the artisan who produced these elegant wares of understated simplicity preferred by the court and by the literati. The imperial family and other collectors compiled catalogs and essays of their ceremonial wares, which were produced according to their specifications, different from the ceramics used by the populace. These ceramics came to be regarded not as cheaper substitutes for articles fashioned from more precious metalware such as gold and silver, but as works of art in themselves.

Fine hard-paste porcelain, which was developed about a century later, became the hallmark of luxury and accomplishment synonymous with the name of China. By the 9th century, tea drinking had been elevated as an art and white ceramics were deemed to be the best vessels for complementing the burnished golden hue of tea.

Tea connoisseur Lu Yue in his famous treatise *Cha Jing* or the Classic of Tea, dating to the mid-9th century, summed up the spirit, appearance and function of the white vessels as the perfect containers for tea. He described them as being 'Bright as Silver, White as Snow', which appropriately served as the title of the year-long exhibition (and catalog of the exhibition) of the Kai-Yin Lo Collection which opened in October 1998 at the Denver Art Museum. The celebrated Chinese art specialist Regina Krahl wrote a fine essay on white ceramics to accompany it in the catalog, as well as all the captions and notes on the fifty-nine items exhibited.

The exhibition catalog also featured three additional essays by leading scholars, illuminating the flourishing material and intellectual culture of the Northern and Southern Song era (960-1276AD). Professor Li Zhiyan of Beijing's Palace Museum wrote an in-depth account on 'The development and background of white and *Qingbai* wares from Tang to Song'. Professor Roderick Whitfield, former Keeper of Asia at the British Museum, explored the 'Material culture in the Northern Song Dynasty: the world of Zhang Zeduan'; and Dr Sören Edgren, the print expert, contributed an essay on 'Hangzhou in the Southern Song Dynasty: perspective through print culture.'

These essays, together with my preface, 'Glimpses of a splendid era: Life in the Song Dynasty,' illustrate that the Song era, despite military

The catalog featuring the Kai-Yin Lo collection of White and Qingbai ceramics at Denver Art Museum from October 1998

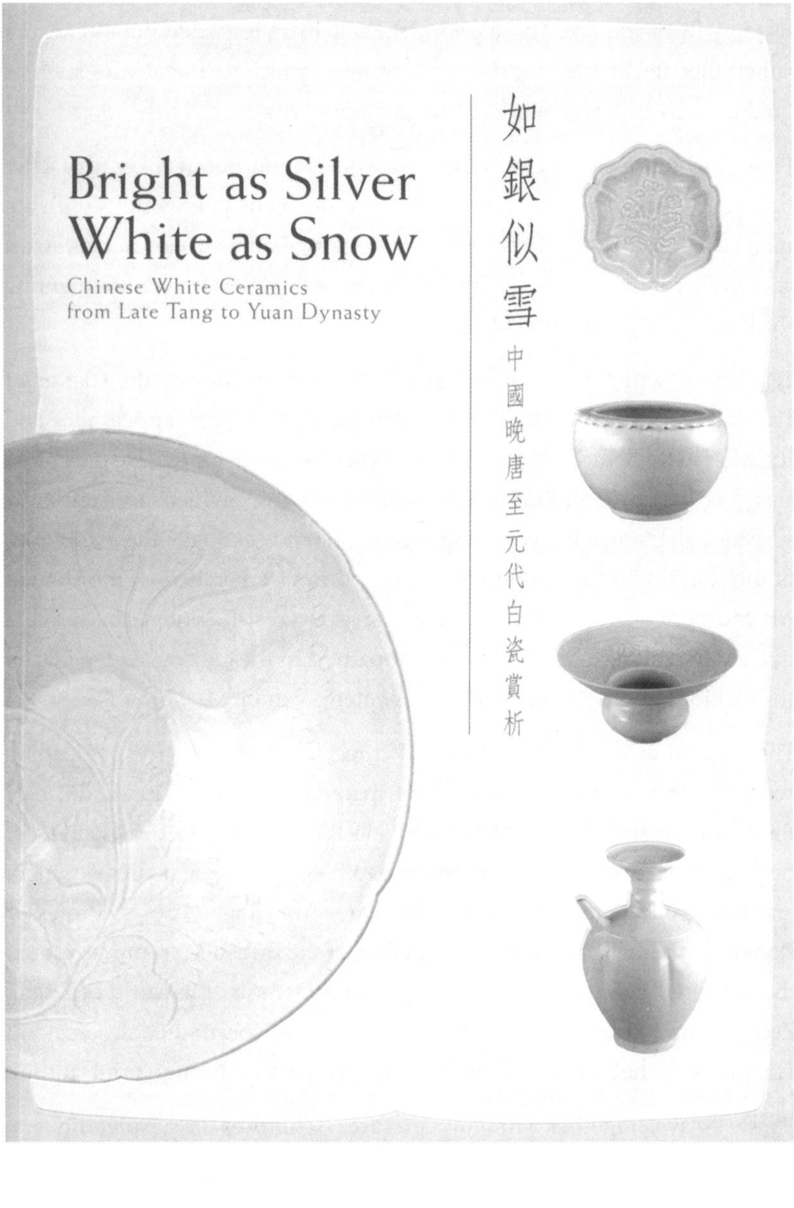

weakness, was a period of flourishing intellectual culture and outstanding development in many art forms — painting, literature, poetry, philosophy and ethics — all of which proliferated by virtue of the important development in printing, which caused a profound change in the social order of China. Printing expanded the range of the educated class, caused accepted values and traditions to be questioned, and stimulated the formation of official and personal libraries. It furthered the transmission of new ideas, especially within the academies that sprang up in communities in both urban and rural areas, and also afforded greater opportunities for women to read and write within the confines of their homes. The printed books also extended the range of content beyond the traditional classics, poetry and prose usually reserved for the elite. They included manuals covering practical topics such as agriculture, health and religious rituals. For the first time, a large number of people had easy access to this kind of information in printed form.

The Song period was an era of economic growth, with marked advances in agricultural productivity, industrial skills, transport, communication and commercial organization. And possibly no other Chinese dynasty was truer to the Confucian model. The population multiplied, cities thrived and society prospered with a vastly improved standard of living. After the Manchus, then called Jurchens, conquered northern China, the Song capital was relocated to Hangzhou in 1127, and this city soon surpassed the old Song capital of Kaifeng in population and economic development. Patronage increased demand and technological advancements accounted for the growth in the traditional industries of ceramics, silk, lacquer and stone carving. The flowering of Song ceramics was mostly due to the artisan makers' mastery over the raw materials and the greater control exercised during the firing cycle. Silk, ceramic and craft workshops, including those operated by the government, prospered. The period also saw the first issuance of paper money anywhere in the world, a significant invention by any measure. And the Cizhou kilns near Hangzhou saw heightened demand for their wares, as well as new impetus for their growth.

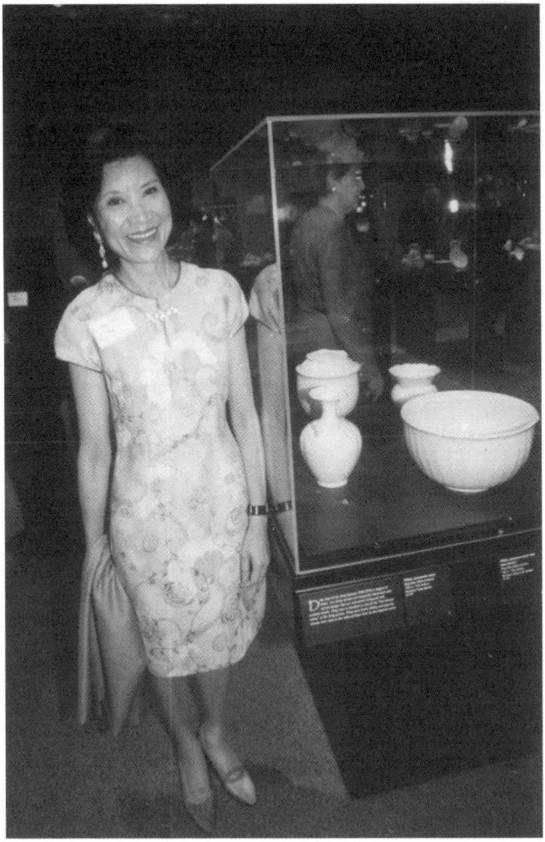

Kai-Yin at the opening of the white ceramic exhibition at Denver Art Museum, October 1998

The dynasty tried to uphold a policy of containment of its aggressive neighbors – the Khitans and the Jurchens – but it fell, for despite its intellectual, social and economic vitality, it was militarily weak.

The Denver Art Museum has for many years benefited by exhibiting Chinese art from Hong Kong collections, providing visitors with an opportunity to see aspects of Chinese art otherwise unavailable to the American public. Exhibitions have included the very distinguished 'Adornment for Eternity: Status and Rank in Chinese Ornament', featuring jewelry and accessories from the great Mengdiexuan Collection, and 'Treasures from the Dr. S.Y. Yip Collection: Classical Chinese Furniture, Painting and Calligraphy'.

The Kai-Yin Lo Collection was on display in Denver from 1998 to 2012, when it returned to Hong Kong. The social environment of Hong Kong provides more opportunities for collectors to share their treasures with one another, creating a stimulating atmosphere which has inspired an array of fascinating exhibitions, conferences and publications. The impact of these private collections has also extended well beyond the shores of Hong Kong via these exhibitions overseas.

Much of the serious collecting impetus was propelled by members of the Min Chiu Society, the distinguished society formed by a group of gentlemen collectors devoted to enhancing appreciation of Chinese art by showcasing their members' acclaimed private collections. The inspiration was drawn from a line in the Confucian Analects, 'I was not born with knowledge, but being fond of antiquity, I am quick to seek it.'

The clean lines and elegant shapes of white and *Qingbai* (or shadowy blue-green) ceramics produced under the Northern and Southern Song dynasties (960-1279AD) are the ultimate expression of cultural maturity and high taste — and these wares were designed for daily use!

To mark the opening of Hotel Icon in 2011, a few of Hong Kong's leading architects and designers were commissioned to furnish special designs. I was one of the chosen designers who furnished a small collection of interpreted white and *Qingbai* tableware for the VIP dining room. As a longtime collector of these genres of ceramics, I have created two porcelain collections called 'Contemporary Song'. The first consisted of a shallow bowl punctuated with a sweeping calligraphic stroke and an anchoring red dot, and a foliated bowl decorated with monochrome dripping lines of color (inspired by the work of American artist Cy Twombly), complete with a dish to form a set. The second collection consisted of *Qingbai* ware crafted in Jingdezhen in south China, the center of this industry since the Song Dynasty, with forms inspired by Central Asian metalware and decorated in raised patterns of the peony, much used as a design motif in the Tang dynasty (618-906AD), and the tulip, a flower of the Middle East, denoting cross-cultural intermixing.

I hope I have also helped to spread interest in, and deepen appreciation of, white and *Qingbai* ceramics, not only for the beauty of the wares, but also for their background and history. In addition to the collection I assembled, what has endured is the book, which embodies the research, knowledge and insight, not only of the ceramics, but also of the social, economic and cultural background that engendered their flowering, capturing glimpses of Chinese civilization under the Song — indigenous and diverse, controlled yet pluralistic. The Song dynasty eventually fell, but the culture survived, and its social strength and cultural identity has proved resilient enough to adjust and transform through subsequent ages to become the unifying characteristics we identify today as 'Chineseness'.

'Contemporary Song' of white and Qingbai ceramic, designed by Kai-Yin Lo, 2012

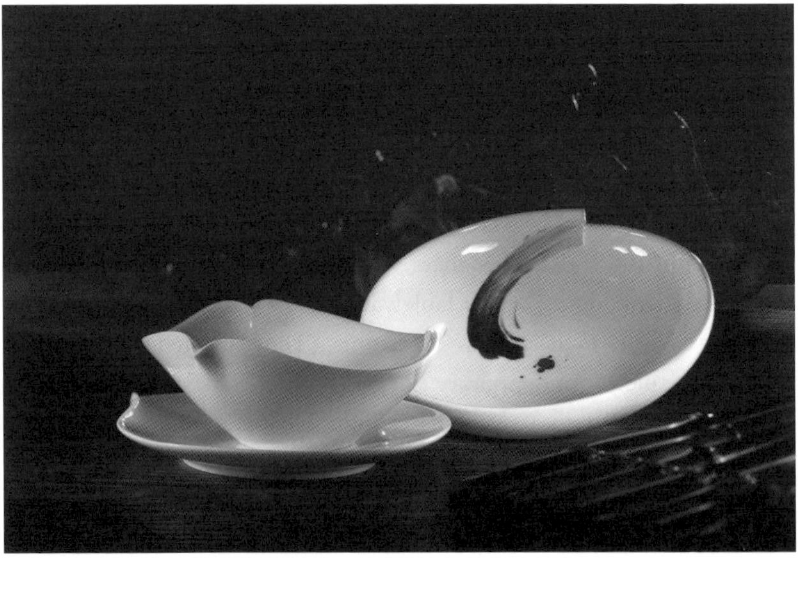

15

Wu Guanzhong & Xu Bing at the British Museum

The British Museum occupies a special place in my life. It was in its august and historic Reading Room, built in 1837, where I spent several years reading and researching Medieval English and European history. Walking through the North Gallery almost every day, I developed my knowledge of Chinese ceramics by looking at the lined cabinets full of Chinese artifacts and ceramics dating from the Warring States period (474–121BC) down to the white ceramics of the Liao and Song dynasties (960 to 1125AD).

I can say that I 'grew up' in the British Museum.

I was also fortunate enough to organize an exhibition there, the first-ever retrospective of a modern Chinese artist, Wu Guanzhong. Entitled 'Wu Guanzhong, A Twentieth-Century Chinese Artist,' the exhibition was staged from March to May 1993, and was also the first one-man show mounted at the British Museum. Later, in March 2011, I played a part in the exhibition of a significant single installation created by the leading Chinese contemporary artist Xu Bing.

My first exposure to the art of Wu Guanzhong was thanks to my sister Marina's introduction. It must have been 1988 or 1989; she was moving into a new flat in Hong Kong and needed something to hang on the walls. Out of the blue, she called me one day and said, 'I'm in an art gallery in Causeway Bay, and there are some paintings here that I would like you to see.' Up to that moment, neither she nor I had been collecting Chinese art.

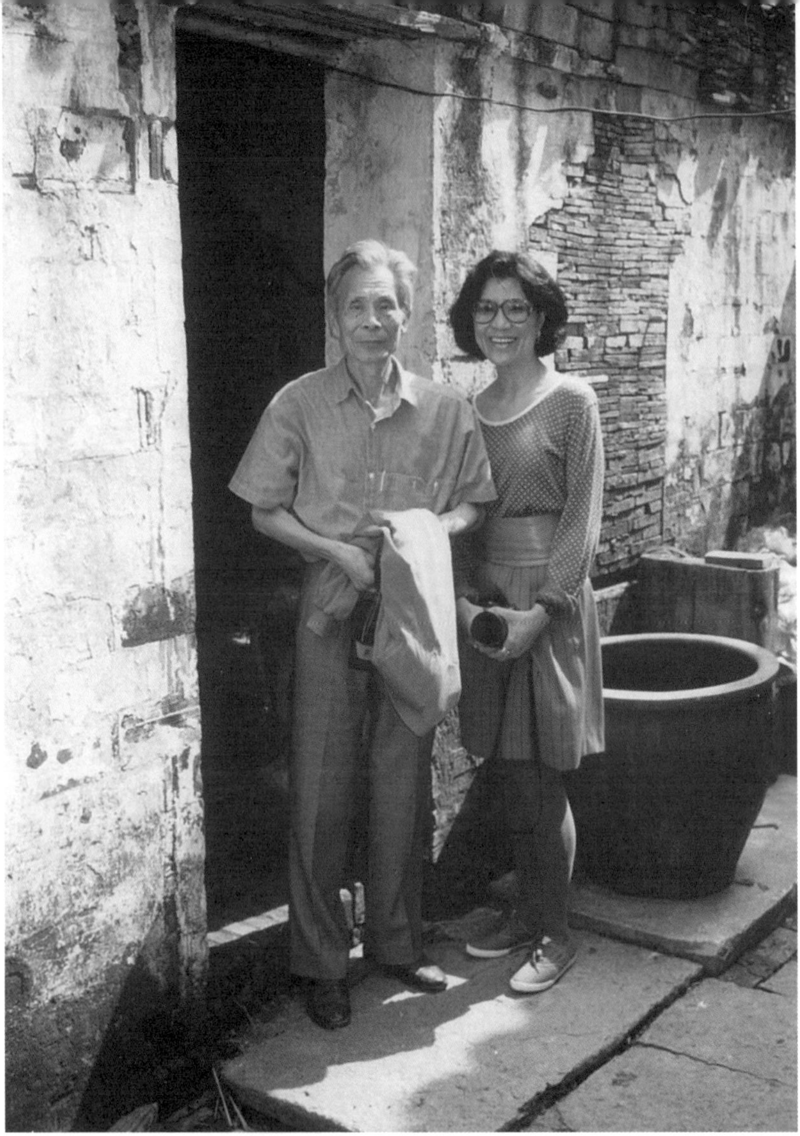

Kai-Yin Lo with Wu Guanzhong in front of his family home in Yixing, Zhejiang province, 1993

That consequential date marked the start of our collecting journey. In the end, she became a much more important collector than me.

In the 1980s, Hong Kong had only two prominent galleries selling modern Chinese art — Chinese Arts & Crafts, and Rong Bao Zhai, but my sister was at a different gallery located on the second floor of a building in Causeway Bay, operated by Xu Lai Peng. I obliged and went to meet her.

The featured artist was Wu Guanzhong. It was the first time I saw his work, and it opened my eyes and my heart. I had never before seen Chinese brush and ink painting rendered with such feeling, rhythm and energy in a style where the generally observed rules seemed redundant.

Today, the term Modern Chinese Art is used quite arbitrarily to describe works, mostly executed in Chinese ink, created between 1900 and 1989. Most of the artists in this category were people who largely painted in the traditional way, although there were important departures that introduced personal interpretations. Some of the most influential artists went to France, most of them to Paris, and enrolled in the Ecole des Beaux-Arts. The last batch included Zao Wou-ki, Chu Teh-Chun, Xiong Bing Ming and other students of Lin Fengmian at the Hangzhou Fine Art Academy, which in the 1920s and 1930s was known as the China Art Academy. Wu Guanzhong also attended this institution one year ahead of the better-known Zao Wou-ki (Zhao Wuji), but as I understand it, the two painters were not exactly friends. Zao came from a wealthy family while Wu was a fisherman's son. In about 2002, I went to a dinner with Wu Guanzhong, Zao Wou-ki and Lin Fengmian, the former director of the Academy. It was remarkable and touching to see the pupils 'kowtow' to the ground before their former teacher. We ate crab, and I watched Lin Fengmian, nearly 90 years of age, devour five crabs in a row!

More than a teacher, Lin Fengmian was also an innovative artist of great accomplishment. He went to live in Paris during the First World War, one of the first of his generation to settle there. Then, in the 1930s, he returned to China to teach and became principal of the Art Academy in Hangzhou. Wu also returned, while Zao and other classmates including Chu Teh-Chun and Xiong Bing Ming remained in Paris. Zao in particular became famous in his own right.

Wu began to exhibit in the early 1980s in Shenzhen and at the annual Canton Fair, the only official commercial exchange outlet between China and the rest of the world in those days. Besides commodities such as foodstuffs and machinery, arts and crafts were also offered, from works in carved ivory and wood to paintings by masters such as Qi Baishi, Lu Yanshao and Li Keran. It was an exposure outlet for a good number of the Mainland artists.

My sister and I both bought our first painting by Wu Guanzhong that day in Causeway Bay. Then, in 1989, Wu was given an exhibition at Plum Blossoms Gallery in Hong Kong, and I bought another of his paintings. I became distracted after that, spending a lot of time in Japan trying to break into the Japanese market with my jewelry. One day while there, I heard that Wu Guanzhong was having an exhibition, his debut, at the Seibu Department store in Tokyo. I had to hustle to the opening! I was staying at the Aso family's ancestral compound in Kyushu. It was a rare treat to have been invited to such a special home. Rushing back to Tokyo to catch the exhibition would mean a trip of several hours. I was new to Japan at that point, and would have become hopelessly lost making the trip, and above all, I felt it was not very polite, having arrived at 5 p.m. the day before, to leave so abruptly at the crack of dawn the next morning! I was very lucky to have the understanding of Kazuko Aso, my host, who did not take offense, and who remains a very good friend and a fan of Wu Guanzhong's works. We both took a train that left at 5:45 a.m. the next day and we puffed our way to the Seibu Department Store to be at Wu Guanzhong's opening at 10 a.m.

When we got there, the very first thing Wu said to me was, 'Ms Lo, I know you travel a lot and you know a lot of people. Please arrange an exhibition for me in Paris.'

It was true, I was traveling a great deal for my business in those days. I took his request to heart and I went to twenty museums, galleries and art institutions around the world on his behalf. Most museums in Europe at that time would mount exhibitions of Chinese, Japanese and South East Asian art only once every three to five years. In America, institutions which would stage such shows included museums in Cleveland, Kansas City and San Francisco, but they all tended to show works by established modern artists of that generation like Zhang Daqian and Xu Bei Hong. An emerging artist would have to wait at least three years for an exhibition opportunity. Finally, I heard that the Victoria & Albert Museum in London was going through some reshuffling of leadership. Director Elizabeth Esteve-Coll said to me, 'Why don't you try the British Museum? They have a new director and have installed a new assistant keeper of Asia who knows something about painting.'

For a long time, an august lady named Jessica Rawson, eminently erudite in jade and ancient artifacts, ran the British Museum's Asian Department and she fortunately agreed that it was a good time to stage an exhibition to introduce new developments in contemporary Chinese art. The department had just hired an assistant curator, Dr Anne Farrer, who was a specialist on early modern Chinese woodblock prints. I worked hard on the project and once again I got lucky, and so did Wu Guanzhong. In 1993, there was a cancellation of an exhibition at the Asahi Shimbun Gallery in the museum that opened up a slot for us. The British Museum that year was exhibiting its rich collection of Rembrandt's drawings to celebrate the 350th anniversary of the artist's death and it was made clear to us that they had no time, manpower nor money to support us. 'You'll do it yourself and please do it well!' they said.

And so we did. We managed to arrange the funds required, and succeeded in mounting the exhibition.

I put a great deal of time and energy into the show, working with a team that included Y.Y. Fong, Wu's son Ke Yu, and my sister Marina, to ensure the exhibition's success because Wu's story really moved all of us. Having traveled from abject poverty to renown as an outstanding and innovative artist, he was an individual completely absorbed and devoted, never thinking of anything but painting. Born in 1919 in the town of Yixing in Jiangsu Province by Lake Tai, west of Shanghai, he was expected to follow his father as a fisherman. He once took me to see his family's one-story house, which consisted of a large room and a kitchen. He had a talent for art and was able to get himself enrolled in the China Academy of Art in Hangzhou. When the Japanese attacked China in 1937, he followed the

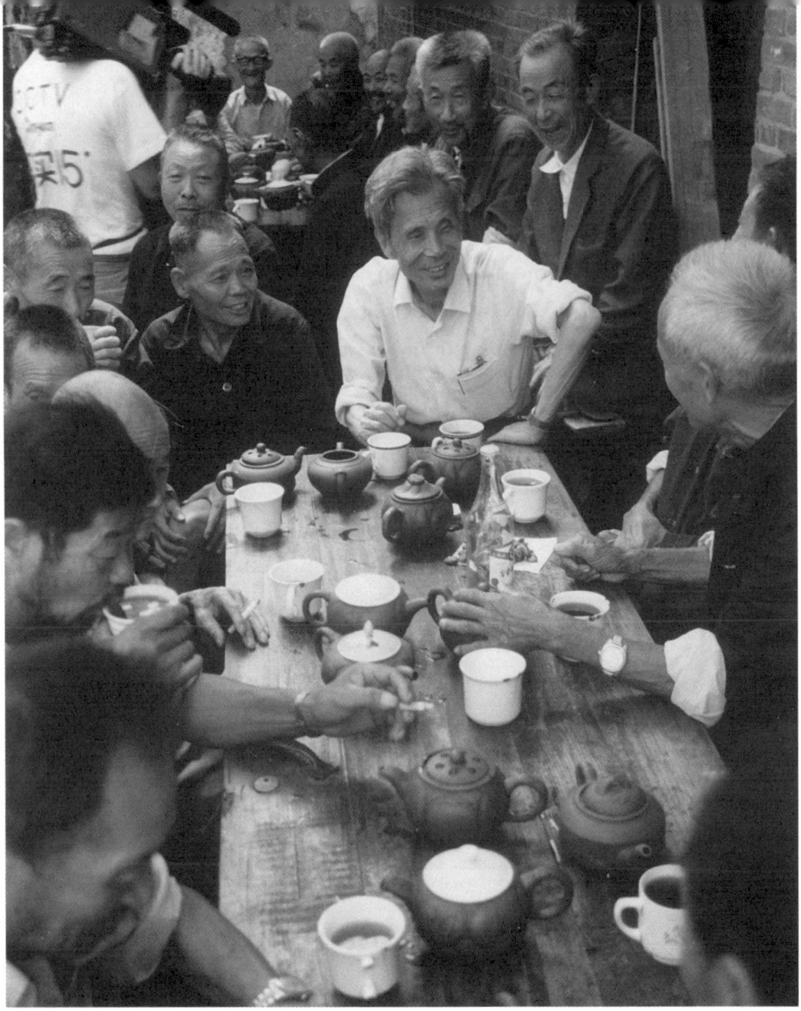

Wu Guanzhong's favorite photograph,
captured during a tea break in Yixing

Academy and moved to Chungking, and then went to Paris on a scholarship. I once asked him how he managed to get the scholarship, and he said the key was that he had learned to speak and read French. There was a French priest in Chungking, and every day he walked three hours to have a lesson with him, and then three hours back. And so, being able to speak French, he secured the scholarship and took a boat to France, a move that changed his life, his way of seeing things, depicting things — everything.

That was why he wanted to hold an exhibition in Paris.

There was the miracle of a cancellation at the British Museum, and we grasped the opportunity. Then the Musée Cernuschi in Paris opened up space for Wu after learning of the impending British Museum exhibition. We had a choice. I asked Wu where to mount the exhibition first, the British Museum or the Cernuschi, and he said the British Museum. It was a landmark show, being the first major exhibition held at the British Museum by a modern artist of any nationality, delineating a significant artistic development in China from the beginning to the end of the 20th century and acting as an antidote to the vociferous development of contemporary art in China that started in the 1970s. The exhibition comprised 44 ink and oil paintings, watercolors and sketches. It remains a landmark moment.

The opening on March 15, 1993 was officiated by the Duke of Gloucester, who at that time was the Patron of the British Museum, and attended by the Director of the British Museum Robert Anderson, Keeper of Asia Dame Jessica Rawson and Curator Dr Anne Farrer, as well as Wu's chums from Paris — Chu Teh-Chun and Xiong Bing Ming, my London friends Simon and Emma Keswick, Glenys Roberts, John Tusa, Lady Mary Rothermere and a host of other friends from the U.K., Europe and Hong Kong. Most important was the attendance of key art critics from the *Financial Times*, *The Times* and the *Spectator* and they produced glowing critiques, the like of which no previous contemporary Chinese artist had received.

The influential *International Herald Tribune's* art critic, however, was missing. But a couple of days later, after I left the museum for a while to attend to a few errands, my sister was anxiously waiting at the front entrance on my return: 'Souren Melikian, the art critic of the *International Herald Tribune*, is here!'

What I then witnessed at the exhibition hall was a poignant and moving scene. As Wu did not speak English, he was using all his powers to rake up whatever French he could muster, a language he had not had the opportunity to speak for years, to converse with Melikian. The resulting review that Melikian wrote in the *IHT* was ecstatic.

In 1995 and 1996, the Hong Kong Museum of Art organized a traveling retrospective of 20th-century Chinese art for which I, together with Victor Lo, Robert Miller and others as lead sponsors, assembled an international symposium in Hong Kong at which Souren Melikian, as well as Kirk Varnedoe, chief curator of the Museum of Modern Art in New York, were speakers. The event marked the start of a four-city exhibition that began in Hong Kong, then toured the Singapore National Museum, the British Museum and the Museum für Ostasiatische Kunst in Cologne. In the end, the last stop — San Francisco — was canceled, as the Hong Kong Handover of 1997 was looming too close. Wu Guanzhong's art was included in this overall retrospective of 20th-century Chinese painting. He was courted far and wide. One very good thing Wu did before his death in 2010 was to gift 460 works — printings, drawings and sketches — to the permanent collection of the Hong Kong Museum of Art which finally devoted special space to permanently exhibiting his works, helped by his older son, Ke Yu, who had lived in Singapore for many years. With the renovation of the museum, a dedicated Wu Guanzhong Gallery will be installed to house the collection donated by Wu and family. That would have pleased Wu immensely as he had always wanted to have a good representation in Hong Kong. Wu also donated over 300 works, drawings and paintings large and small, to the Asian Civilizations Museum in Singapore.

Despite the high recognition and the escalating prices his paintings fetched, Wu remained modest in his lifestyle. He bought himself a larger apartment not far from his old place in Chaoyang District, Beijing. But he found that he was not inspired to paint there, so he moved back to his old abode, where he resumed his way of spreading paper and painting on the floor.

Sometime in the mid-1990s, on behalf of the Land Development Corporation of Hong Kong, a government body, we invited Wu to paint some scenes of our city. He captured a few aspects of the side streets off Queen's Road East below the Lo family's ancestral home, which was by then demolished. I cherished those wonderful sketches as they serve as valuable records of the now very changed district, even though the sketches belong to a government department.

Thanks to supporting the epochal art of Wu Guanzhong, I was pleased to be given another opportunity to help promote innovative contemporary

Chinese art at the British Museum. The opportunity was offered by Jan Stuart, Keeper of Asia, who commissioned Xu Bing, the celebrated conceptual Chinese artist, to install a site-specific work to be exhibited at a highly visible position near the front entrance of the museum from May 1 to July 10, 2012.

This impactful work, 'Background Story 7,' was made up of a large-scale shadow-and-light box nearly five meters tall with a wooden frame and a panel of frosted acrylic. It was lit from behind, giving the illusion of a traditional Chinese landscape. Unlike the previous six renditions of 'Background Story' created by Xu Bing since 2004, which were all in a horizontal format as with most traditional hand scrolls, this one, a depiction of a lofty mountain scene by the Ming dynasty painter Wang Shimin, dating to 1654 and drawn from the collection of the British Museum, was vertical. The contemporary and the original works were exhibited in close proximity following the time-honored Chinese practice of artwork and viewer entering into a 'dialogue.'

Xu Bing's work explored the relationship and tension between art and illusion, intentionally challenging the correlation between the image and the medium. It purposely stimulated the viewer to look at objects in a different way. He had created a work that looked like a landscape painting but was neither a landscape nor a painting. He used three-dimensional materials to imitate two-dimensional brushstrokes, questioning perception and the limitations of how we see things. He told me he had initially been inspired while passing through an airport in Valencia, Spain in 1997, where he saw images that were highly distorted, becoming another reality, when seen through a thick panel of glass.

With 'Background Story 7', viewers look from the front at what seems to be a brushstroke landscape painting of high artistic accomplishment. From behind, viewers see the reality; a composition of hemp fibers, dry plants, corn husks, crumpled paper and debris sourced from sites all over London, glued or loosely placed onto the back of the acrylic light box! From the front these materials depict a beautiful traditional landscape. The telling photographs show this well.

The Xu Bing installation was part of the visual program commissioned by the leading Japanese newspaper *Asahi Shimbun,* a long-time sponsor of exhibitions at the British Museum (they were one of the sponsors of the Wu Guanzhong 1993 one-man exhibition). 'Background Story 7' was completely dismantled after the exhibition and preserved for posterity on a website in English and Chinese that I was proud to sponsor.

Xu Bing, originally from Chongqing, is on any list of China's three to five best-known international contemporary artists. He received a grant in the 1980s from the Asian Cultural Council that took him to New York where he became well-known for producing a monumental work of calligraphy that features 4,000 'made-up' Chinese characters, meaningless symbols that were intended to explore the nature and use of language. He called the controversial and experimental work 'Book from the Sky' and it brought him international fame. In 2001, he was the first non-American artist to exhibit at the Arthur M. Sackler Gallery at the Smithsonian Institution in Washington D.C., the national museum of the United States. And he was the winner of the prestigious MacArthur Fellows 'Genius Grant' in 1999 and also the Artes Mundi prize in 2004.

Advancing from exploring the relationship between reality, words and thought in 'Landscript' to the relationship and tension between art and illusion, Xu Bing has been creating 'Background Story' since 2004, as a response to the traditional horizontal hand scrolls last shown at the Museum of Art and Design, New York in 2010.

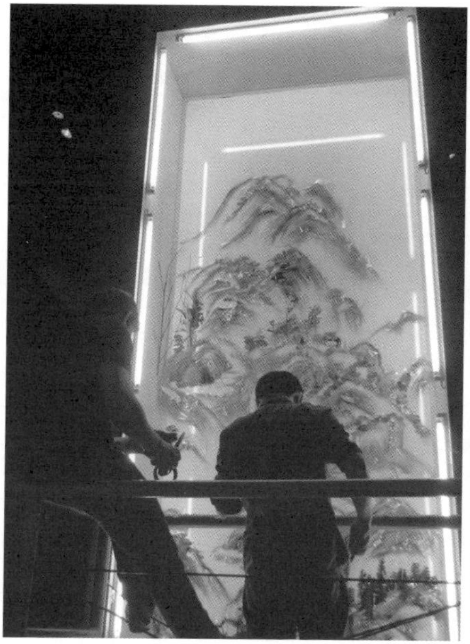

Front view of "Background Story 7" – Xu Bing's interpretation of the landscape by Ming dynasty master, Wang Shiming, dated 1654

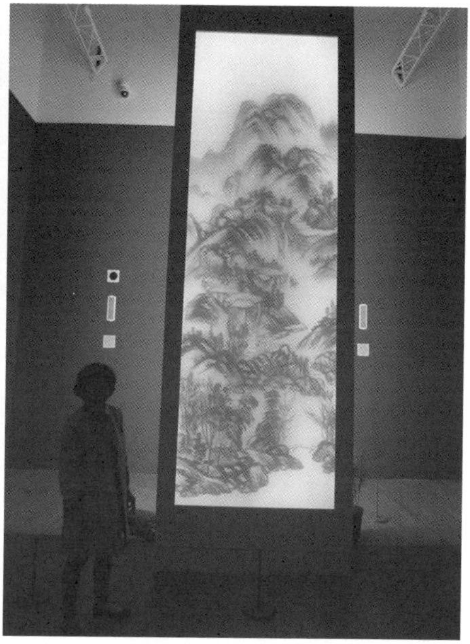

Back view showing the trompe l'oeil painting composed of hay and straw

MY SILK ROAD

16

My Silk Road

It was Charles de Gaulle who said, 'China is not a country, but a civilization.' History has repeatedly proved the resilience and influence of the unique Chinese civilization, and nowhere is it more evident than in the cross-cultural exchanges between China, Central Asia, and parts of the Mediterranean world dating from ancient Rome to early modern times. These commercial and cultural interactions were facilitated by what is now known as the Silk Road, the ancient trading routes that stretched from Asia through the Middle East to Europe. Past interactions between China and the worlds that were foreign to it have shown the country's ability to absorb, transcend and regenerate itself vigorously and to adapt to new influences and forms. My personal journey of exploration and exchanges along the Silk Road has encompassed all the pleasures, enlightenment and challenges of a determined quest.

The term 'Silk Road' came into general parlance only a little more than a century ago. It was coined originally in German, 'Seidenstrasse', in 1877 by the German explorer Ferdinand von Richthofen, who made seven expeditions to Central Asia and to China from 1868 to 1872. One could say the name was a misnomer, for the 'road' was not one route but a vast network of land and maritime trade routes between Asia and Europe, and the merchants who used them carried a wide variety of commodities, not just silk. The long caravans were loaded with herbs, ginseng and 'elixirs' of immortality, exotic woods and ceramics, herbal medicines and gunpowder, which was invented in China in the 7th century, first used for military purposes in the 8th century and exported to Europe in the 14th century. Also included in the westbound traffic from Asia were gemstones and other goods from India and Southeast Asia. But the most prized commodity was silk from China, which first reached the West probably via the Kushan Empire originating in Afghanistan in the first century BC. Records show silk first arrived in the Roman Empire in 46BC and caused a sensation. So sought-after was the commodity that by 4AD, its price was the same by weight as gold, straining the finances of the aristocracy to the extent that Emperor Tiberius had to ban its trading.

Commodities from the West that were transported by land and sea eastwards included carpets, textiles, Baltic amber, Mediterranean coral, perfume and opium that reached India from about the 7th century.

Silk Road trade over land and sea impacted the flow not only of commodities but of ideas in art and culture as well. For three millennia — across time and space, religion and ideas, confluence and exchange from western China via Central Asia to the Mediterranean, and back again — the Silk Road has left cross-cultural footprints and residues in art, design and religious practices that are still visible today. The Buddhist and Islamic designs that have prevailed along the Silk Road for centuries have furnished me with ample inspiration. These influences are much evident in my thinking, research and designs, which reflect history and its continuous expression and interpretation as a cultural statement.

The Silk Road has special meaning for me. I have been to Dunhuang several times, and I have long been fascinated by the connections between 'Zhongyuan' culture — the culture of the Han Chinese — and the cultures on the fringes. I have been to Turfan and Kashgar, and to Hetian, which for centuries has been the source of the best white jade, serving as a connection that makes up my designs from pebbles big and small, the larger size serving as luxurious paperweights — and the smaller pebbles carved into beads. An indelible impression of a Silk Road symbol is the wonderful and imposing bronze sculpture in Wuwei, one of the first garrison towns in the narrow Hexi Corridor that runs through Gansu Province. It is possibly my favorite piece of sculpture in the whole of China. Coated in green patina, with mouth open, ears pricked and nostril flared, the steed charges at full tilt with its mane swept back. What is remarkable is the small swallow that appears under one hind hoof of the galloping horse, as if to support its tremendous weight. It stands as a fitting memorial to the quest for the 'Tian Ma' or the long-legged strong breed of 'celestial steed' from Fergana in Central Asia, so sought after by the Chinese from the days of the Han Emperor, Wudi (141-87BC).

The Heavenly Horse supported by a swallow is kept in Wuwei Museum, Gansu province. Dating to the 3rd century BC, it is China's emblem for tourism

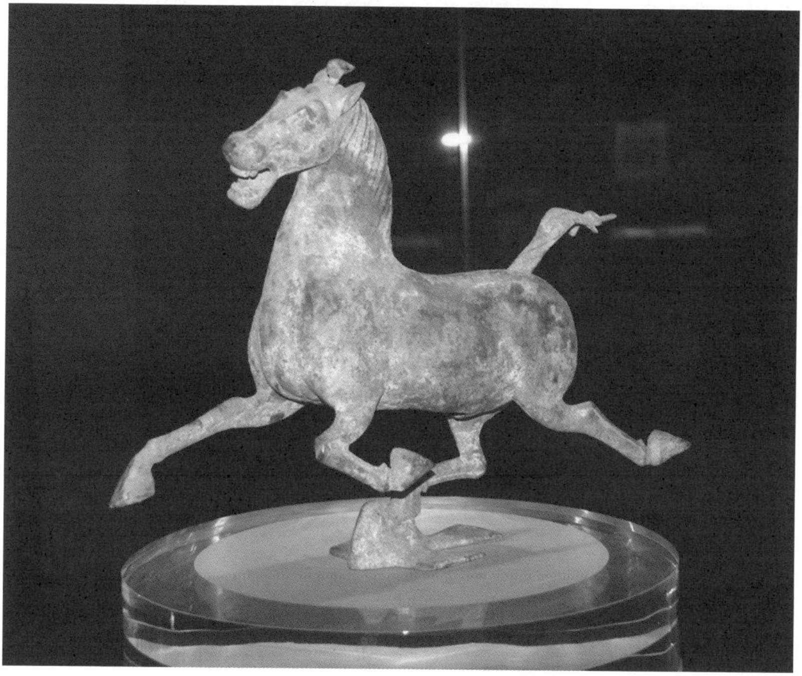

As one journeys on, north of Jiuquan City, towards the end of the Hexi Corridor in Gansu, is a group of tombs of an aristocrat — either a duke or a marquis — of the Northern Liang Kingdom, dating from between 386 and 441AD, the era of the Sixteen Kingdoms. Seven remarkable murals on the walls of one tomb are preserved in fresh and vivid colors. Surviving because of the dry environment, they illustrate Han culture, illuminating the celestial and the Confucian-based worldly realms, the latter depicting facets of daily life — agriculture, hunting, forestry, sericulture, music and dance. The rhythm, unbridled power, and the naïveté contained in this tomb, which measures ten square meters yet contains thirty square meters of illustrations, make it a memorable artifact of Han culture and aristocratic life outside the confines of Imperial China.

The desert oasis of Dunhuang was an important link on the ancient trade routes, a vital point in East-West communication, and between 1994 and 2009, I visited it six times, each via a different approach — by plane or train to Urumqi, or by car along the Hexi Corridor from Tianshui in Gansu Province — passing through the ancient garrison towns of Xiling, Wuwei, Zhangye, Jiuquan and Anxi, first set up in the Western Han Dynasty (206BC-9AD) to safeguard this strategic route from the barbarian Xiongnu hordes beyond the desert.

The Mogao Caves near Dunhuang were among the first Chinese sites to be recognized by the United Nations' World Heritage Center in the 1980s, along with the Great Wall and the Forbidden City. A total of 735 caves created from the 4th century AD onwards, spanning a period of 1,000

Parts of the Great Wall of China in Xinjiang, on the Silk Road, are now no more than a few meters high

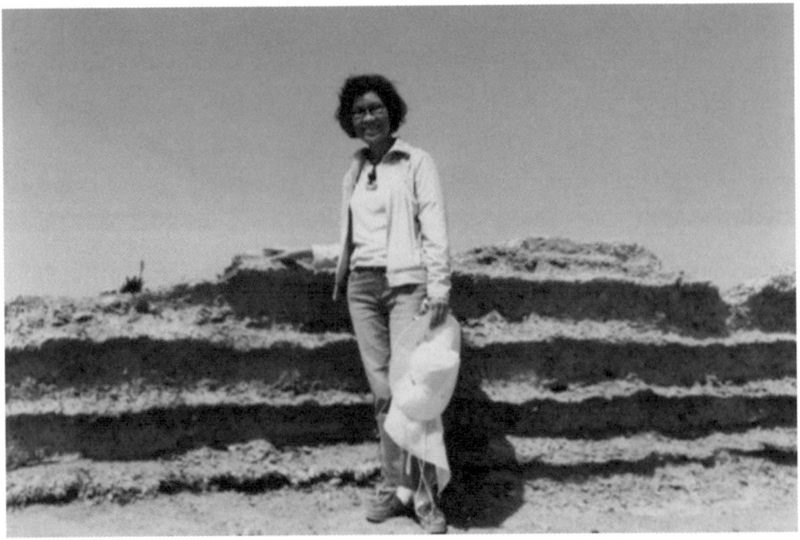

years, have been preserved nearby, serving as a depository for Buddhist art for about a millennium. The caves contain 45,000 square meters of wall paintings and 2,000 colored statues. Dunhuang has a profound culture, is deservedly valued for the colorful murals depicting earthly and heavenly scenes which fill its caves, and I was pleased to contribute a donation to the Dunhuang Academy to support the digitization and preservation of two Tang Dynasty (618-907AD) caves: no. 329 and the small but highly

Funding for the restoration and digitization of the Dunhuang Caves, initiated by past Director Fan Jingxi (middle), and supported by Hong Kong's Elsie Leung Oi-sie and me

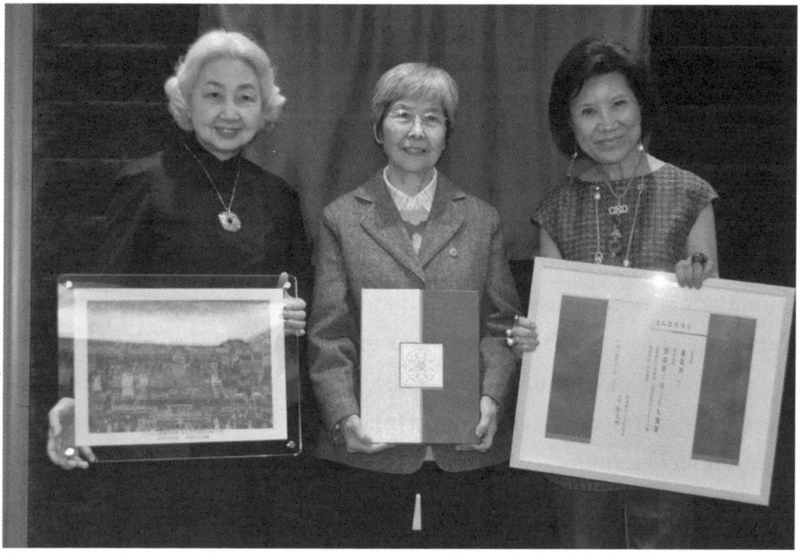

important no. 17. The former was filled with valuable early manuscripts in Chinese, Uighur and other languages. I am gratified that I have been given the opportunity to preserve for memory and record this important chamber, to perpetuate and illuminate Chinese heritage.

It was Sir Aurel Stein (1862-1943) who purportedly paid 320 pounds of silver to custodian Abbot Wang to restore his temple and took away 35 cartloads of manuscripts from cave no. 17 which were eventually housed at the British Museum. French explorer Paul Pelliot (1878-1945) arrived at the same secret chamber three months after Stein in 1908. With his grasp of classical Chinese and several Central Asian languages, Pelliot purchased what he considered the most valuable of the ancient scripts for 500 taels of silver (about US$11,000 in 2014). It was not until 1912, when Aurel Stein published his book *Ruins of Desert Cathay*, that Pelliot's work was finally recognized. The manuscripts are now housed in the Musée Guimet in Paris.

Dunhuang Academy is a pioneer among Chinese cultural institutions in its substantial achievements in digitization, 3D scanning and virtual reality representation of the Dunhuang relics, promoting greater awareness of cultural heritage through the Internet and multimedia programs. A lesser known aspect of the Dunhuang caves are the murals depicting music-playing scenes and a rich archive of ancient musical scores. Music-related images documenting the development of Chinese music are found on murals in over 200 caves, and 3,000 players and more than 4,000 musical instruments are depicted in the paintings, which means every musical instrument that appeared throughout China's history can be found in the Dunhuang cave paintings. While Chinese music has developed and evolved, the music of our time is often rooted in ancient melodies, allowing very old and contemporary music to coexist. The music ensemble Gaudeamus Dunhuang, formed by ten young Hong Kong musicians, has a mission to promote Dunhuang culture and Chinese music through adopting and interpreting ancient musical scores and related elements found at the Dunhuang Mogao grottoes. The group, initiated by Ms Leonie Ki and supported by New World Group Charity Foundation, aims to recreate and enliven the musical scenes of over a thousand years depicted in the Dunhuang murals.

At the extreme eastern end of the old Silk Road, thousands of miles away, is Hangzhou, one of the main centers of China's silk production then and now, and the site of the China National Silk Museum, a UNESCO World Heritage site. For over two thousand years, the West Lake in Hangzhou, blessed with natural and man-made islands, has been regarded as the Garden of China, memorably described by poets and literary giants.

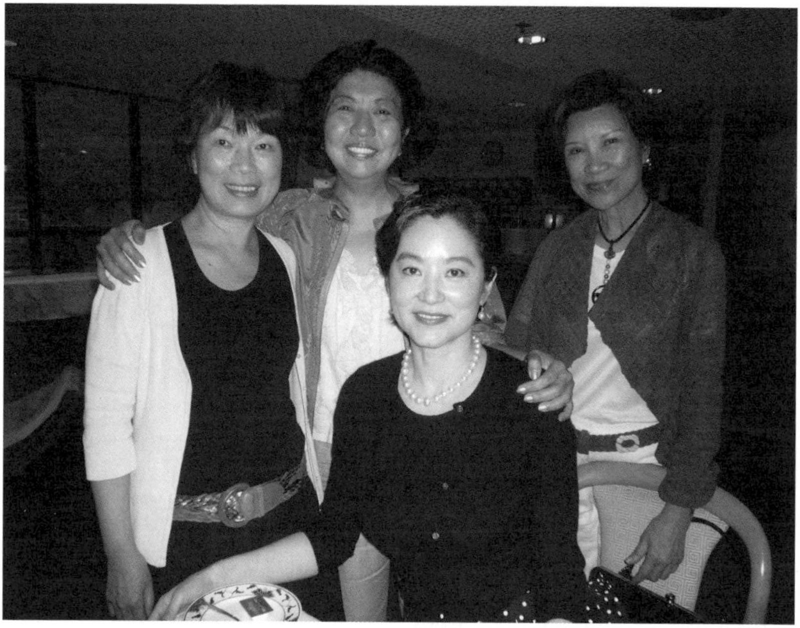

Leonie Ki (center rear) with celebrated Taiwanese writer Lung Yingtai and actress Lin Ching-hsia

One of my most cherished experiences was a stay by the West Lake in early April at the Hangzhou Xihu State Guesthouse, which occupies a wonderful location opposite the famous Su Ti (Su Causeway), constructed under the guidance of the great poet, Su Dong Po of the Song dynasty (960-1279AD), who immortalized the scene with famous verses. It was at this guesthouse that Premier Zhou Enlai met with President Richard Nixon in 1974 and achieved an historic diplomatic breakthrough. This state guesthouse has a choice location bordering the lake, which is lined with weeping willow trees that screen the ferryboats as ducks glide by. Dawn on the Su Causeway, situated just across the Lake, is considered one of the top ten scenic draws in China. Colorful flora intermixes — early yellow daffodils sit under the last of the flowering plum blossoms — late spring and early summer entwined. In 2015, when I visited with friend Rodman Primack of Design Miami, I secured for him the suite formerly occupied by Chairman Mao. The sitting room juts out onto the water below, surrounded by willows. I hope this secluded compound will maintain its tranquility and quietude, as Hangzhou grows prosperous as a technology center, attracting more and more people.

Near Hangzhou are two destinations of importance. The Liangzhu Museum is dedicated to displaying the artifacts of Neolithic Liangzhu culture, discovered in 1931 and dating back to 3000BC. It was a major discovery revealing a new aspect of Neolithic China. The draw for me, as much as the artifacts, was experiencing the structure built by eminent British architect David Chipperfield.

Another destination in the vicinity of Hangzhou is an educational and cultural center developed by Chinese real estate giant Vanke. I was very impressed with a building designed by Japanese architect Tadao Ando. Constructed mostly of wood, with interiors of clean lines and simplicity, it must be amongst the most outstanding buildings by the Japanese master.

I have always attempted to translate the past, and to synthesize its essence into new forms and applications in my life and work. The repurposing of antiques of different origins into arrangements and designs of my own ordering, thus 'making history wearable', and at the same time incorporating these 'embodied relics' as part of everyday life, has been a key part of what I have done since the 1980s when I was first drawn to seek better understanding and definition of the essence and merits of cross-cultural history and interchange between China, Central Asia and the West.

As time has passed, ongoing research has offered greater insight and advanced our knowledge of the complex area of accurate dating and provenance of items by allowing us to identify and authenticate their origins. From the early days of anecdotal knowledge of provenance to the cutting-edge science of today, scholarship has advanced to the point where we know that many of the pieces I have come across or collected throughout the years are linked to the Silk Road trading routes, which means that while they are a part of Chinese heritage, they also display influences and visual links to other cultures across Asia and the Middle East.

My line of contemporary jewelry, incorporating predominantly colored stones, ivory and ox bone — and metal, usually silver — calls for at least one key motif that is both eye-catching and meaningful. As an example of these links, I chose the knot. I use it in many different configurations and derivations that have served as the accent features in necklaces and pendant formations interpreted with a wide variety of materials, from stones to metals.

The story of the knot representations bears witness to the cultural exchange between China and its border regions, through Central Asia (present day Iran, Iraq and Lebanon) and Constantinople (present-day Istanbul) across the Mediterranean to Rome and Venice, traversing France, England and all the way to Ireland, with exchanges and influences that transcend time, place and faith.

It was in the mid-1980s that I came across the images of biscuits (yes, biscuits) made of flour dough, dug up from a 9th-century tomb in Astana, near Turfan in the Xinjiang region of northwest China, and now housed in Turfan Museum. The very dry climate of the region has enabled their remarkable preservation. The arresting shape of the interlocking knot with which they are decorated inspired me to seek similar shapes to interpret as accent elements in jewelry and accessories. Islamic designs and their variations, which carry no depiction of facial interpretations and instead focus on graphic signs and their variations, have been a particularly significant source of my inspiration.

Many of the colored stones such as crystals, agate, turquoise, amazonite and lapis lazuli, used in carvings and ornaments collected by museums, originally come from Central Asia, brought through China's western border provinces by itinerant traders. Agate and amazonite, as well as ancient gold and silver beads and small sculptures, may well have originated from the Siberian steppes and the Atlas mountain regions as demonstrated in the pathmaking exhibition first held at Denver Art Museum, "Adornment for Eternity: Status and Rank in Chinese Ornament", curated by Julia White and Emma Bunker, which ran from October 1994 to September 1995.

The next significant exhibition documenting the impact of cross-cultural interchange was the magnificent "Adornment for Body and Soul, Ancient Chinese Ornament," which showcased the Mengdiexuan Collection belonging to Kenneth Chu and Betty Lo, held at the University of Hong Kong Art Gallery for several months in 1999. The extraordinary gold suits and ornaments worn by the deceased royals of the Liao Dynasty opened a new consciousness and direction for exploration.

Some of the pieces in my collection or assembled in my jewelry date from between 500BC and 1300AD, proving that there were extensive movements and interchanges across Eurasia dating back more than 3,000 years. The impact of cross-cultural exchanges has always been at the core of my thought process and practice.

One motif I regularly use in my design is configurations of the Knot of Destiny, or the Eternal Knot, one of the Eight Buddhist emblems, a design that has no beginning and no end. It is a design that transcends borders and time. Due to its harmonious presence, it has become a familiar symbol adapted for commercial use and we tend to overlook its significance and meaning. Over the years, I have traced the presence of this knot all the way from Tibet to China, depicted in Buddhist and Tantric art and in the Dunhuang caves, and across Central Asia; it is prevalent in Iran as a

A marble wall decorated with variations of the infinity knot in Iran

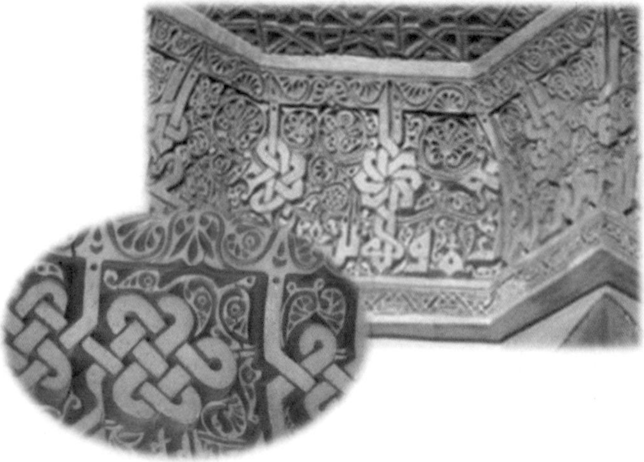

decorative motif, depicted in books and manuscripts as well as on carved marble walls. These motifs are also evident in Venice and its surrounds, in northern and southern Spain and all the way to Ireland.

Persia and Syria were both important parts of the Silk Road, and I am lucky to have visited both. I still feel guilty about the small marble piece I picked up during a visit to Persepolis. My trip to Syria in 2008 was a journey of discovery and a mind-opening adventure that enhanced my horizons both as an historian and designer. What I saw there reinforced much of my thinking about the melting pot of ideas, art and decorations inspired by linked cultures, religions, folk traditions and practices which the Silk Road represented and connected. I could see the footprints and links, the mingling of layers of traditions and influences accumulated over many centuries of trade from China all the way to Venice, arguably the western terminus of the medieval and early modern Silk Road. I was so excited to see the 'Knot of Destiny' pattern carved as a central motif decorating the front banisters of six principal balconies on the inner central court in the Doge's Palace in Venice, dating from the 16th century.

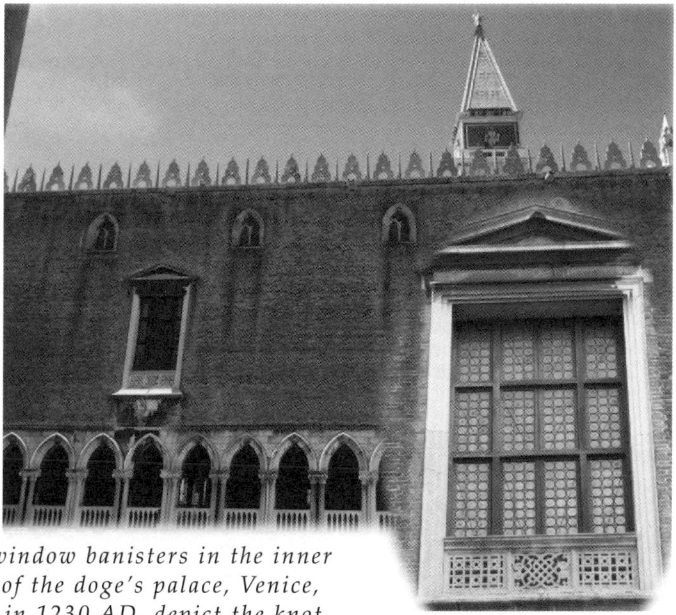

All eight window banisters in the inner courtyard of the doge's palace, Venice, first built in 1230 AD, depict the knot of destiny design

In addition, I have seen majolica plates bordered with these 'Knots of Destiny', with the Duke of Mantua's crest in the middle, in the Rothschild collection on display at Waddesdon Manor in England, and the same style of plate with more elaborate decorations displayed at the Hermitage Museum in St Petersburg. Both plates (dated 1545-50) once belonged to the collection of the Duke of Mantua, who was a cousin of the Pope. Only nobles with high connections in Europe had access to Chinese ceramics at that time and would draw inspiration from designs transported via the Silk Road trade routes, including those referenced in their local productions. It certainly was proof of the importance of the artistic influence and the high regard for ceramics in Europe transported via the Silk Road. In the archives of the Victoria & Albert Museum in London, I saw embroidery incorporating a knot with open ends terminating with serpent heads made by Mary Queen of Scots in 1570 and presented to her good friend, Countess Bess of Hardwick.

Embroidery by Mary Queen of Scots, 1570

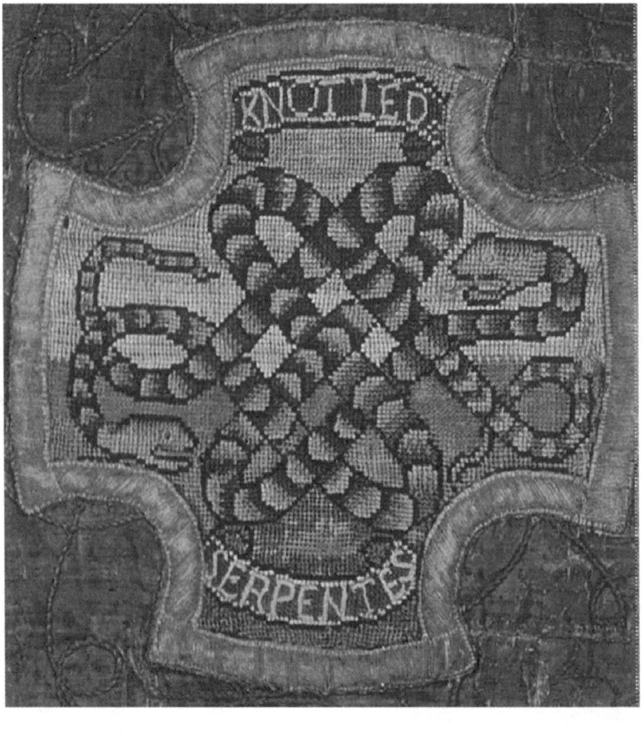

There are other depictions of knots with a different configuration that I have seen in Iran and Syria. Having spent years working out variances of the knot, I thought I had explored and created sufficient new shapes. Little did I know that similar ones were to be found in the Damascus Museum dating from the 5th century. There was another knot configuration that I thought was my original design that I later saw carved in an ancient stone plaque at an arena in Bostra in southern Syria. And I have observed friezes containing a key pattern that was a much-featured decoration in the Far East, used on many stone slabs in Roman temples near Baalbek.

As a designer with no formal training, I draw knowledge and inspiration from history and culture. On the same trip to Syria in 2008, I went to the magnificent 10th-12th century castle built by the Crusaders, Krak Des Chevaliers, situated outside Damascus. I saw that an interior chamber was decorated with meandering knots. But I had no awareness of these connections when I made my basic design choices in the 1970s and 1980s. In Syria, I was consciously looking for symbols that inspired me, and I found many, especially knots, the most impressive of which was the continuous frieze of endless knots high on the upper wall all the way around the Umayyad Mosque, renovated in 710AD. High up near the ceiling of the Hagia Sophia in Istanbul, knots of another configuration, not unlike the shapes I saw in Bostra, southern Syria, encircled the lower frieze. Isnik tiles from Turkey, dated to the 17th century, are decorated with borders connected by knots.

Some of the necklaces with antique beads (agate, amazonite and other stones) that I have created look remarkably like ones dating from the 3rd century displayed at that great exhibition, 'Gilded Dragons', held at the British Museum in 1999. At a recent exhibition in Hong Kong, 'World Heritage Along the Silk Road', organized as part of the city's 'Return to China' 20th anniversary celebrations, wonderful artifacts in gilt bronze, including a rendering of the silk worm dating to the Han Dynasty from the collection of the Shaanxi History Museum, were on display. Also on display were two necklaces made from turquoise, amazonite, agate, crystal and gilt beads, drawn from the Shanxi Chingu Museum, and dating from

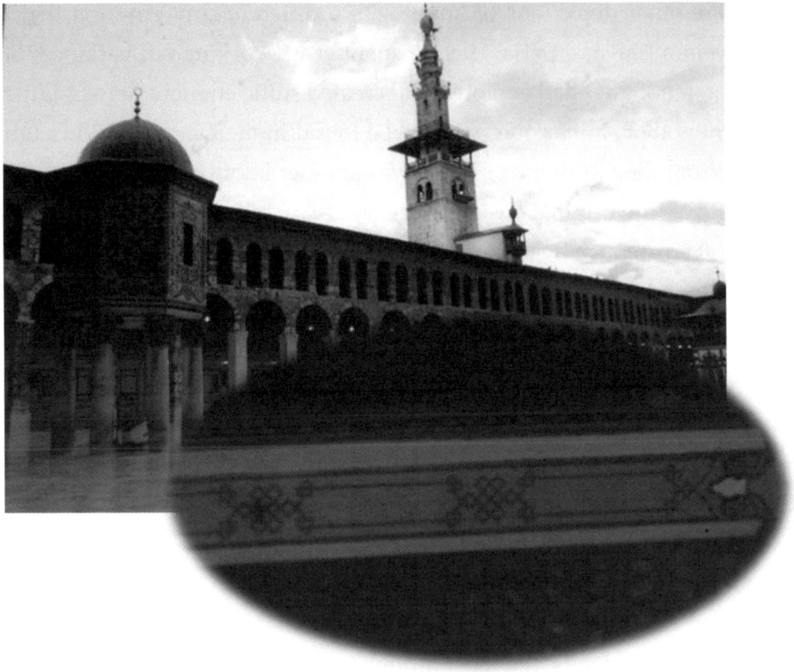

Ceiling beams of the 7th century Omayyad mosque in Damascus, built in 710 AD, are strewn with the infinity knot sign

around 3000BC — they did not look dissimilar to some of my creations!

In Syria, the wonderful knots I saw were what resonated. I saw them in Turkey too, the same basic designs which are found in Tang Dynasty decorations from the 8th century. I saw the same renditions of the knot on inlay marble floors in Venice at the Doge's Palace. I saw knots of many shapes carved around decorated columns in a Catholic cloister in Leon, northern Spain, dating to the 9th century, and also in the grand cathedral in Leon.

The same intricate knot has long been used in Tibet too, where it is one of the main Buddhist emblems, except the shape was placed upright, not horizontally as elsewhere. It appears to have first come to China in the 1st century AD, when China adopted Buddhism.

That knot has really done the rounds. I cannot tell why it was so popular. I have always used knots because they are part of a universal language and at the same time personally appealing. The classic knot design is symmetrical, which doesn't quite fit with my interest in asymmetry. But in my designs, symmetry is needed in knots for them to begin and to end. If you have a specifically Chinese symbol as part of jewelry design, Americans and Europeans cannot relate to it. But a knot is something that everyone can understand. There are knots that I thought I had invented, and then I found them on some parts of the Silk Road, extending to different parts of the world.

China is now promoting the ambitious "Belt and Road" policy, a reinterpreted, contemporary version of the Silk Road as a way of implementing its global ambitions. The policy is reshaping its external

Columns strewn with knots showing Islamic influence in the cloister of Leon Cathedral, northern Spain

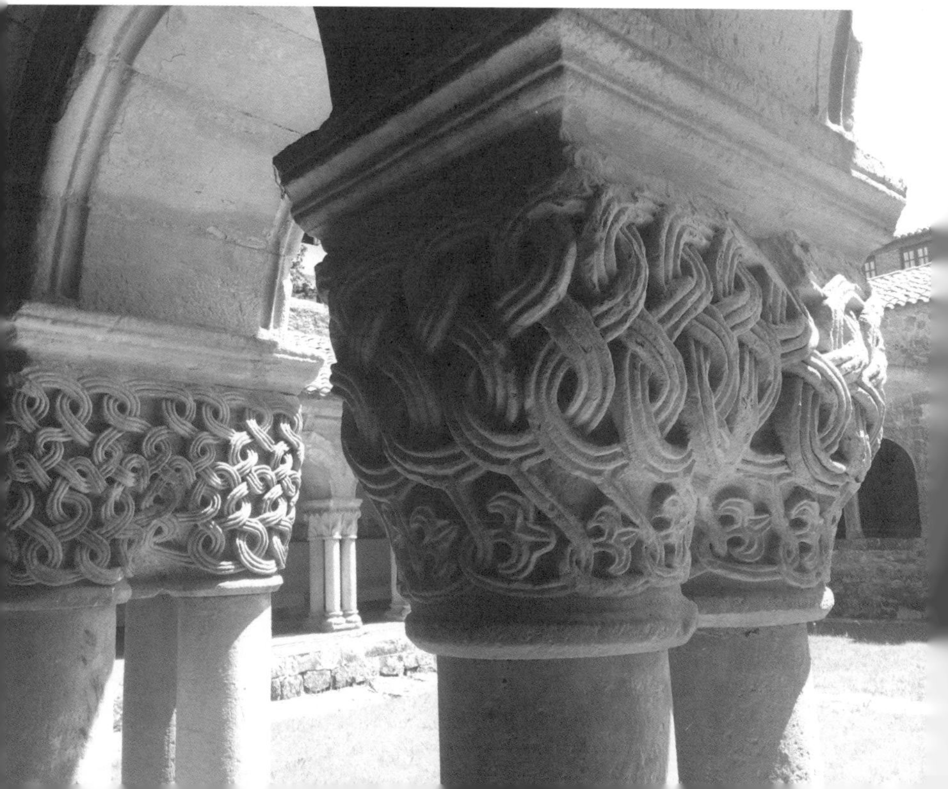

environment and repurposing the ancient concept of *tianxia* or 'all under heaven' that traditionally placed China at the center of power and civilization. 'Mutual dependence and respect' are hailed as the basis of obligations in the Belt and Road initiative by Chinese leader Xi Jinping.

The present heavily promoted China-centered network stretches far and wide. It employs manpower on construction sites, secures raw materials, and creates a global economy with China as a major player. In the five years since the implementation of the Belt and Road program, an historic cross-cultural initiative has been undertaken, consisting of ambitious infrastructure development including pipelines, roads, transcontinental railways, fiber-optic cables, ports and bridges, buildings and manufacturing zones.

They represent China's new quest to spread soft and hard power with unprecedented scope, outreach and intensity.

FURTHERING CREATIVE VISIONS

17

Furthering Creative Visions

Cross-cultural exchanges, and the fusion of ideas leading to new expressions in art, design, social development and innovation, have been so important in my mind, heart and practice. I gained knowledge and understanding of their development and relationship not so much from textbooks and traditional academic study, and not from the prevailing 'Zhongyuan' or 'Heart of the Kingdom' culture, but from observing traditions, customs, practices, interchanges and development in arts and crafts, many of which trace their beginnings to the border regions adjacent to Central Asia. For me, examining their beginnings and development has given rise to an understanding and awareness of the roots of cross-cultural exchanges, stimulated new insights, and spurred further inquiries. Oxford historian Peter Frankopan, in his influential 2015 bestseller, *The Silk Roads: A New History of the World*, rightly questioned the accuracy of the long and widely held premise that 'the Mediterranean' in its literal meaning was correctly considered the center of the world, and a cradle of civilization. 'The center of the world was not a sea separating Europe from Africa, but right in the heart of Asia,' he asserted.

Of all the recognition accorded to me as the result of my inquiries and exploration of cultural connections and interactions, be it academic, civic or commercial, two accolades have uniquely special meaning for me. The first was to have been named in April 2018 as the first Visiting Professor, Cross Culture, at Central Saint Martins College of Arts and Design, University of the Arts, London. This appointment is validated by College Principal Professor Jeremy Till endorsing my long-held belief in the importance of the pursuit and exploration of cultural connections and of seeking new understanding through these interactions.

The second honor was to have been acknowledged as the 'World's Leading Chinese Designer, 2007' by the Hong Kong Design Centre. The citation read, '(Kai-Yin Lo's) understanding of China's rich legacy avoids imitation and she constantly reinterprets China's heritage in entirely contemporary terms'. Both accolades acknowledged my contribution to the deeper understanding of Chinese civilization, the impact of cross-cultural fertilization, and the importance of generating new creative directions and energies.

Jane Rapley, former Head of Central St. Martins, interviewed Kai-Yin Lo at the first Cross Culture Lecture series in London, March 2013

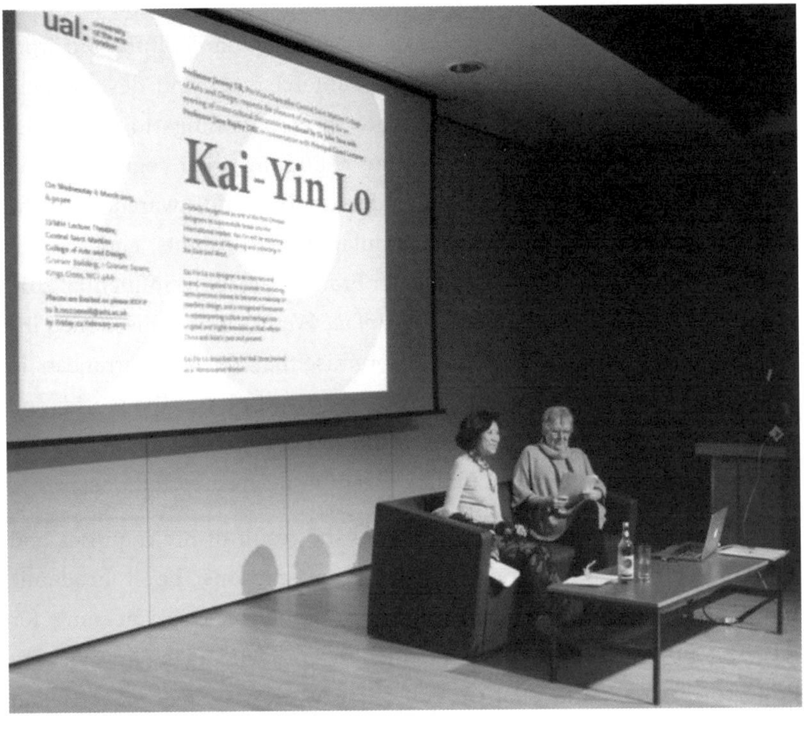

It was in 2012 that Jane Rapley, then the Head of Central Saint Martins, who had made great contributions to enhancing the quality and international reputation of the school and had at the same time groomed so many world-famous fashion designers (Alexander McQueen, Phoebe Philo and Stella McCartney, to name a few), proposed that my cross-disciplinary and cross-cultural understanding of East and West interchange would open up further windows of thought and inquiries. Thus, a course of lectures was set up, and I found sponsorship for the first three lectures from Hans Michael Jebsen, whose family firm Jebsen and Company started trading with China in the early 19th century, setting up a base in Hong Kong in 1895.

The 2014 lecture, 'Bridge of Aspirations — Connecting East and West,' was given by Thomas Heatherwick, the maverick designer/creator, whose practice defies categorization, embracing design and architectural work in highly creative expressions ranging from the prizewinning U.K. Pavilion at the Shanghai Expo (2010), the London Olympic Cauldron (2012), the new London bus, and the Learning Hub Centre in Singapore's Nanyang Technological University (2015), to the 2,500-step Cauldron at Hudson Yards on New York's West Side (2019), the planned new Google headquarters in Mountain View, California, and the new airport in Singapore. He has been a frequent visitor to Hong Kong since the 1990s. From the first retrospective of his design held in 2010 at the Victoria and Albert Museum, I have followed his work with admiration and awe, and am honored and pleased to call him a friend. He is also very fond of Hong Kong, having made many visits to see friends and to oversee his projects, the most high-profile of which is the renovation of Pacific Place near Central and the façade of the adjacent Upper House Hotel.

Heatherwick is one of today's most celebrated and in-demand designers. Imagine our surprise and thrill to have him recently bring his twins to Hong Kong for a break to see old friends! He surprised me by bringing a wonderful cake with the inscription 'Happy Afternoon, Kai-Yin' and it was wonderful to see that his twin boy and girl had grown so much. The next day, I arranged a lunch at Government House, hosted by our Chief

Executive Carrie Lam and attended by Keith Kerr, Thomas's good friend, Duncan Pescod, Chief Executive of the West Kowloon Cultural District, architect Ole Scheeren and others. It was a convivial welcome back for Thomas, who I believe has made 65 trips to Hong Kong. Do come back again often, Thomas!

The 2015 Central Saint Martins lecture focused on the merits of public art. Themed 'Sculpture and the Animation of Collective Space,' it offered the first view of a large-scale placement of sculptural works by the renowned British sculptor Antony Gormley. This latest edition of 'Event Horizon,' featuring Gormley's high-profile display of public art that had been successfully mounted in London, Amsterdam, New York and Sao Paulo, was the first large-scale exposition of public art ever staged in Hong Kong. The panel discussion that followed was authoritatively and adroitly moderated by Jeremy Till, the distinguished critic and opinion leader of the built environment. The exchange between Gormley and a select panel that included promoter of creativity Ada Wong was a rewarding exploration of the role and merits of the first city-wide public art exposition, and an eye-opener for the people of Hong Kong. As a reminder and commemoration, a Gormley statue was permanently installed on the roof of the Asia Society Center, looking onto the harbor and the horizon beyond, heralding optimism and good fortune.

The Central Saint Martins lecture held in November 2016 was chaired by London-based creative guru John Howkins, author of the bestselling books *Creative Economy* (2001) and *Creative Ecologies* (2010). He found a worthy vis-à-vis debatee in Hong Kong's own pioneering technology entrepreneur Yat Siu. It took place on a memorable evening when core Central Hong Kong was taken over by hordes of 'Occupy Hong Kong' protagonists. Yet Victor Fung, our distinguished business leader, braved obstacles and barricades to arrive at the auditorium to deliver the introductory remarks as he thought that the topic under discussion was of great relevance to Hong Kong's creative development and he wanted to add his weight to further its course. It was a memorable gesture that one would not forget.

Singtao Education 星島教育 二〇一五年十二月三日 星期四 星島日報 SINGTAO DAILY F2

首個海外夥伴 導師來港任教

英國中央聖馬丁 香港首辦藝術碩士

專訪

英國重量級藝術學府中央聖馬丁藝術設計學院即將與香港大學專業進修學院合作，開辦藝術及文化企業文學碩士，是該校首次在倫敦以外開辦碩士課程，更會派導師來港親身任教。該院院長Professor Jeremy Till接受本報專訪時表示，選擇香港成為首個海外合作夥伴，是因為香港是亞洲區的創意樞紐，加上即將落成的西九文化區，相信香港未來的藝術文化發展會更加蓬勃。

記者 羅環

英國中央聖馬丁藝術設計學院(Central Saint Martins College of Art and Design)有逾一百五十年歷史，屬於倫敦藝術大學其中一個學院，在藝術界享負盛名，世界多位著名藝術界人物都在該校畢業，該校將與香港大學專業進修學院(HKUSpace)合辦藝術及文化企業文學碩士課程，是該校首次在倫敦以外開辦碩士課程，該院院長Professor Jeremy Till接受本報專訪時表示，香港是亞洲區重要的創意樞紐，因此選擇香港作為首個海外合作夥伴。

獲兩學院學歷證明

Professor Till指，新開辦的碩士課程是兩年兼讀制，結合藝術及商業的理論，針對培訓藝術文化事業的管理人才；而課程最大的特點，就是修畢課程的學生，可同時獲得到中央聖馬丁及HKUSpace發出的學歷證明；為了確保課程質素，中央聖馬丁的導師更會親身來港任教，亦會與英國的學生在網上互動學習平台一同進行導修。他更稱，若果香港學生願意的話，歡迎他們親身到倫敦的中央聖馬丁完成部分課節。

收生着重藝術熱誠

課程全期總學費十六萬港元，申請人須擁有學士學位之外，亦需要兩年藝術相關工作的經驗，但Professor Till指，只要申請人能夠證明他對藝術充滿熱誠亦可，「不一定要有設計系的學士學位，亦不一定要有藝術背景，但一定要對藝術有興趣。」

他透露，課程接受報名近兩個月以來，已經取錄十多名學生，大部分是專業人士，包括律師、藝術家，亦有來自商界的企業人員。他指，畢業生出路相當多元化，可以在文化機構、藝術館工作，甚至是政府文化管理的部門、大企業旗下的藝術部門等。

為了令課程的內容更加切合香港的情況，上課時會邀請業內人士分享他們的藝術管理經驗，其中一位就是中央聖馬丁藝術設計學院首席客席講師、西九文化管理局博物館委員會委員羅啟妍。她會在課程中，分享她曾在大英博物館及香港策劃藝術展覽的經驗。

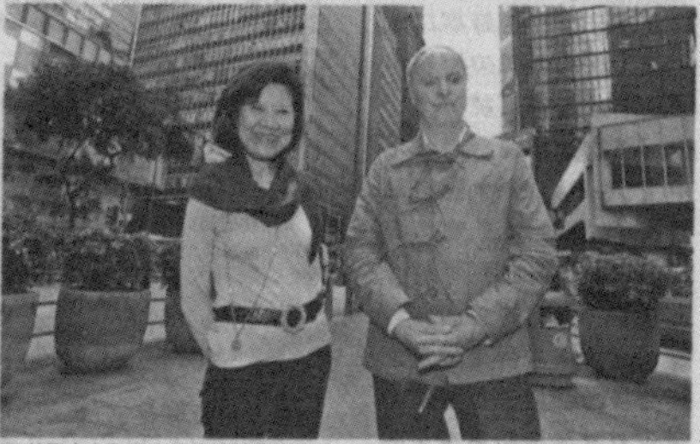

■英國中央聖馬丁藝術設計學院院長Professor Till(右)與首席客席講師羅啟妍(左)。 陳鎮基攝

Jeremy Till, Head of Central St. Martins, was in Hong Kong in December 2015 to initiate the CSM MA Arts and Cultural Enterprise course

In November 2016 I organized a Central Saint Martins forum at the University of Hong Kong with all the speakers under forty years of age, all successful technology entrepreneurs, to explore the constructive role of 'Creative Capital — Hard Power or Soft Power?' i.e. the government can exercise supportive policies and initiatives to build 'creative capital', thereby helping to unleash the 'soft power' generated by the creative drive, energy and ingenuity that reside in individuals and in the community culture at large.

To date, the most significant development of the Central Saint Martins initiative in Hong Kong is the establishment of the 24-month Master of Arts 'online' course, 'Arts and Cultural Enterprise', in which Central Saint Martins tutors conduct face-to-face intensive exchanges for three days over a long weekend with students based in Hong Kong. I have enjoyed conducting lectures at these sessions. The first graduation of the two-year course took place in June 2018. It was officiated by the distinguished and highly approachable Vice Chancellor of University of the Arts London,

Nigel Carrington. Witnessing the graduation ceremony filled me with pride and reassurance, to see that Hong Kong has become a hub not only for art transactions, but also importantly, is developing into a center of creative education and critical practice. More courses with UAL colleges are to be installed, envisaging collaboration with West Kowloon Cultural District constituents, destined to be the largest cultural hub in the Asia Pacific region.

I have also enjoyed and benefited from my long association with the Hong Kong Design Centre, the organization established in 2001 by Create Hong Kong, a division of the Commerce and Economic Development Bureau for funding creative industries. The Centre's mission is to promote design awareness among business, public and service communities, to nurture 'design-preneurs' and start-ups, to cultivate appreciation and expertise in design and design projects, and to spread awareness of design excellence – and importantly, to enhance networking and interchange. I can say that I have grown up with the institution as a member of the board since 2007. My recruitment could have been facilitated by the fact that I was a member of the Arts and Cultural Commission, formed in the year 2000 by former Chief Executive Tung Chee-hwa as an attempt to assess the cultural and identity position and outlook of Hong Kong people after reversion to Chinese rule. The commission, regrettably, did not yield any conclusions or any effective recommendations, due to ineffective leadership.

As a board member of the Hong Kong Design Centre, I have found it rewarding and invigorating to participate in driving its vision and mission. In turn, I myself have expanded my own vision, outreach and experience while taking part in the planning and realization of some of its programs. Its broad areas of work can be summed up as celebrating excellence in design; nurturing design entrepreneurs and start-ups; enhancing networking activities for members of the design community; and endeavoring to raise the profile of Hong Kong as a design hub.

These goals are pursued with funding support from the Create Smart scheme of the Hong Kong Government. It is invigorating and reassuring to see that the many educational programs have yielded encouraging results in stimulating skills, education and design thinking. The two flagship annual events — BODW (Business of Design Week), established in 2002 and held during the first week of December, and KODW (Knowledge of Design Week), scheduled in mid-July — have become weighty international forums of knowledge and experience sharing for individuals, communities, enterprises and cities.

The vision, cultivation and growth in outreach and reputation of the Hong Kong Design Centre, especially in the proliferation of its international programming and consequent recognition, have been encouraged and effectively fostered under the ten-year (2007-2017) chairmanship of Victor Lo, whose training in industrial design at the Illinois Institute of Technology in Chicago groomed him to be one of the earliest advocates for driving the development of Hong Kong's industrial sector from competitive volume factory production to the culture of value-added innovative product and systemic design. His vision and grasp of advancing cutting-edge design and design thinking are relevant and visionary, and his support of the annual Business of Design Week has made Hong Kong the hub and draw for discussing and showcasing the best and cutting edge of design thinking and practices.

Under the present chair Professor Eric Yim, and Executive Director Edmund Lee, the Hong Kong Design Centre continues its impactful work of organizing design forums and exhibitions and educational sessions headed by William To at PMQ and at a new venue on Mallory Street, Wan Chai. The two major events — Knowledge of Design Week and Business of Design Week — are recognized as Asia's premier creative design forums and exchange platforms for design thinking and exposition.

My personal favorite moments of past BODW presentations include the delivery at the second Forum in 2003 by Terence Conran, who drove home the notion that 'design is no big deal' — it is rather a requisite to improve the quality of everyday living, and this philosophy is well evidenced in the lifestyle products offered at Conran shops and restaurants. Dieter

Rams (2011), the revered German industrial inventor/designer, echoed the same philosophy. Kazuyo Sejima, the Pritzker Architecture Prize-winning architect, arrived in Hong Kong from Paris two hours before presenting her concept for building in Japan and Europe, and left to head back to Paris after spending no more than four hours in Hong Kong, demonstrating the importance of Hong Kong as a worthy platform of design advocacy. Then there was the refreshing 38-year-old Danish architect Bjarke Ingels who spoke memorably in 2012, introducing his bold scheme of installing a ski run on the roof of a museum under construction in Oslo. Another stately Pritzker Prize-winning architect, Tadao Ando, whose work I admire, came with his own team including a translator. However, moments before his presentation, I saw him sorting out the sequence of illustrations himself.

Quite apart from educating the local design and related community, the aim and residual value of these flagship programs of the Hong Kong Design Centre is also to enhance networking activities and to successfully raise the profile of Hong Kong as an international design hub. I am happy to say I have grown up with the Hong Kong Design Centre, and I am privileged to have served on its board for thirteen years.

Between 1984 and 1994, I spent from four to six months a year based in New York, maintaining an office at 57th Street and Fifth Avenue, and later at The Galleria, at the corner of Park Avenue and 57th Street, in close proximity to my retail outlets. It was a period of intensive activity — attending to design and production in Hong Kong and Dongguan on the Pearl River Delta, and merchandising and promoting my brand of semi-precious jewelry in New York. Life was more than full. My clients became good friends as well, and ties with them and their families are maintained today. In Texas, I had the great support of good friends like Ann Symonds, Judy Allen, Nanette Finger and their offspring, whose connections are further sustained by the founding of an Asia Society Texas Center in Houston that was established by oil magnate Roy Huffington. The present imposing edifice erected by Japanese architect Yoshio Taniguchi was opened in 2012. I was thrilled to have journeyed there for the festivities celebrating the opening of the first Asia Society regional center in North America. Imagine my excitement and joy when I saw that Nancy Allen, the chief fundraiser of the Center, wore the necklace she had purchased from me seven or eight years before at the official press conference, and kept on wearing it during the next few days!

In New York, I have greatly benefited from the education and social networking provided by two non-profit educational, cultural and policy institutions — the China Institute and the Asia Society, both of which I joined as a member in the late 1980s. The first, founded in 1926 by eminent Chinese reformers Hu Shi, K.P. Wen and John Dewey, is the oldest bi-cultural non-profit organization in America to focus on China.

The photographic exhibition, 'Living Heritage, Vernacular Environment in China,' drawn from the collection taken by Chinese mainland photographer Li Yuxiang during trips we undertook in the mid-1990s, was assembled and curated by me and architect and historian Dr. Puay Peng Ho of Hong Kong Chinese University. After an exhibition at City Hall in Hong Kong it traveled to the China Institute in New York where it was exhibited from January to June in 2001. The very successful show was visited by students

Curators Fumio Nanjo (third left) and Kai-Yin Lo (third right) at the first art/design exhibition, "Imminent Domain", at the Asia Society Hong Kong Center, pictured with Carrie Lam, at that time Chief Secretary of Hong Kong (center), Ronnie Chan, Chairman of the Asia Society Hong Kong Center (second left), and Executive Director Alice Mong (second right). William Lim (first right) and Amy Chan also participated in the exhibition

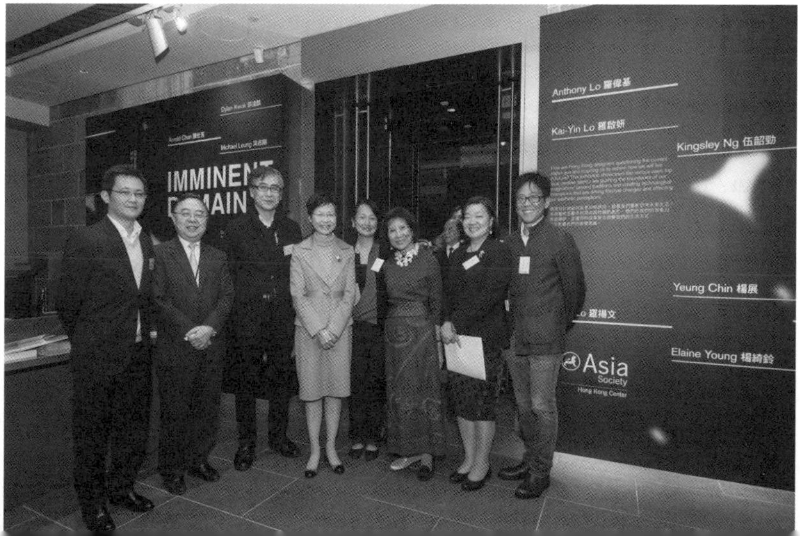

from schools all over the USA, many of whom had never seen Chinese vernacular architecture or had any knowledge of Chinese rural living.

The next significant event on Chinese living styles was the one-day symposium held on April 28, 2001 to accompany the book *House, Home, Family: Living and Being Chinese,* jointly edited by Professor Ron Knapp, the vernacular living specialist, and myself. The event was co-organized by the China Institute and the Asia Society. The list of speakers read like a who's who in the field of Chinese vernacular living and lifestyle culture. I still recall the impressive insight and scholarship expounded in the speeches delivered by Professor Knapp, the respected Professor Wen Fong, Nancy Steinhart, Cary Liu and Craig Clunas.

A footnote: *House, Home. Family: Living and Being Chinese* was selected in 2012 as one of 'the fifteen great books for understanding China' by the Association of Art Museum Curators, USA, spearheaded by curators of the Peabody Essex Museum in Salem, Massachusetts. Others on the list included celebrated tomes such as *Ten Thousand Things: Module and Mass Production in Chinese Art* by Lothar Ledderose and *The Gate of Heavenly Peace: the Chinese and their Revolution 1895-1980* and *The Chan's Great Continent: China in Western Minds,* both by Jonathan Spence.

Another cultural institution that has been close to me, and which has supported me in so many ways, is the Asia Society, a distinguished educational institution founded in 1956 by the Rockefeller family to promote greater appreciation of Asia in America, and to encourage cross-cultural partnerships. In the aftermath of the Second World War, John D. Rockefeller III recognized the dangers of sustained animosity from the decimated Japanese nation. As he put it, 'We can only heal it through soft power.' In the 1950s and 1960s, he worked with Sherman Lee, a renowned expert on Chinese art, putting together an extraordinary collection of Asian art that is now regarded as the world's single finest private collection of Chinese, Japanese, Southeast Asian and Indian art. In an example of the largesse that Americans often exhibit, the family donated the entirety of this substantial collection to the Asia Society.

From 1995 or thereabouts, I would often attend lectures and briefings on Asian politics, business, education, arts and culture and mingle with other like-minded people at the Asia Society. In 2004, I founded the Kai-Yin Lo Lecture Series at the Asia Society after quoting the *New York Times's* comment to its president, Nicholas Platt.

"*The New York Times* describes your programs as 'oppressively educational!' You need to introduce more programs dwelling on the livelier soft power of arts and culture, their interaction, influence and interface to create greater mutual understanding. The cultural link with Asia needs to be better explored and presented," I suggested. So Platt invited me to found a lecture series, and through an endowment, nine lectures covering subjects on arts, dance, music design, innovation and employment of cultural space were conducted in the Society's New York headquarters, and one at the Asia Society Hong Kong Center in 2014, probing the application and employment of 'Creative Capital — Hard Power or Soft Power.'

For the inaugural lecture 'Transcending Borders — Music, Dance, Design' (October 2004), held at Asia Society New York, I was queried as to who

The ongoing Kai-Yin Lo Distinguished Program Series at Asia Society New York in October 2017, with stellar speakers

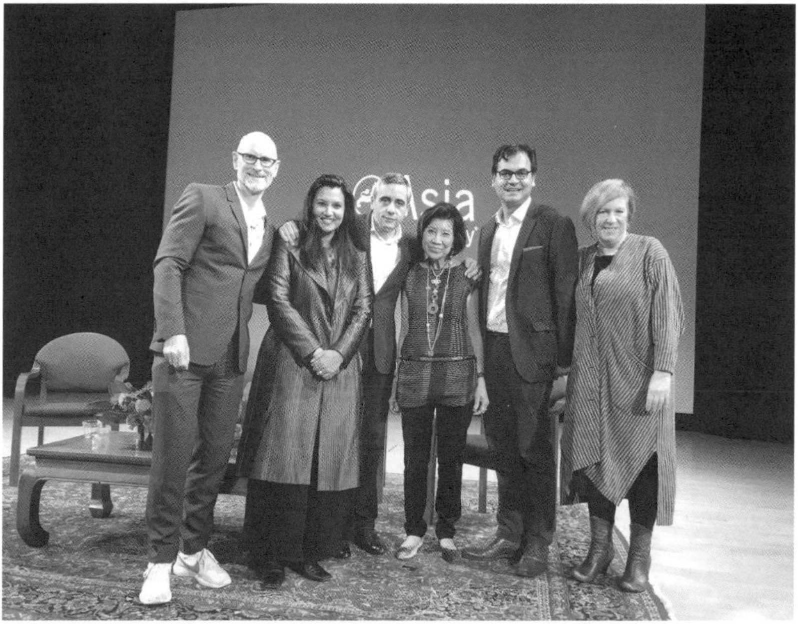

the relatively unknown dancer Shen Wei was, and whether he would be well-known enough to be featured. I replied, 'He will be very much in our consciousness very soon.' Sure enough, four months later, he and his dance troupe were written up in many media as the new expression and force of dance, and he has since remained a notable innovative and creative power appreciated all over the world.

The Kai-Yin Lo Lecture Series has featured great creative talents like Shen Wei, Tan Dun, Xu Bing, and recently Alex Poots, artistic director of The Shed, Suhanya Raffel, executive director of M+ Museum, and Nicholas Baume, director of the Public Art Fund, New York.

The most recent edition of the Kai-Yin Lo Distinguished Program Series took place at the Asia Society New York on October 19, 2017. Entitled 'Creative Spaces Empowering the City', it focused on the goals, plans, realization and further development of M+ in Hong Kong, and The Shed, the new creative hub at Hudson Yards on New York's West Side. These are both creative spaces offering a new perspective.

Looking to the future, I am thrilled at the recognition that Hong Kong has earned as a center for international cultural exchange, as demonstrated by the West Kowloon Cultural District. The concept and planning of West Kowloon drew from the work of the Culture and Heritage Commission, set up by former Chief Executive Tung Chee-hwa in May 2000, following the handover of Hong Kong to China. A man with a strong belief in the validity and importance of mainstream Chinese and regional culture and heritage, Tung wanted to preserve a good measure of Hong Kong culture and identity. The Culture and Heritage Commission was chaired by Professor Chang Hsin-kang, former president of City University, an academic with a broad vision and a deep understanding of Chinese and Western cultures. The commission, of which I was one of ten members, met for two years and submitted a wide-ranging report, making recommendations on identity definition and exploration, on educational and cultural issues for Hong Kong, and on the development of West Kowloon as an arts and culture project.

The commission insisted that 'what the West Kowloon Cultural District ought to reclaim is not only land but also Hong Kong's history, identity, and creative spirit.' The commission proposed the establishment of seventeen core arts and cultural venues, as well as a space for arts education. After revisions and the abandonment of several schemes, three core concepts remain: enhancing the quality of life of the people of Hong Kong, fostering a sense of belonging and cultural identity among the public, and developing Hong Kong into a center of international cultural exchange.

M+ embodies these ideas, as a museum that builds on Hong Kong's historic balance of the local and the international to define a clear voice in contemporary conversations on art, design, architecture, and moving image. The name is significant: 'M+', or 'museum plus', encapsulates the vision, collecting activities and operations of this new institution. I recall the lengthy discussions at committee meetings to choose a name that would frame the growth and inclusiveness that define M+'s ambitions, to provide for a wide scope and an emphatically cross-disciplinary approach.

M+ is firmly rooted in Hong Kong and also looks outward to Asia and beyond. This perspective is articulated through the M+ Collections, which consist of more than six thousand objects and continue to grow. The museum's programming is just as important, providing ways to connect with diverse audiences and to establish local and international collaborative relationships. M+'s learning and interpretation programs emerge from the conviction that participation in arts and culture empowers individuals and transforms society — public programs complement exhibitions on view, and also bring the museum learning experience into schools and communities. M+ engages in collaborative projects and partnerships with cultural institutions and artists in Hong Kong and around the world, ensuring that curatorial initiatives reach the broadest possible audiences.

M+'s base in Hong Kong is located in the West Kowloon Cultural District. Following an international competition, Herzog & de Meuron was selected to design the building, collaborating with TFP Farrells and Ove Arup &

Partners Hong Kong. Currently in the final phases of construction, the building offers seventeen thousand square meters of exhibition space, a lecture theater, a learning center, shops, performance spaces, three cinemas, cafes, a médiathèque, and a public roof terrace with views of Victoria Harbor and the Hong Kong skyline. After its opening, scheduled for late 2020, M+ will take an important position in a rapidly developing global hub of art, design and culture, and will make an immense contribution to the cultural life of Hong Kong and the region.

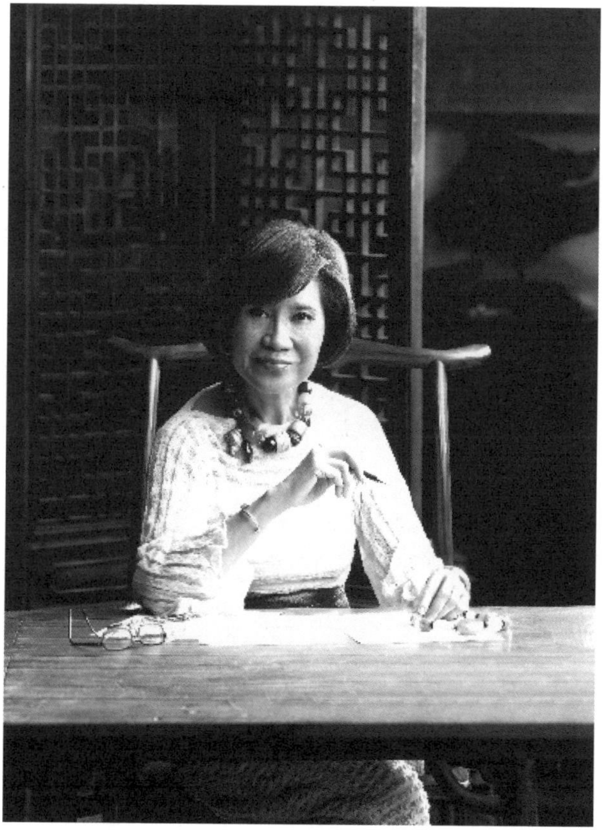

Consciously or unconsciously,
I create living culture
for everyday life to be shared

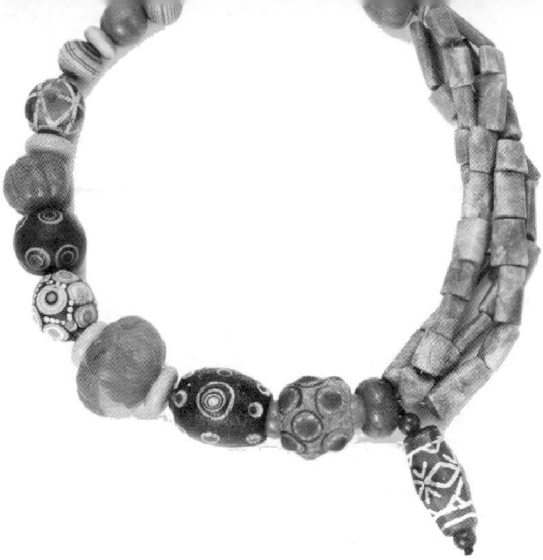

PART III

'Show me and I will forget
Tell me and I may remember
Involve me and I will understand.'

—Confucius

A RICH TAPESTRY

18

A Rich Tapestry

My story is, I think, about going from one world to another and becoming a success in something that was completely unexpected. From my era it was Vivienne Tam and myself who achieved international recognition. We both saw the need to infuse our work with the essence of Chinese design sensibility and to interpret that essence in a way that would be appealing and understood by a contemporary public. She drew her inspiration more from colorful folk culture and I was inspired by the cross-fertilization between Han culture and influences from across the desert and the Middle East. Those were pioneering times. These days, fashion designers from Mainland China and fine jewelry designers, among them Wallace Chan from Hong Kong and Cindy Chao from Taiwan, both based in Hong Kong, enjoy international renown. More than a designer, I think of myself as a cultural specialist who expresses personal philosophy and aesthetics through jewelry and accessories design.

The crux of my story is not necessarily of business success. It is about being independent and taking the road less-traveled — my own road, striking out, searching for something different and creating something that ushered in a new concept and a new trend that would last. That endeavor has value independent of any money that results, or not. Suzy Menkes, the leading fashion critic, saw that what I introduced was a new direction for adornment using less expensive colorful semi-precious stones, one that was affordable and easy to wear, aimed at giving people self-confidence and satisfaction. The success it garnered was not to be measured in financial terms even though it did provide a good income. But I think I did create a new design concept that, in its way, presented a new perspective and at the same time altered the existing mindset regarding the concept and use of jewelry.

Learning something as 'esoteric' as Medieval European and English history seemed like an error when I was young, but it enlarged my perspective of Chinese history, the development of its civilization, and cross-cultural interactions. This was one of the factors that led to the recognition of my work by Central Saint Martins College of Arts and Design, a key part of the University of the Arts London. I am thankful to the College for this recognition of the importance of cross-cultural fertilization.

The Silk Road, representing over 3,000 years of interaction, is the fount and inspiration for my designs. The markings, carvings and symbols of Buddha's association that I have observed along the Silk Road often reflect Islamic influence, whether found in Central Asia or northern or southern Spain. To me, they were universal and easy to adapt for the contemporary lexicon. Dunhuang would mean more to me and many others than to Aurel Stein and the adventurers who both plundered and helped to preserve China's heritage. Returning to my own culture via Chinese antiques, immersing myself in Chinese living patterns, and following their gradual evolution into our present mode of living, incorporating chunks of heritage into our everyday life, is in a way adapting scholarship to the living world.

I ride on observations of East-West exchanges, but none of my jewelry is particularly Chinese. That's the whole idea. It transcends being Chinese. My jewelry and accessories have been worn by many famous people, but besides my contribution to design in jewelry, I would like to think that through my books I have played some role in the advancement of knowledge and understanding of the role of Chinese furniture and the Chinese traditional living environment, from family to community, to the idea of nation and civilization — the whole ecology and belief of being Chinese.

Courage and taking chances get harder as time passes. Going out on the streets of New York with my bag of samples in the 1970s, going to Japan and finding a way to become the first non-Japanese Asian jewelry designer to be accepted in that market; these were tough, but vanity and courage helped.

I now show and sell my designs at exhibitions — in Hong Kong, New York and London where I am recognized by a small and loyal following, and also in Beijing and Shanghai where I am acknowledged as a brand that has succeeded in the West and in Japan. But I'm not that ambitious anymore. There is a bell curve to life, and I no longer have the stamina nor drive to undertake the marketing, or to host events to maintain the positioning of the brand. I spend my energy learning, and enjoying things that will stimulate and enhance life and experience — I travel and serve on museum and design committees — and that occupies good enough time!

But I am still designing. It is both work and a pastime. I find designing and assembling — particularly antique pieces that contrast, harmonize and coordinate in highly striking and distinguished looking accessories — stimulating, edifying and satisfying. I have come across some clear glass beads and large crystal rings from the Warring States period so finely chiseled in layers; and round, clear and opaque glass beads, known as 'dragonfly eye', a style that originated in 1400BC in Egypt, and spread to Central Asia and then China. And I have found small long glass tubes with raised decorations usually in yellow and blue that are unique in China. The melding of cross-current influences of artifacts and decorations of East and West dating back over thousands of years, juxtaposed and coordinated into everyday adornments with vivacity and allure, looking so contemporary and à la mode — that is my passion.

I have designed so many things. Apart from jewelry and ornaments, I have designed plates and bowls inspired from white and *Qingbai* Chinese ceramics of the 9th to 11th centuries, a favorite period that I collect, and fashion including clothes and cashmere shawls. Looking back, what I have done is a reflection of what Hong Kong is capable of. I gained an understanding of the lifestyle in the United States, and that stimulated me to find a new direction in accessories for women who live and work a fast-paced life and need convenience and want to look good. I saw blocks of semi-precious stones appearing on the market in Hong Kong and I merged that with the skills of the stone and ivory carvers to create items to sell in New York and other American cities. And I built it for a while into a global business. Things have come full circle — designs with antique components are now significant because the Mainland Chinese buyers today appreciate them much more than the Americans and Europeans ever did, and they now have the money to purchase them. As a historian, and designer, I provide style and context in making antiques wearable.

I am now finally, amongst other things, a teacher, as fate has propelled me to be. Also a lecturer, interacting with design students and specialists in Hong Kong, Beijing, London and New York. Aside from being the first Principal Lecturer, Cross Culture at Central Saint Martins, London, I was Visiting Professor at CAFA (Central Academy of Fine Arts, Beijing) from 2012 to 2014 and Visiting Professor at Tsinghua University, Beijing from 2004 to 2010. In China, they all call me Teacher Lo, which I find reassuring and flattering!

I am blessed with a close-knit and loving family of two brothers, their spouses and their four children, four lovely grandchildren and a sister full of common sense. They provide me with needed advice and much valued support. The younger adults and the third generation, just being what they are, recharge my life.

My brother Robert and sister-in-law Sally and their two daughters Emma and Melissa, and now their families, have for some forty years spent part of the summer at their farmhouse in the village of Salabes in Lauzun, located in the sleepy and rural Lot-et-Garonne region in southwest France. When elder daughter Emma married John Brunner there in 2006, it was a country wedding of rustic color and beauty which remains vivid in my memory. The pre-nuptial dinner occupied a good part of the village square of Monflanquin in Aquitaine, and the wedding was held in the 13th-century church nearby. It is a region closely associated with my study of Medieval English and French history, as the monarchical ties and interactions of the two countries were so entwined, especially in Aquitaine. King Henry II of England (1133-1189) was married to the greatest landowner in Europe, Eleanor of Aquitaine (1124-1204), and the rivalries and battles waged between the two and their eight children were legendary.

Little seems to change in the sleepy village of Salabes where Robert and Sally have kept their farmhouse all these years. I recall the sight of the farmland covered with giant sunflowers interrupted by fast-moving streams, and the weekend fairs with offerings ranging from bread, cheese and wine from local vineyards to embroidered pillow cases and coverlets which I still use. Rural France does not change.

Robert, who has a long affiliation with Thailand that goes back to his days working there in the 1980s, together with other brother Anthony, also built a lovely development of four compounds, each with four Thai-style bungalows graced with individual gardens and a large central garden with a swimming pool, on what must be one of the longest beaches in Phuket. The story started at Christmas in 2000 when Robert and his family were sailing near the Similan Islands on the Andaman Sea nearby. Robert got off the boat, and a man resting in the shade was bold enough to ask if he was interested in buying parcels of land along the beach. And fortunately Robert obliged! By 2006, after massive installation of infrastructure, the four compounds with bungalows in the modern Thai style were constructed and equipped with all amenities for modern comfort. Two are now owned by Robert's friends, the other by brother Anthony, his wife Audrey and two sons: Jonathan, who has finally returned to the East after a long spell working in South America, and Benjamin.

I have spent many happy days at their villas enjoying a complete withdrawal from worldly woes — walking that long beach which stretches as far as the eye can see, and relaxing in a compound that is a cloistered web of tranquility. It is a great joy playing with my young grandnieces and nephews and seeing how much they have grown each time we meet there during Christmas and New Year holidays. Being able to enjoy them in relative peace before losing them to a world I might not know has been such a gift. And also updating myself with what is new and trendy with my other two grown-up nephews, sons of Anthony and Audrey. It is precious time to catch up with the many articles and books I have not read and joining up with the clan for meals that are feasts of fresh seafood and vegetables. Great pleasures and such a good way for regeneration! I do hope this peaceful way of life will not be eroded by the increasing pressures of development that have impacted much of Phuket town.

Over the years, I have spent equal lengths of time in London and New York, the former when I was at school in the U.K. and the latter as my North American base for jewelry distribution and marketing. These days, living in Hong Kong, I try to visit New York and London at least once a year — New York usually in the autumn when the city is bursting with fall colors and great art and design shows and music performances. It is also when I take the opportunity for a personal appearance at the Asia Society Store where my jewelry is sold. At the same time, it is usually when the Kai-Yin Lo Lecture on Arts and Culture at the Asia Society has been held intermittently since 2004.

I usually visit London after the annual Art Basel Fair in June, or after the Venice Biennale Opening in May every other year. I know the Kensington/Holland Park area well as I used to live there. It is a special treat for me these days to go to Holland Park and visit the Design Museum headed by the distinguished Deyan Sudjic, who has done so much to promote design to be important and relevant in life and society. I stay in a small hotel across the street from the entrance of Kensington Gardens, and it is a great pleasure when early in the morning, I run across the road into the park, past Kensington Palace and follow one of two routes — either to the Round Pond to rest in the shade or to do my exercises or read, or walk as far as the Serpentine, where at the end of July there is an exciting installation of a temporary design pavilion erected by a candidate selected by a jury. All the big names in architecture, art and design have been featured, and it is a highly regarded honor to have been chosen by the organizers, now headed by current Managing Director Yana Peel and a distinguished panel. I recall my favorite pavilion, the Toyo Ito/Cecil Balmond steel pavilion by the Serpentine in 2002. I wanted to amass the capital required to buy the distinguished multipurpose structure and hoped to move it to Hong Kong, but I did not succeed, and the pavilion now serves as a cafe in the South of France.

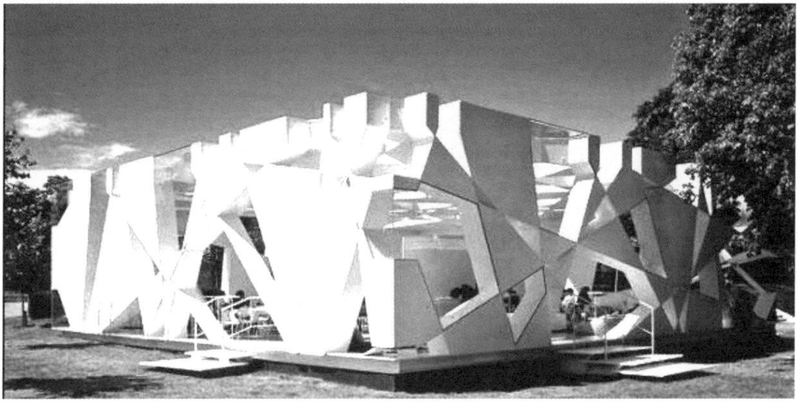

The Toyo Ito/Cecil Balmond steel pavilion, erected by the Serpentine in Green Park, London, in 2002

Another memorable structure was the sinuous curved brick wall designed by innovative Danish architect Bjarke Ingels in 2016. Ingels, born in 1974, won the *Wall Street Journal* Innovator of the Year award in 2016, and is one of the most in-demand architects in the world. Among his many projects are Two World Trade Center in New York, and the Google headquarters in Mountain View, California, working in collaboration with that maverick, Thomas Heatherwick.

A lovely private garden I have often visited these many years is the spacious grounds with unusual flora and fauna in the house of dear friends Sir Sydney and Lady Lipworth in North London. The open gardens adjoin a spacious atrium where I have held several exhibitions of my jewelry and accessory designs over the years. Gregarious and generous, the Lipworths are regular hosts of musical and cultural events.

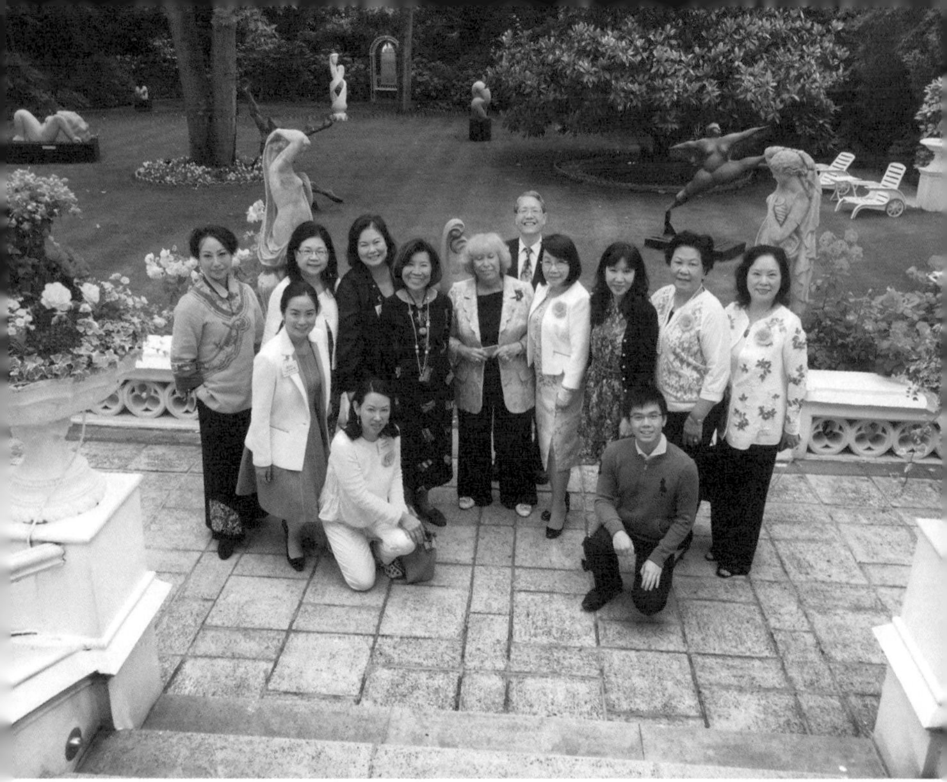

The Hong Kong / Tientsin Women's Delegation enjoyed the lovely garden of Lady Lipworth (center with leader Janice Choi and me) in north London, June 2018

One memorable encounter took place in a car outside the Lipworth house, when elderly Sir Ronnie Grierson, a friend since the 1970s, came to visit my exhibition. As he was too frail to get out of the car, I sat with him and chatted for some thirty minutes and was joined by Rosa Lipworth and Tessa Keswick who had just arrived. It was such a happy meeting and it was the last time I saw him. That brings to mind David Tang, whom I introduced to Ronnie and the two became inseparable friends. Supposedly they talked to each other by phone wherever they were, every day for thirty years. Think of their telephone bills!

I also introduced Ronnie Grierson to my sister-in-law Sally who founded the Hong Kong Cancer Fund in 1987. Sally has been the guiding angel of this worthwhile institution providing free information and support for cancer care to improve the lives of people in Hong Kong touched by cancer.

As for New York, Central Park is a favorite spot, a true oasis in the middle of Manhattan. In the 1980s, I would frequent the lower part of the park,

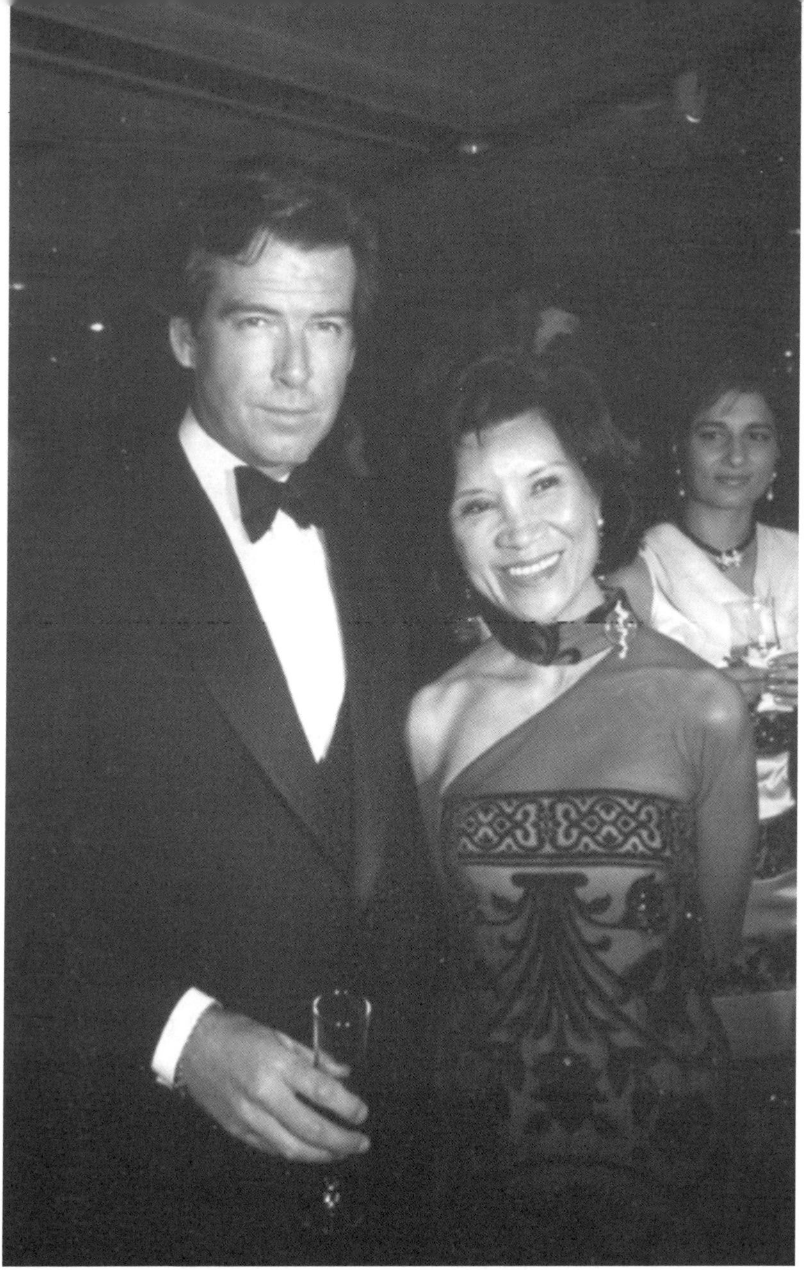

With Pierce Brosnan at the Cancer Fund Ball, Hong Kong, in 2000

from 57th to 72nd Streets. Recently, thanks to my good friend Cristina Heeren, I have been staying in her uptown triplex apartment in a building offering unobstructed views of Central Park. One recent November, we were blessed with wonderful weather, and it was a treat to see New York

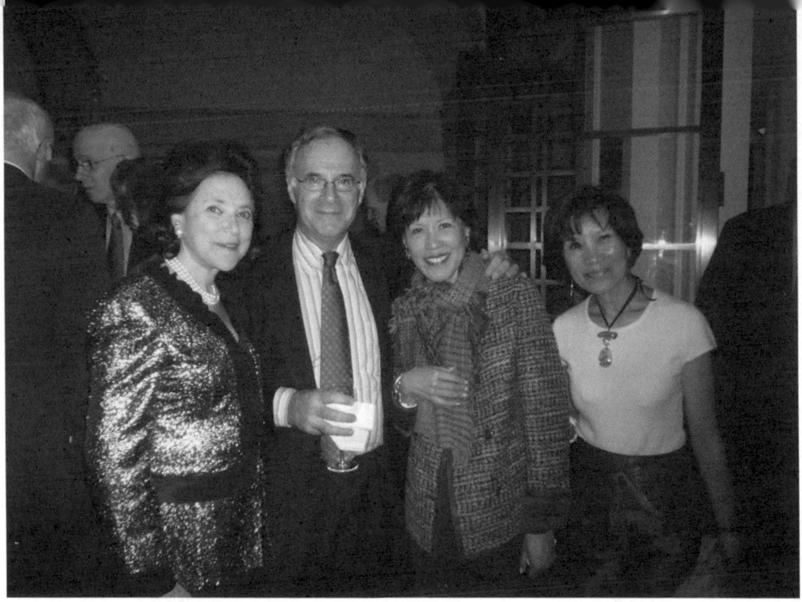

Movers and shakers in art and music - in New York with Marina French (left), Sir Clive Gillison, Artistic Director of Carnegie Hall, and Patty Tang

looking its best. Running in the park with Cristina and her three dogs of varying sizes, we were soon surrounded by a pack of dogs sniffing and befriending one another as the owners also got acquainted. I, meanwhile, was introduced to the manners of canine culture in the fall sunshine!

Further south, I like to visit the Cooper Hewitt Smithsonian Design Museum on East 91st Street and was fortunate in September 2017 to catch the exhibition of the works of Joris Laarman, whose display of twenty chairs of the same shape, all constructed in a different pattern, and all designed and realized by digital calculation, formed an impressive display.

At the Guggenheim Museum, at 89th Street, I caught the last of the exhibition featuring 'Art and China after 1989 till the Olympics 2008 – Theater of the World' organized by Alexandra Monroe, assisted by Philip Tinari of Beijing's Ullens Center of Contemporary Art, with works by a new generation of Mainland Chinese artists aiming to forge reality free from ideology to define the contemporary Chinese experience. I concur with the general opinion that the exhibition was rather academic, but the curled dragon made of crushed metal and rubber tiles by Chen Zhen, titled 'Precipitous Parturition', looming from atop the rotunda gave it an impressive yet menacing panache.

Memories flooded back with the Guggenheim Museum's great 1998 exhibition 'China 5000', the first mega show of Chinese artifacts collected from all over the country, including a good few from the provinces of Sichuan and Yunnan shown for the first time, whose unusualness caused quite a stir. Still vivid in my memory is the exhibition's opening, when I was asked to act as the gala evening's official presenter when the dignitary from China did not turn up. Imagine making a speech at short notice to announce the opening of such an important event!

Further down on my familiar route along Fifth Avenue, at 86th Street and the Park, stands the Metropolitan Museum of Art, the repository of artifacts from many lands and the site of so many distinguished exhibitions. In 2017, I had the good fortune of a reunion with Maxwell Hearn, the highly-respected Douglas Dillon Chairman, Department of Asian Art, to discuss future plans and reminisce over wonderful past exhibitions, one of which I particularly recall, the 2010 'The World of Kubilai Khan: Chinese Art in the Yuan Dynasty.' It featured exhibits assembled from all over the world and included some of the greatest paintings ever produced in China, dispelling the premise that the Mongols excelled only in military feats. Indeed, they demonstrated the revolutionary changes in art and science wrought during the hundred years of the dynasty. Other exhibits ranged from archaeological finds to ornaments worn by men, which greatly interested me. I can recount so many wonderful exhibitions I have attended at the Met, including 'China: Dawn of a Golden Age, 200-750AD' (October 12, 2004 to January 3, 2005) and 'China Through the Looking Glass: Fashion, Film, Art', a well-deserved blockbuster (August 19, 2015 to February 29, 2016).

The last stop for me on my usual Fifth Avenue tour would be Bergdorf Goodman on 59th Street and Fifth Avenue, a top retail emporium that for some twelve years was the premier outlet for my jewelry, and whose endorsement and exposure helped make me into a brand name in America. The pattern of retail has now changed but I still relish those bygone days not that long ago when it was my most high-profile retail base in the USA, where I enjoyed good business and fame. Now I can look at the store and the showcases with detachment and retain fond memories.

When I was based in London way back, I cultivated a liking for classical music and opera. As a student, I shared a ticket with a friend to take turns to occupy the one seat purchased. I vividly remember one memorable performance by Maria Callas as Tosca in one of her final performances in a full-scale opera. It was magic! There were also two memorable performances with Placido Domingo interpreting Otello.

But it is Salzburg that is the Mecca of opera. In the mid-1990s, for three years I was fortunate enough to be part of the entourage of Gordon and Ann Getty, occupying a small room in their house just outside Salzburg. These days it is thanks to Thaddaeus Ropac, gallerist and art promoter, who helps me to purchase seats at the opera and secure my accommodation at the Blaue Gans, centrally located at colorful Getreidegasse. I so enjoy looking out of the window to see the throngs of pedestrians below. As a devoted fan of the Bavarian tenor, Jonas Kaufmann, a super good-looking and engaging actor with an interpretive voice, I relished his performances in *Carmen* and *Don Carlos*, and also soprano Anna Netrebko's appearance in *Il Trovatore* with Dmitri Hvorostovsky, whose unfortunate death is much-lamented.

Before Salzburg, I will have a health checkup at the clinic run by Dr. Claus Martin and his son Nicholas Martin in the village of Rottach by beautiful Tegernsee, the resort of the wealthy. Now it is not unusual to see Mainland Chinese, accompanied by their guides, nesting there. As a result of their presence, many more boutiques selling fashion and souvenirs have surfaced.

The other joy of Salzburg is the beautiful lakes. I never tire of taking the ferry boat for yet another tour to Fuschl and the other islands. I recall, some years ago, the large gatherings of visitors from all parts of the world in the gardens of the affable Princess Marianne zu Sayn-Wittgenstein-Sayn, grande dame of Salzburg.

Opera is costly to mount, and some argue that it is a bygone art form and that the expensive scenery should be dispensed with. The drama, it is true, is found in the music and the interpretation, and I advocate keeping the singing, the prime factor, and the drama alive in concert presentation, especially the operas by Wagner. The Hong Kong Philharmonic's performances of the four-part Ring in concert form have been a triumph and more such realizations should be adopted. It's the music and the interpretation that count.

In 2001, my good friend Shirley Young, the music enthusiast and promoter, invited me to attend the premier of composer/conductor Tan Dun's concerto *The Map,* inspired by the sounds and folklore of his home province, Hunan. It was a pleasure and an eye-opener to journey to Fenghuang, where people are endeavoring to preserve their indigenous culture. It was indeed a big production by the river, with the orchestra lit by powerful floodlights and Tan Dun conducting with finesse and aplomb. There was a choir recruited locally and the lead singer with a powerful voice was adept at singing *shan ge,* or 'mountain tunes,' a local way of communicating by projecting singing voices across the mountains. Old practice has it that voices that harmonize would lead to acquaintance and later marriage. This event remains vivid in my mind — it was a joy to see and hear contemporary music inspired and harnessed by traditional native culture.

Now, as Tan Dun has firmly established himself as a leading composer and conductor in the world, high expectations awaited the Asian premiere held on March 2, 2018 in Hong Kong of his latest work, *Buddha Passion.* The score, the performance by the soloists, baritone Shenyang, soprano Maria Chiara Chissoni, mezzo soprano Zhu Huiling and tenor Wang Kang, and especially the 200-member chorus, were all excellent and inspiring. It was a memorable evening especially to see that a Chinese musician, Tan Dun, has attained the first ranking in musicianship.

And so, to today. I am still living in the proximity of Kennedy Road, where our family house once stood. I moved to my present home in Hong Kong recently and one of the joys is to be able to visit the nearby Hong Kong Zoological and Botanical Gardens. Space is at a great premium in Hong

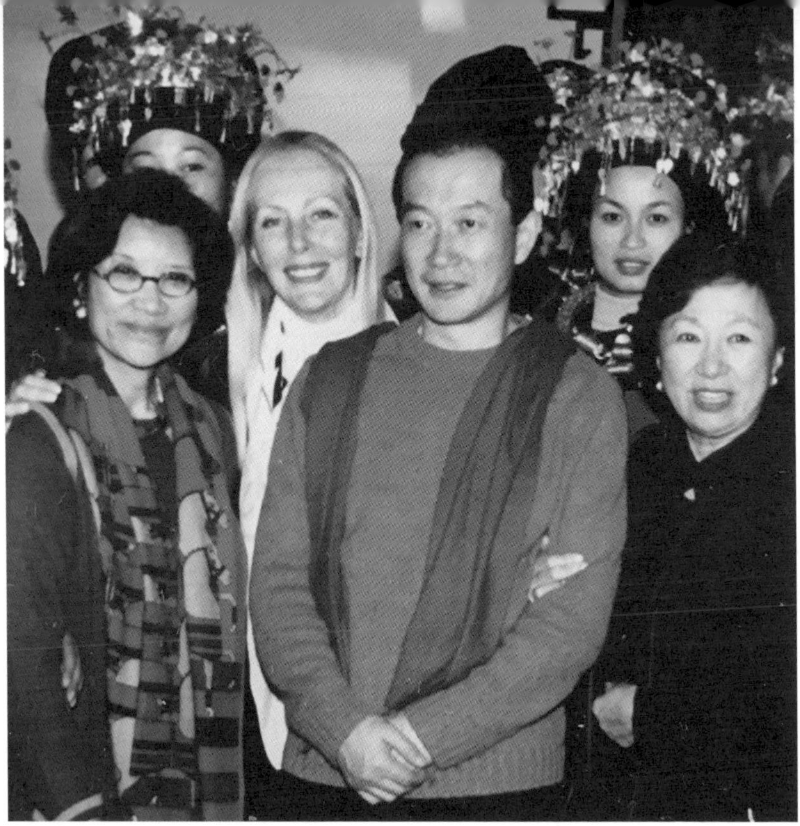

Tan Dun (center) flanked by me and Shirley Young (right), now a celebrated conductor/ composer, at the premiere of "The Map" in Fenghuang, 2008

Kong, but the Botanical Gardens that I frequent remain a long-established oasis, well-groomed with flora and fauna, allowing us to sit leisurely on a bench and read a book, or watch birds from flamingos to egrets, and animals from monkeys to squirrels and dozens of other species, or do what I prefer to do — energetically conduct a brisk fifteen-round walk during the cooler season of October to April and feel the better for it!

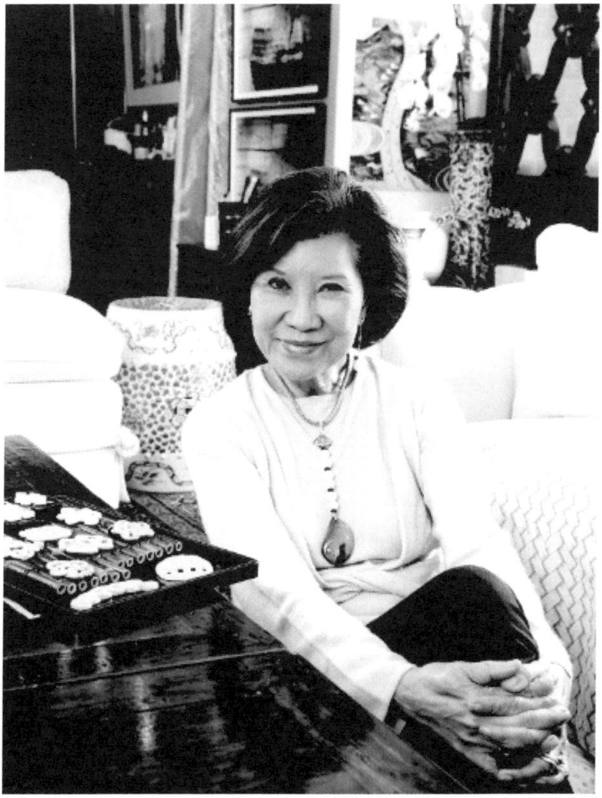

Balance with imbalance
is a device and a way of
freeing yourself from constraints

EPILOGUE

EMPOWERING OUR CREATIVE FUTURE

'History enriches minds and educates hearts — a lifetime of curiosity, critical thinking and intellectual pleasure.'

These lines, which I came across recently, were posted in the History Department of Cambridge University and resonated deeply with me because they reflect my own experience, aspirations, and the rewards of my life's journey.

Through good fortune, my personal 'Silk Road' of pursuit and confluence spanning East and West started with my first post at the Mandarin Hotel where I was fortunate to be exposed to a new international horizon and opportunities, while at the same time being enlightened into new aspects of learning about Chinese heritage when all kinds of antique pieces, big and small, the likes of which we had not seen before, appeared on the Hong Kong and Macau markets. I was blessed with more luck when I was offered a job in New York.

Looking back, I was fortunate to have spent those years at school and at university in the U.K., and fortunate to have found jobs at an international hotel — The Mandarin — and then at Time Inc., which enabled global exposure while seeking to make a new living. During those years, life in the West influenced, nurtured and broadened me with new knowledge, insights and values all rolled into an amalgam that found expression in what I did and do.

Belief in one's creativity lies at the heart of innovation. Daring to try is the first step leading to a new expression and to action. At the core is creative confidence that expresses itself if we are brave enough to tap into it. Believing in your ability and expressing your creative vision with belief,

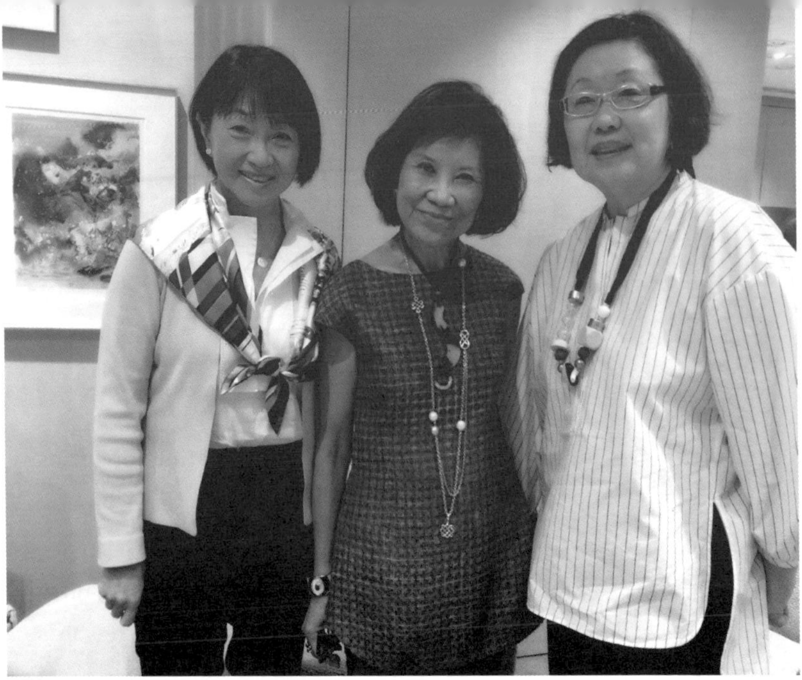

With good friends of over 30 years, Nancy Lee (left) and Virginia Yee (right)

self-assurance and flexibility are necessary preparations, but first you need to have a good grasp of your skills before you are in a position to initiate changes in the world around you. This is my advice to young people: have the courage to try, but first do your homework! It may take a while to harness your energies or excavate that latent creative sparkle, but stay the course. Many have a day job and can only indulge in personal pursuits in their own time. Nevertheless, proceed with the belief that with research, observation, trial and refinement, there will be a breakthrough that will lead to opportunities, recognition and fulfillment.

Tom Kelley, the CEO of the celebrated design think tank Ideo, in his book *Creative Confidence*, cites many valuable observations and advice about creativity, among which is an illustration he encountered some years ago in Shinjuku, Tokyo — when he saw a young Japanese woman wearing different-colored sneakers, one turquoise and one pink. I have been wearing mismatched shoes, socks and clothes with front and back in different colors and sleeves in contrasting colors in one form or another for as long as I can remember. It was induced by having to simplify my wardrobe and lighten my luggage to allow room for carrying samples of jewelry and

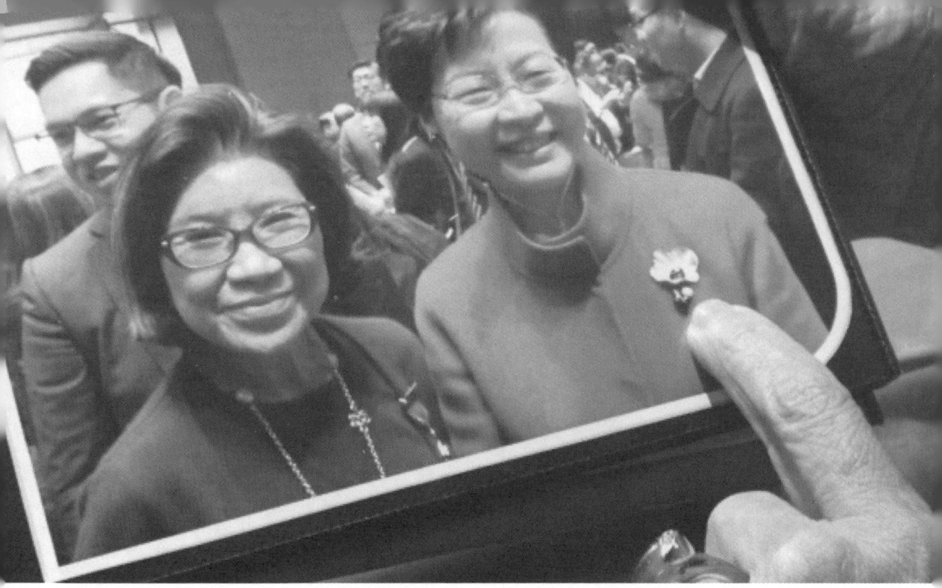

Chief Executive Carrie Lam, wearing a Kai-Yin Lo brooch, is a long-time supporter

accessories. Taking three shoes to enable two combinations was a way to save weight! With my design, I do not describe my earrings with different colors for the left and right ear as being mismatched — I regard this rather as coordination with a different harmony. The asymmetrical treatment creates harmony in its own way.

Creativity resides in everyone. We need not declare that we are creative — it is self-evident. And creativity can be cultivated. My wearing of mismatched shoes and trousers is harmony expressed in a different and practical way. It shows an approach for solving problems and for establishing new aesthetics. Besides, I can buy less expensive remnant materials to fashion into clothes that are original! In a similar way, my semi-precious jewelry design — colorful, genuine, versatile and affordable — delivers a solution to fill the gap between precious and costume jewelry. You can call it an expression of creative confidence.

I have elsewhere cited examples that document the remarkable influence of Chinese design and culture in the West through the ages. First there was silk, then porcelain. What I find particularly extraordinary is a Chinese ceramic cup depicted in the 15th-century painting 'The Adoration of the Magi' by Italian master Andrea Mantegna (1495-1505). The painting features a blue-and-white cup of the Ming dynasty presented to the newborn Jesus, a gift

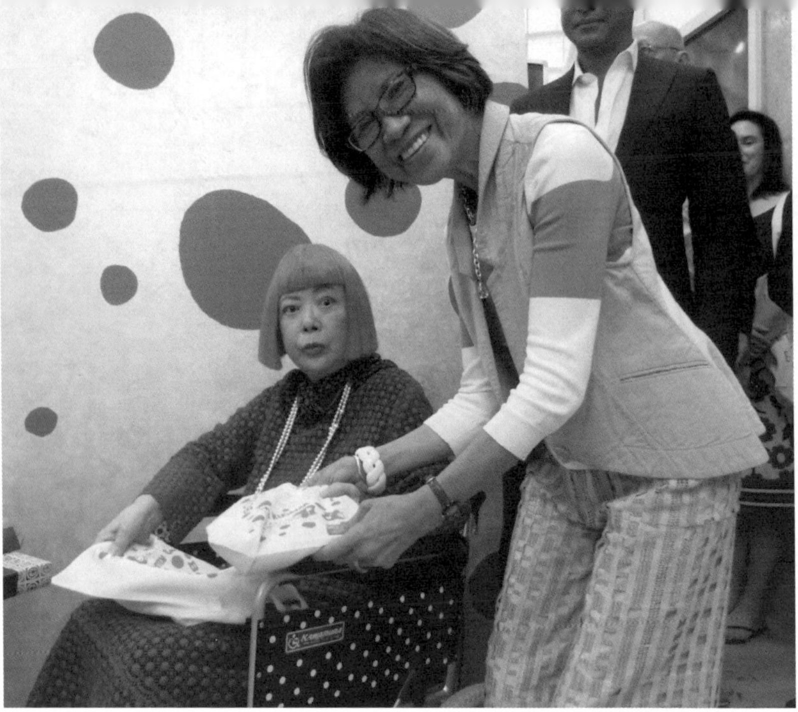

Kai-Yin Lo with Yayoi Kusama, taken at her studio in Tokyo in September 2011 with the Tate Modern Asia Pacific Art Acquisitions Committee.

from one of the three magi, and serves as a compelling acknowledgement of the preciousness of Chinese ceramics in the West in the 15th century.

It is the quest for knowledge and greater understanding which has always been my added reward. I reflect, consider and perform as best I can. I truly enjoy the process of inquiry and sharing with peers and experts from other fields. I am an historian whose focus encompasses art and design as well as societal and economic developments covering narratives of history and humanity. I am thankful to have had the freedom and flexibility to grow and develop. I value the company and interchange with friends, experts and a wider public — these are different ways and rewards of empowerment. And I acknowledge and respect the inter-influence generated from East to West, and more recently from West to East.

My loving family includes older and younger nieces and nephews who, being what they are, acquaint me with new observations and ideas, and inspire me to lead the full life that I do. I have been asked umpteen times why I never married decades back when it was more the norm to find a partner and have a family. Am I an odd ball, or an original thinker and player? Of course I had the chance, but somehow I never undertook the 'plunge' in order to have security or companionship. More than ever, this is now a time when women are empowered to exercise to the fullest their capabilities in work, while also running a family and focusing on self-development. The glass ceiling has long been smashed by women of proven ability, talent and the knack for grasping opportunity — from business to technology to politics to the varied expressions in art, design,

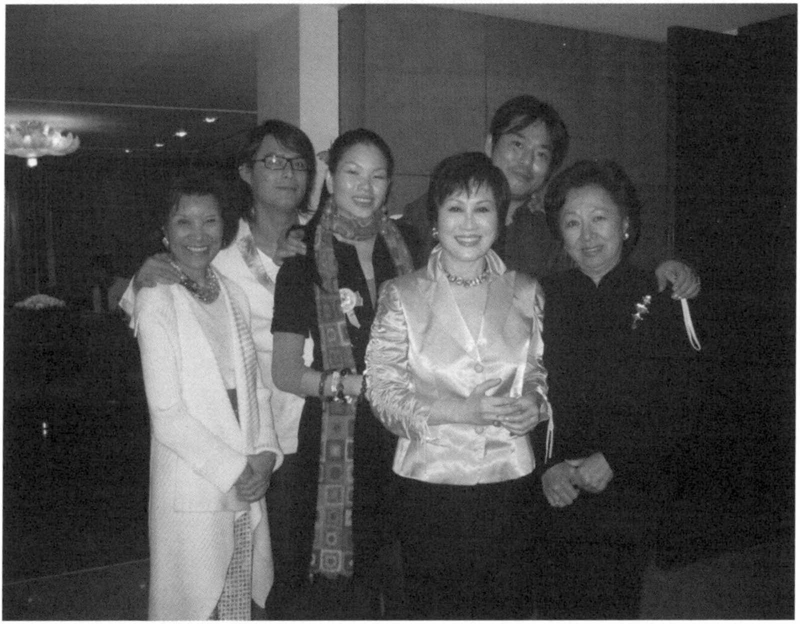

With powerhouses Yue-Sai Kan (front) and Shirley Young (far right), both based in Shanghai and New York

performance and multimedia engagement. Women also bring to the workplace emotions, realizations and skills that balance work, home, family and personal development. From innovative business leaders including Mary Barra, CEO at General Motors and Sheryl Sandberg of Facebook, to politicians, among them Carrie Lam, Chief Executive of the Hong Kong Special Administrative Region and Angela Merkel, the long-reigning Chancellor of the Federal Republic of Germany, and to groundbreaking

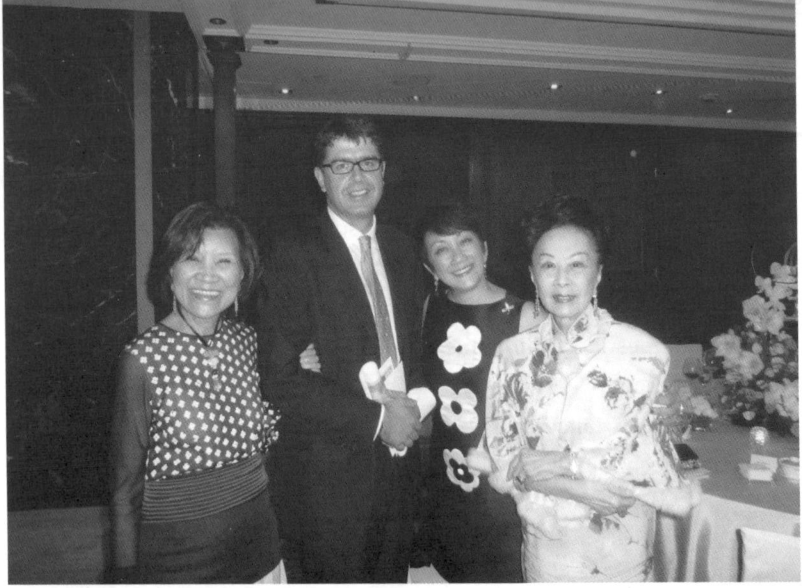

Adam Keswick and daughter Irene Lee at the 90th birthday dinner of Christina Lee at The Mandarin

artists like Yayoi Kusama, Haegue Yang, Tracey Emin and Mona Hatoum — and the list goes on — it is a well-established recognition that women are empowered to create, lead, grow, excel and remain feminine.

Creativity and self-expression require the freedom to think, experiment and give voice. We in Hong Kong have enjoyed freedom and protection under a "rule of law" with an impartial judiciary.

This bedrock of liberty and protection needs to be guarded and maintained as our city becomes more integrated with China as one of the five connected units in the scheme of the Greater Bay Area.

Hong Kong remains uniquely placed to start or partner with companies in the adjacent Pearl River Delta, where with improved connectivity any major centre can be reached within three hours' travel time. According to Victor Fung and Professor Michael Enright, leading experts on Pearl River Delta development, Hong Kong should focus its strengths on better connections with global finance, with digitization capability provided by nearby Shenzhen and Dongguan.

And Hong Kong can be the binding force in the Greater Bay Area, a scheme advocated by paramount leader Deng Xiaoping two years before 1997, when Hong Kong reverted to China.

We firmly believe it is freedom of thought under the protection of law that is the bedrock of confidence and trust, and that it must be maintained. The people of Hong Kong, especially the young, are defending what we consider fundamental to our way of life under the 'One Country, Two Systems' framework.

As the Bay Area grows with an inner ring of core cities and an outer ring of satellite cities, each with specializations of labour, skills and industries, Hong Kong must maintain its relevance as the credible financial connector with international outreach.

I advise young people of Hong Kong to be more adventurous, however, to travel and to tap into the resources and opportunities of the Pearl River hinterland and embrace a broader horizon. After all, it is no more than three hours to any destination within the Delta via the new network of fast trains.

If financial skills and connectivity are Hong Kong's forte, another area we can excel in is development in design and design thinking.

I have been on the board of the Hong Kong Design Centre for twelve years and am very encouraged that the Hong Kong government is providing more resources for cultivating 'design thinking' through workshops, a practitioner certification program, conferences and exchanges. In addition, awareness of this need is projected to the business sector, to encourage and help generate new solutions for unleashing creative energy and engendering a 'creative confidence'. Not long ago, it was thought that creativity was vested in the arts; now creativity manifests itself in multiple aspects, not only in the arts and design, but in the business world and technological innovation, as witnessed in the creation and growth of the most valuable businesses in the world.

Creativity is too often confused with newness. As Einstein said, "creativity is seeing what others see and thinking what no one has thought." In other words, seeing old things with new eyes. Understanding the past is the basis for assessing the present and exploring new possibilities. Therefore, it is essential that an arts and design education should include the humanities, with history and culture as the foundation on which to build and to groom the "complete human being who leads a life of fullness and contribution," in the words of former US president Barack Obama. As Japanese design master Issey Miyake once said, "I go deep into my heritage and come up with something brand new." That resonates with me and should provide inspiration for the next generation of designers in a new economy such as China. For me, the successful fusion of old and new, East and West, is a synthesis of culture, sensibility and aesthetics for the global present. Hence, the acknowledgement from James Pomfret of Reuters that I was "one of the first to do what is commonplace today — taking Chinese culture and re-working it into an original, modern form" — is a most rewarding recognition.

I am of course interested in the status and influence of Chinese civilization, from the way silk and porcelain mesmerized the Western world for millennia, the residues of military triumphs of the Mongols' relatively short-lived sweep through Asia deep into the heart of Europe in the 13th and 14th centuries, and the lasting influence of the Islamic conquests from Asia to the borders of Europe and North Africa.

The ascendancy of European civilization since 1500AD, dominating the world economically and igniting scientific awareness and a cultural renaissance, was due to new discoveries in science and medicine, and gave rise to a new development — competition within society — as pointed out by historian Niall Ferguson in his influential tome, *Civilization: The West and the Rest* (2011).

A more recent perspective is provided by another noted historian, Peter Frankopan, in his perceptive and deservedly best-selling books *The Silk Roads: A New History of the World* (2015) followed by *The New Silk Roads: The Present and Future of the World* (2018). "We see how the world was connected not as a series of periods and regions that are isolated and distinct, but linked by rhythms of history for millennia as being part of a bigger, inclusive global past ... We are now living in the Asian era — and once again witness the rise of China as a dominant power."

Indeed, China, is now a global player. It is hoped that the country is respected not only for its economic and commercial power, but also for its cultural and technological achievements and influence, with outstanding practitioners in the arts, music, moving images and new creative expressions, as well as innovation in science and technology, as a living matrix of cross-fertilization towards a new civilization.

The direction is swift and Asia will regain the economic position it held 300 years ago, before the Industrial Revolution. We want to see Hong Kong integrate with mainland China as the metropolis of the south, a leader in Guangdong's Greater Bay Area development, but maintaining its individual taste, character, creative and entrepreneurial panache — connected to the global pulse and very much an integral propeller of the Chinese phenomenon.

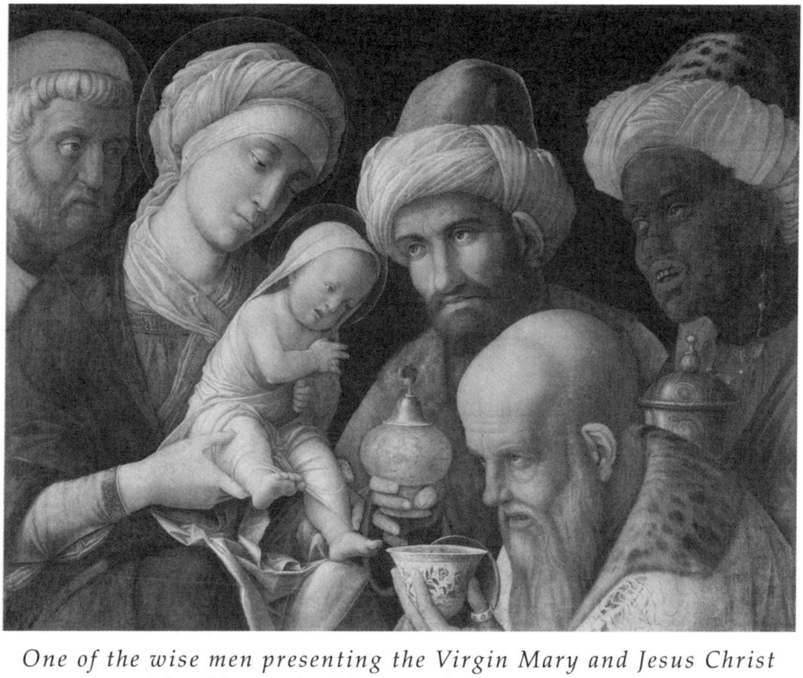

One of the wise men presenting the Virgin Mary and Jesus Christ with a blue and white porcelain cup as depicted by Italian artist Andrea Mantegna (1431-1506)

Afterword

Kai-Yin is one of Hong Kong's iconic jewelry designers. Her ingenuity, sense of style, and gifted sensibility have empowered her vision of the future – a future where East and West are connected through heritage, art and design.

I have known Kai-Yin and her family for over three decades. Over the past fifteen years, I have had the opportunity, and pleasure, to work quite closely with her through my involvement with the Hong Kong Design Centre (HKDC) and also the establishment of the M+ Museum of the West Kowloon Cultural District. She has always been a key contributor to both projects, pretty much from the early planning stage.

Over the years, Kai-Yin has helped the HKDC curate important design exhibitions internationally, and also helped us edit key publications. In all our work in advocating design, she has never failed to remind us of the importance of the perspective of culture and heritage. And she has deep appreciation for craftsmanship as well. In 2007, I was one of her fans who nominated her as a "World's Outstanding Chinese Designer", an important annual award by the HKDC.

Kai-Yin is truly a cultural ambassador and has invested much of her time and energy fostering exchanges globally and locally and promoting good design and art as core to the new economic future and societal well-being. She is very generous in sharing her design philosophy and cultural insights, which are uniquely blended with her impressive international network and extensive travels, globally and along the Silk Road.

Kai-Yin has always strongly supported the HKDC in championing the design movement for our city. She knows dearly that art, design and technology play a crucial role in weaving a healthy, inclusive and harmonious society. We are grateful to a genuine companion's devotion to our public mission as we STEAM Hong Kong forward with creative thinking, good design and enterprising creativity, never forgetting the importance of culture and heritage.

I am so delighted that Kai-Yin is publishing her memoir. An inspiration for so many, Kai-Yin is an amazing self-made designer and self-made businesswoman. Selfless in promoting good design, she is very Asian and very global at the same time. I treasure our friendship.

Victor Lo
Chairman of the Board, M+ Museum
West Kowloon Cultural District Authority

Acknowledgements

Many thanks are owed to those who have helped me to put this book together. For family history, and for cautioning me not to write 'meandering trivia,' I am indebted to sister Marina and sister-in-law Sally, and also to Audrey, and indeed my brothers Robert and Anthony and cousin Kenneth. Thank you to Joan Foo Mahoney, a publisher friend dating from the 1980s who counseled me to bring to life the ups and downs of my journey; to Frank and Liz Newman, Shirley Young, Stephanie Stokes, Leonie Ki, and Virginia Yee, all of whom have encouraged me to share my life with others; to Victor Lo, who has enlisted me to contribute and participate in many commissions locally and internationally, advancing design and creative development; to the Asia Society New York and Hong Kong for providing an entrée and platform for the Kai-Yin Lo and Central Saint Martins Lectures; to Professors Puay-Peng Ho and Ronald R. Knapp for furthering my understanding of the traditional and changing way of 'Living and Being' in China; and to Carrie Lam, Chief Executive of the HKSAR, for being such an outstanding role model, and for validating my jewelry design concept, and for proving it is as good for everyday wear as it is for ceremonial occasions.

I would also like to offer my sincere gratitude to all those in my office who have provided invaluable assistance, and who have helped me umpteen times compiling information and images. Thank you to Veronica Chan, Sally Lam and Marcelo Bukid Malihan.

And my thanks to the history departments at Girton College, Cambridge University, and King's College, London University, which opened up my horizons and showed me that 'history enriches minds and educates hearts – a lifetime of curiosity, critical thinking and intellectual pleasure'; to Jane Rapley, former Head, Central Saint Martins, University of the Arts London, who encourages me to share the inspiration for my design; to Jeremy Till, Head, Central Saint Martins, and Nigel Carrington, Vice-

Chancellor, University of the Arts London, for endorsing the importance of cross-cultural fertilization by installing me as the University's first visiting professor in this discipline, validating that understanding the differences, linkages, exchanges and shared commonalities of East and West stimulates new awareness and developments of vital importance; to Professor Pan Gong Kai who appointed me as visiting professor of the Central Academy of Fine Arts at School of Design (CAFA), Beijing (2012-2014); and to Prof. Li Dang Chi, who installed me as visiting professor, Tsinghua University, School of Design (2003-2010).

And finally, I would like to acknowledge with thanks the support I received in providing direction and focus in producing this book from Kevin Mulroy, and from my publisher Pete Spurrier.

APPENDIX 1

BOOKS EDITED OR CO-EDITED BY KAI-YIN LO

Classical and Vernacular Chinese Furniture in the Living Environment 中國古典家具與生活環境: 羅啓妍收藏精選. Maudsley Catherine 毛岱康and Lo Kai-Yin 羅啓妍. Hong Kong: Yungmingtang 雍明堂, 1998.

Bright as Silver, White as Snow: Chinese White Ceramics from Late Tang to Yuan Dynasty 如銀似雪: 中國晚唐至元代白瓷賞析. Maudsley Catherine 毛岱康, Mok Kar Leung Harold 莫家良and Lo Kai-Yin 羅啓妍. Hong Kong: Yungmingtang 雍明堂, 1998.

Living Heritage: Vernacular Environment in China 古承今襲: 中國民間生活方式. Ho Puay-Peng 何培斌 and Lo Kai-Yin 羅啓妍. Hong Kong: Yungmingtang 雍明堂, 1999 ed., reprint 2002.

House, Home, Family: Living and Being Chinese. Lo Kai-Yin and Knapp Ronald G. Honolulu: University of Hawaii Press; Beijing: China Architecture and Building Press; New York: China Institute in America, 2005.

House, Home, Family: Living and Being Chinese 家: 中國人的居家文化. Lo Kai-Yin 羅啓妍and Knapp Ronald G 納普. Beijing: New Star Press 新星出版社, 2011.

Hong Kong: Creative Ecologies: the Shaping of a Design Culture 香港: 創意生態: 設計文化的塑造. Lo Kai-Yin 羅啓妍. Hong Kong: Hong Kong Design Centre 香港設計中心, 2010.

APPENDIX 2

THE KAI-YIN LO DISTINGUISHED PROGRAM LECTURES

HONG KONG

"Creative Capital – Hard Power or Soft Power?" 2014

Speakers:

- John Howkins, business leader and author who has pioneered new ideas on creativity and innovation
- Yat Siu, Founder and CEO of Outblaze, Director for TurnOut Ventures (Hong Kong)
- Chan Koon Chung, cultural critic and author (Beijing)

NEW YORK

"Creative Spaces Empowering the City" 2017

Speakers:

- Nicholas Baume, Director and Chief Curator, Public Art Fund New York
- Alex Poots, Founding Artistic Director and CEO, The Shed
- Suhanya Raffel, Executive Director, M+ Museum, West Kowloon Cultural District

Moderated by Cassim Shepard, urban planner, filmmaker and writer, founding editor-in-chief of Urban Omnibus

<u>"Creating Space for Culture – Hong Kong – Chicago – New York" 2010</u>

Speakers:

- Edward Uhlir, Executive Director, Millennium Park, Chicago
- Hugh Hardy, architect of BAM Annex & Lincoln Center Theater, LCT3, H3 Collaboration Architecture
- Rocco Yim嚴迅奇, architect and urban planner, Hong Kong and China

Moderated by Kristy Edmunds, Consulting Artist Director, Park Avenue Armory, New York

<u>"Looking Ahead – Art and Music" 2009</u>

Speakers:

- Tan Dun譚盾, leading composer
- Gu Wenda 谷文達, international artist (New York and China)

Moderated by Melissa Chiu, Director, Asia Society Museum and Global Cultural Programs

<u>"Chinese Spirit, Global Design" 2008</u>

Speakers:

- Eric Chan陳秉鵬, leading New York-based Hong Kong-born industrial designer
- Calvin Tsai曹覲文, leading New York-based Hong Kong-born architect/interior designer

Moderated by Susanne Szenasy, editor-in-chief of Metropolitan Magazine

Event in partnership with Hong Kong Design Centre

"Chinese Art Outside China, November 2007

Speakers:

- Xu Bing徐冰, leading international Chinese artist (China and New York-based)
- Ji Yunfei季雲飛, leading international Chinese artist (China and New York-based)

Moderated by Melissa Chiu, Director, Asia Society Museum and author of "Chinese Art Outside China"

"Fashion and Stage Design, East and West" 2006

Speakers:

- Han Feng韓楓, Chinese stage, film and fashion designer (Shanghai and New York)

"Building for the World" 2005

Speakers:

- Edwin Chan陳日榮, Hong Kong-born and at that time partner of Gehry Partners, LLP, world-famous architectural firm (Los Angeles)

"Transcending Borders – Music, Dance, Design" 2004

Speakers:

- Bright Sheng盛宗亮, composer (China and Michigan, USA)
- Shen Wei沈偉, choreographer/dancer/artist (China and New York)
- Douglas Young 楊志超, architect and designer (Hong Kong)

APPENDIX 3

CENTRAL SAINT MARTINS LECTURES, LONDON

"Harbour Arts Sculpture Park, VIP Talk" 2018

Presented by Hong Kong Arts Centre (Hong Kong)

Speakers: Alex Schady, Tim Marlow, Kacey Wong and Michael Craig-Martin

"CSM's MA Arts & Cultural Enterprise Distinguished Evening Forum" 2016

Presented by HKU SPACE (Hong Kong)

Speakers: Jerry Liu, Yat Siu, Dr. Tommy Tse, Andy Amm, Ed Tam

"Sculpture and the Animation of Collective Space" 2015

Presented by British Council (Hong Kong)

Speaker: Antony Gormley

"The Bridge of Aspirations – Connecting East and West" 2014

Co-Presented by Asia Society and British Council (Hong Kong)

Speaker: Thomas Heatherwick

Evening CSM Kai-Yin Lo Panel Discussion 2013

Kai-Yin Lo interviewed by Jane Rapley, Professor Emerita, Central Saint Martins UAL

APPENDIX 4

POSITIONS

- Visiting Professor, Central Saint Martins, University of the Arts London
- Visiting Professor, School of Design, Central Academy of Fine Arts, Beijing
- Member, Board of Directors, Hong Kong Design Centre
- Member, Board of Directors and Acquisition Committee, M+ Museum, West Kowloon Cultural District Authority, Hong Kong
- Member, Asia Pacific Art Acquisition Committee, Tate Modern, London
- Member, Global Leadership Council, Museum of Arts and Design, New York
- Committee Member, Global Council, Asia Society, New York
- Member, Arts and Culture Council, Asia Society Hong Kong Center
- Member, the International Women's Forum
- Member, Women Entrepreneurs Committee, Hong Kong Federation of Women
- Museum Expert Adviser, Leisure and Cultural Services Department, Hong Kong SAR Government

APPENDIX 5

ACCOLADES

"Kai-Yin Lo was probably the first Hongkonger to successfully turn her own name into a luxury brand in the 1980s... She is also a cultural historian who has curated a number of major exhibitions in Hong Kong and abroad, edited several scholarly books on Chinese ceramics, furniture and the traditional Chinese home... and wields a lot of influence in shaping Hong Kong's cultural sectors."

Enid Tsui, *South China Morning Post*, Hong Kong, 10 December 2016

"She interprets culture and heritage into original and highly wearable art that reflects China and Asia's past and present, and heralds the future."

Asia Society New York website, 12 June 2015

"Making history wearable... Kai-Yin is the first to interpret the cultural past in a contemporary sense."

David Pillings, Former Asia Editor, *Financial Times*, 3-4 May 2013

"Her aesthetic concept and treatment, 'balancing with imbalance', has made her world-renowned. East and West convergence in her style of design also represents a way of life."

Vogue China, Autumn, 2013

"Your books are so very impressive – the way you look at art, design and life in a holistic fashion is very special, and that you do it with a historical understanding and true connoisseurship makes you rare indeed."

Jan Stuart, former Keeper of Asia, the British Museum, 2011

"A renaissance woman"

***Wall Street Journal*, 2011**

"Her understanding of China's rich legacy avoids imitation and she constantly reinterprets China's heritage in entirely contemporary terms."

Citation for naming Kai-Yin Lo the "World's Best Chinese Designer" by the Hong Kong Design Centre in 2007, recognized as the highest honor given to a designer of Chinese nationality

"She bridged the gap between precious and fashion jewelry – and set a new direction. She is a pioneer."

Current international editor of *Vogue*, former fashion editor of *International Herald Tribune*, Suzy Menkes, 7 May 1992